Claire wa[...]ld kill her that she took o[...] insurance policy the day she saw a lawyer about a divorce.

A DAUGHTER MAIMED
Natasha's beautiful face and skull had been crushed by the crowbar's blows, but her mind refused to forget who had done it.

A LAWYER THREATENED
Victoria Doom had no idea that taking on Natasha's case would make her the target of a hit man.

A COP DETERMINED
Steve Fisk was haunted by the fates of Natasha and Claire, sworn to find the perpetrator, and determined to put him away.

A PSYCHO ON THE RUN
Robert Peernock had money, a plan, plastic surgery, and a girlfriend to help him escape . . . but his twisted brain had left one damning piece of evidence behind.

QUANTITY SALES

INDIVIDUAL SALES

A CHECKLIST FOR MURDER

Anthony Flacco

A DELL BOOK

Published by
Dell Publishing
a division of
Bantam Doubleday Dell Publishing Group, Inc.
1540 Broadway
New York, New York 10036

ISBN: 0-440-21790-3

Printed in the United States of America

Published simultaneously in Canada

September 1995

10   9   8   7   6   5   4   3   2   1

RAD

Contents

Monsters in the Dark

TORTURE: An extreme physical and mental assault on a person who has been rendered defenseless.

—*Amnesty International*

CHAPTER

1

She lay in the seat listening to the metallic sounds as he tinkered under the Cadillac. Was it safe to move?

She still had a little physical control left, despite her cuffed hands, her bound ankles, her blindness inside the canvas hood. But long hours in captivity being force-fed a combination of alcohol and some kind of an unknown drug had served to take a severe toll. Even though she was a healthy eighteen-year-old and had always been athletic, by this point it took all her effort just to make her slim body obey her.

She reached out over her mother's unconscious form. Slowly, she ran trembling fingers down the steering column until at last her fingertips brushed the ignition. The key was still there, but she pulled back. Could she start the car even though her hands were cuffed in front of her? Could she shift the transmission into reverse even though she couldn't see, stomp on the gas even though her feet were tied? Most of all, could she do it fast enough to run the car over him before he heard her and scrambled out of the way? She had to try. There was no longer any doubt that he was about to kill them both. Once again she leaned over her mother, stretching her cuffed hands out toward the key.

But just as her fingertips finally reached the ignition, she realized the sounds under the car had stopped.

Sometime before 4:00 A.M. on July 22, 1987, a motorist named John Dozier pulled over to the side of a desolate road. He peered into the early morning darkness and struggled to

3

focus on a jumble of twisted wreckage off the right-hand shoulder. It seemed to be a single car wreck; no one was moving at the scene.

He looked closer. A thin wisp of smoke was rising from the undercarriage of an old Cadillac resting near the side of the road. The rear of the car was still on the gravel shoulder, but the front straddled the remains of a wooden telephone pole. It appeared that the heavy '71 sedan had rammed the pole with such force that it had splintered and collapsed. The front of the car had come to rest on top of the remains of the pole as it lay on the ground.

Dozier realized that the wreck must have happened only moments before and that he was the first to come along. He knew that on an isolated strip of road like this one, it might be hours before anyone else chanced by in the darkness.

He hurried over, opened the driver's door of the Cadillac and discovered a petite woman lying inside. She gave no signs of life. He tried to pull her free but she was jammed under the dashboard beneath the steering wheel. On the floor beside her he could hear a female passenger moaning softly, but the door on the passenger side was jammed in place and there was nothing he could do to free the second victim either.

Then he remembered the thin wisp of smoke rising from under the car. He realized an explosion could happen at any second.

Dozier hurried away to find a phone and call for help.

At 4:25 on that same July morning, Paramedic Clyde Piehoff was sleeping through the quiet hours of a twenty-four-hour shift at Fire Station 89 in the North Hollywood area of Los Angeles when he received a radio dispatch over his hotline. The call came from the main dispatch center in downtown L.A., located five riot-proof floors below ground level. The order directed him to proceed to San Fernando Road near the Tuxford intersection in the neighboring town of Sun Valley. Clyde was a supervisor with the rank of paramedic 3, serving all county municipalities, so the call was within his jurisdiction. He summoned his partner, Paramedic 2 Todd Carb, and their trainee, Paul Egizi. Within moments they were rolling toward the scene.

Clyde's problems began immediately; there are two San Fernando Roads that intersect Tuxford. He made his best guess and arrived shortly afterward at what he considered the more commonly traveled of the two locations: the new strip of road, where most of the traffic could be expected to go.

There was nothing there.

Knowing he was losing precious seconds, he and his crew rushed toward old San Fernando Road, a lesser used strip of dead-end road running slightly north of a set of railroad tracks. There they finally spotted the "dispatch incident."

Four minutes had elapsed since their call came in.

Clyde saw the first body before he and the crew had even exited their ambulance. The woman lay on the floor under the steering wheel, her back against the driver's seat and her head slumped against the door frame. Her knees were jammed up under the dashboard, with her right arm on the floor and her left arm trailing out of the open driver's side door and onto the ground.

He did not notice the missing section of the underside of the dash or the exposed brackets for mounting stereo equipment, because in his mind, the woman became Clyde's patient the moment he arrived on the scene.

Visibility inside the car was a problem; the dome light was not on, even though the driver's side door was open. His attention was already fixed on assessing her condition. But he suspected that once he reached the woman his check for vital signs would be useless; in addition to clear evidence of massive blood loss, Clyde's patient had sizable portions of brain matter exposed just above her eyes.

After his first quick check of the woman hanging out of

the doorway, Clyde saw a second body on the floor of the passenger side. The second passenger, also a female, wasn't moving either. He called for Todd and Paul to circle around the car to look after the second passenger while he knelt by the driver's side passenger to continue his preliminary assessments.

The smell of gas is typical in bad car wrecks, but Clyde noticed that the odor from this wreck was unusually strong. Glancing around the interior of the car, he saw puddles of fluid on the floorboards. Alarmed that they could be dealing with an active fuel leak, Clyde quickened his pace.

In that first brief moment he had also noticed that blood was also splattered across the inside of the windshield and over the gearshift area. But there was, oddly, no damage at all to the windshield itself or the steering column.

In fact, with the exception of all that blood, the interior of the car did not appear damaged at all. At that moment he couldn't tell if the splattered blood was from one or both of the women. But when Clyde spotted a thin leather strap, several feet long and knotted at both ends, lying across his patient's face, he immediately began conducting his movements so as to disturb things as little as possible. He had been trained to do it that way whenever something about a simple wreck indicated that it might be a crime scene.

Meanwhile Todd and Paul were having trouble getting the passenger's door pried open. The point of impact was on the right front of the car, but the shock had distorted metal all along the car's right side. Quickly retrieving a manual retractor called a hayward from their unit, they began working to free the second patient.

While Clyde was occupied with his examination of the woman on the driver's side, other details of the scene continued to strike him as strangely out of place. A partially empty bottle of whiskey lay in the driver's footwell, but the odor inside the car was more like gas than alcohol. The driver's clothing was soaked, but there again the odor on the clothing was that of gasoline and not alcohol. Most of all, the driver's head injuries were so severe, her face so bloodied and distorted, that he couldn't even guess her age. Clyde couldn't imagine what she might have collided with inside the car that would tear her up so badly without also showing some sign of damage to the impacted object itself.

The urgency of the situation, with the car's interior puddled with gasoline, kept him from continuing his trauma evaluation. With nothing else to go on but his initial impressions, he noted that the driver was small and trim, with no visible signs of aging. He estimated her age to be around thirty while he quickly checked her vital signs.

At 4:35 A.M., Clyde pronounced his patient dead at the scene.

On the passenger side, Todd and Paul called out to Clyde that the second victim showed faint signs of life. As soon as they began to check her, leaning in the window to determine her condition, they confirmed what Clyde had already noticed; there was a strong odor of gas inside the car. It was pooled on the floor around the second victim, soaking through her clothes.

John Dozier had returned to the scene and stood off in the background watching the action, and at that moment he called out a warning to the driver of a street sweeper from a nearby gravel company who had pulled his rig over to protect the scene from traffic. Dozier directed the driver's attention to the source of smoke under the car. When Clyde hurried around to assist his partners in removing the survivor, the street sweeper's driver relayed the warning of fire danger to Clyde.

Clyde dropped to his knees and peered under the car. A piece of rope that he would later describe as looking like a "wick" hung from the undercarriage below the gas tank area. The rope had been partially burned. The end of the rope still smoldered.

The smoldering rope made it imperative to immediately get the surviving young woman out and away from the car. It was also vital to get an engine company on the scene for fire-related backup. The deceased driver would have to remain in the car. Clyde ran to his unit and put out the call for additional aid, then rushed back to help Todd and Paul remove the survivor.

Given the severity of her injuries, they moved her out as quickly as they could. But like the woman on the driver's side, the passenger had suffered massive trauma about her head and face. It took extra precious seconds to handle her with extreme care as they got her strapped to a backboard with her arms and legs fixed in place and a cervical collar stabilizing her neck. Such precautions are standard under the circumstances, but careful handling of the surviving female became more urgent when they found what appeared to be brain matter on her clothing. The paramedics didn't know yet if the brain matter was hers.

They rushed the surviving passenger away on the gurney to begin first aid at a spot behind their ambulance, which had been parked away from any possible flow of gasoline from the wrecked car. They knew it would be a fight to stabilize her enough for the ride to nearby Holy Cross Hospital. With an apparently severe skull fracture and the resulting possibility of coma, the traumatic shock of moving could kill her.

The surviving female groaned softly and muttered a few delirious words. Head-injury patients tend to go in and out of consciousness, so whenever a victim seems alert enough to speak, paramedics will take the opportunity to attempt a few basic questions to determine if the patient is oriented. Clyde asked her name, but got no intelligible answer.

All three paramedics were struck by the fact that even

away from the accident scene the young woman's clothing still reeked of gasoline.

While Clyde directed the treatment and the gentle questions, he noticed an engine company arriving in response to his call. Fire fighters used a two-and-a-half-gallon water gun to soak down the smoldering rope under the car. Then they pulled a hip line over to spray off the accumulated gas under the car, reducing the danger of explosion. Amid the flash of emergency lights, the typical noise of an accident scene was beginning to drone in the predawn darkness. Idling engines rumbled under the crackles of dispatch radios.

Todd and Paul continued with the surviving passenger while Clyde asked the fire fighters to leave the deceased woman in place after the fire danger was controlled. He knew that police investigators would not want anything disturbed more than necessary.

Meanwhile Todd and Paul were unable to orient the survivor. She couldn't identify herself, tell what had happened to her, or even say if she knew where she was. Her breath smelled slightly of alcohol, but it seemed unlikely that alcohol could be the cause of her incoherent condition.

Natasha Peernock was in the place dreams come from. Dreams, or nightmares. Her eyes could register forms moving. Her ears could register sounds. But her conscious mind had been knocked aside and the messages coming in through her senses were getting lost somewhere deep within her. They mingled with the rest of her unconscious, with memories, with hallucinations. Whatever was taking place in the three-dimensional world around her, or even in that tiny part of the world right outside her own skin and bones, it would all have to go by without her help, without her attention, without her even taking notice.

• • •

Arson investigators Michael Camello and Derrick Chew responded to the 8600 block of old San Fernando Road between 5:00 and 5:30 that morning. They saw a fire engine, a patrol car, and a paramedic ambulance already there, plus a handful of onlookers.

The hood and trunk of the car were open. Fire Captain Gene Allen told them that when he had arrived on the scene he'd found both lids closed, but that his men had had to open the hood to check for possible sparking. The fire fighters had also taken the trunk key from the ignition in order to open the trunk and make the same check there.

Camello and Chew had been summoned to determine if this was a crime scene. Had someone intended this car and the people inside of it to explode in flames? In those first moments they learned that a surviving passenger had already been removed from the car and was being given preliminary treatment in the ambulance, but that she was in no condition to offer them any information.

The heavy car was built like a battle tank. Despite a collision severe enough to tear down a telephone pole, most of the damage to the car was in the area of the right front fender. Other than having the one front wheel collapsed, the car was, incredibly, almost drivable.

Inside the passenger compartment, Camello and Chew shared the reactions of the others, amazed that there was no observable damage to the interior other than a minor ding in an air-conditioning vent and a thin crack in the lower right portion of the windshield. Even that small fracture was a single stress crack, not the sort of spidery impact lines that distinguish a blow to the glass from the inside. They observed the deceased woman still in her original position on the driver's floor of the car. Camello spotted a single brown work glove on the floor next to the body, and a capped bottle of Seagram's 7. In his experience, it seemed odd for anyone to drive with a large bottle of such hard stuff. But he also knew that people are completely unpredictable in their drinking habits.

Camello and Chew noted a large amount of blood on the dash and on the floor. Camello suspected that some of the residue was brain matter. Like the paramedics, he and Chew agreed that the deceased woman was in terrible shape for being in such a well-preserved automobile.

Camello looked inside the open trunk. He saw a gas can, scraps of paper, rags, and a wooden stick. It appeared that they had all been burned recently; the rags still felt warm to his touch. He directed photos to be taken while he checked to see if there were any exposed wires that might have ignited the trunk contents in some accidental way. But although he knew that anything is possible with explosive liquids, the trunk fire had already struck Arson Investigator Camello as being incendiary in nature.

The sight under the vehicle was also consistent with a crime scene. He noted that the rope "wick" near the gas tank was wrapped around some type of metal bar. The bar had a sharpened edge and was pointed toward the gas tank with the tip of the point about half an inch from the fuel supply. The other end of the bar was secured to the car's undercarriage by a single screw. Even though everything under the car was dirty, the single screw holding the pointed bar was shiny and clean. Camello noted some darkening on the underside of the gas tank, appearing to be a hydrocarbon burn residue. The location of the partially burned rope added to Camello's suspicions of attempted arson. But with a dead woman in the front seat and a delirious female pulled from the wreckage, the scene left no doubt in his mind that it revealed arson for the purpose of murder.

Somebody had gone to a great deal of trouble to turn this car into an elaborate, self-destructing death machine.

Camello then began searching for the source of the gasoline leak. Despite the strong, persistent odor, he could find

no ruptures in the tank itself. He untied the end of the rope
from the pointed metal bar and pulled the bar's pointed end
down, away from the fuel tank. Once the pointed bar no
longer blocked his view of the tank, Camello noted that there
was a tiny area of the tank's surface that had been scraped
clean. It looked as if the point had momentarily brushed the
metal, such as it might do in a collision of insufficient force
to actually cause a rupture. Thus, it was possible to speculate
that if the big Cadillac had not been stopped by the telephone
pole, and if the car's huge V-8 engine had gone on building
momentum until the car hit the retaining wall at the road's
dead-end, the metal bar could have rammed and punctured
the gas tank. With the rope "wick" still burning and attached
to the metal bar secured under the fuel tank, there could have
been an explosive, extremely hot fire. With the amount of
gasoline pooled inside the heavy car's interior, Camello
knew that the county coroner would have been lucky to be
able to identify the car's two passengers through dental records.

Paramedic 3 Clyde Piephoff climbed in the back of the ambulance to prepare to load the patient with Paul, the trainee.
Todd got in front to drive them to the hospital. After repeatedly asking the patient if she could tell him the name of
the other woman in the car, Clyde finally got a momentary
response from the young woman. She was able to murmur
the name "Patty," but did not give a last name. Clyde went
back to check the car for IDs and found two purses, one with
a driver's license in the name of Claire Peernock. He assumed the other purse must belong to Patty, whom his patient
had identified as the deceased woman. If the disoriented
woman in his ambulance was Claire Peernock, she certainly
didn't look like she was over forty years old, as the California driver's license indicated. In fact, neither of the two
women looked that old, but their faces were so bloodied and

distorted by the trauma that anything was possible. There was no time to sort it out. One of the paramedics tossed Claire Peernock's purse into the ambulance while they all got ready to roll.

As the first pale light of predawn began to show, supervising paramedic Clyde Piephoff greeted the day knowing he had just received a hard-core illustration of the need to be prepared to deal with anything, at any time on his twenty-four-hour shift.

"Do you know your name?"
   "Do you know where you are?"
   "Do you have any idea what happened to you?"
The gentle questions of the paramedics drifted in Natasha's ears. They stirred reflexes in her brain, even elicited a few partial responses. But those responses, the words and the pieces of words, didn't come from Natasha as anyone knew her. They didn't even come from Natasha as she knew herself. They were spatters from her unconscious thought stream, bubbling up through her vocal cords like sprays of some nonsense conversation held with a sleepwalker.

Because Natasha was hovering in a place where things she had done long ago were occurring over and over on a never-ending loop, while things she had only planned to do in the future seemed to have already taken place. Any response that people in the so-called real world would get from her now would only come from far down inside of that place, where dreams and memories and plans and fears all jumble up like brightly colored bits of glass shaken together in a box.

The paramedics did everything they could to get her to fight her way back to a semblance of consciousness, but Natasha was wandering the darkness down where the nightmare factory likes to crank up its assembly line deep in the night. Where familiar shapes can turn into monsters and strike out at you, then snap back into harmless images, all in the blink of an eye. She was alone in the innermost chamber of some dark cave where the paramedics, the police, the doctors, could not go. They couldn't even summon her back.

If Natasha returned at all, she was going to have to come back on her own.

CHAPTER

2

It was after midnight on July 23, more than twenty hours after the crash was discovered, when Natasha's consciousness slowly returned. She fought to open her swollen eyelids, but the torn, puffed flesh around her eyes barely let in any light. Overhead lights were on; there was nothing around her to indicate time. Her contact lenses had been removed, leaving a haze she could only see through well enough to realize that she was lying in a hospital bed. She got the impression that she was the only patient in the room, but had no idea yet that the severity of her wounds and the intensity of her treatment had dictated a private recovery environment. In fact, she had awakened earlier, just long enough to be approved for transfer from the ICU to a private room, but she had no memory of that.

Moments later, while she fought back the groggy remnants of anesthesia, she became aware of a nurse puttering about her bedside, adjusting IV drips, monitoring her vital signs.

When the nurse saw Natasha's eyes flutter open she smiled down at her with a detached, professional gaze. "Do you know where you are?" the nurse asked softly.

Natasha had to struggle to make her lips form a word, to make her throat push out a sound. "A hospital." Her voice rasped out in a dry whisper.

"That's right," the RN said, never dropping her trained smile. "How does your head feel? Do you think you could answer a few questions?"

"What—what hap—what happened?" She pushed the

whisper a little harder, but her vocal cords weren't ready to come back on-line.

"Well, it seems that you were in some kind of an accident. A car accident. So can you tell me your name?"

"Natasha." She quit pushing her voice and let the whisper do the work. Her mouth was too dry. Her tongue felt thick and heavy.

"And your last name?"

"Peernock." The moment she pronounced her family name, Natasha felt a small shock wave go through her. She wasn't sure why.

"Good, and what year is it, Natasha?"

Natasha's first name sounded odd, coming from this woman. People who know her usually just call her Tasha, sometimes shortening it simply to Tash. To hear the formality of her full name as she lay helpless only emphasized to her that she was in a strange place.

But a moment later she realized that she couldn't answer the question. She didn't know what year it was. At first it felt kind of funny to find a piece of her memory gone. It wasn't like anything she had ever heard about amnesia. After all, she knew who she was. And when the RN told her that this was Holy Cross Hospital, she recognized the name; she had driven by the place in the past. But her memory had been Swiss-cheesed and little pieces were simply missing. She got her street address right, but she couldn't remember the name of the current U.S. President. She could picture his face but the name was blank.

And now another shock wave jolted her. This one was stronger. It shot through her like an icy wind and suddenly she didn't feel like answering any more riddles. Her right hand rose absently to her forehead and sent strange messages to her brain: her hair was gone—there were sutured gouges all across her face and head.

But the messages were too much to deal with at the moment.

"My mother was with me." As Tasha spoke the word *mother* it caught in her throat. She didn't know why. She knew, but she couldn't focus on the thought.

"Where's my mother?" She kept her voice quiet, almost timid.

The nurse was well trained and her smile hardly wavered. "You can see your mother later." She started for the door. "Rest now. You've just come out of surgery. We were concerned about you there for a while. I'm sure your mother would want you to rest."

"My mother—" she began again, but the nurse was making good her escape. She was nearly all the way out the door as she turned back to offer one last polished smile. "We'll be coming in and out to check on you," she chirped as she disappeared.

But those last words and their artificial assurance didn't matter anyway. Natasha barely heard them. Distant images, sounds, and voices suddenly overwhelmed her: a revolver's chamber spinning next to her ear, over and over and over . . . crashing sounds of a violent struggle coming from the other side of a bedroom wall . . . the cold feel of steel handcuffs . . . the suffocating panic as thin straps tightened around her throat . . . ropes being pulled tight around her ankles . . . a voice assuring her that she was going to be killed.

The second registered nurse to check on Natasha that evening was just making a routine stop. She didn't know much about the patient. She knew the young woman was a severe head-trauma victim of an auto accident earlier that morning. She knew that an ER test had indicated that there was a .053 blood alcohol level hours after the accident. The odor of alcohol had still been on her breath. Traces of some form of narcotic had also been in her bloodstream. Most likely another drunken car wreck.

The nurse also knew the hospital had been notified that shortly before 11:30 that evening a neighbor named Carl Rowe had come down to the coroner's office and positively identified the fatality as being this patient's mother. But the RN wasn't about to be the one to get stuck with breaking the news.

So she walked into the room determined to do no more than make sure the patient was awake and remaining alert. The nurse would check the IV drip rate, the vitals, assure that the patient's orientation was returning. She would leave the emotional confrontations to somebody else.

But the moment the RN stepped inside, the patient turned to her and began to display great anxiety. It's common for head-trauma patients to register inappropriate levels of emotion as a side effect of their injuries, so the nurse began her routine and answered the questions with matter-of-fact professionalism.

"Where's my mother?" The young woman moaned. "Where—"

"You can see her later," the nurse replied in the prescribed line that had been carefully crafted to tell the truth even while concealing it.

"My father, then. Where is he?" The young woman's voice was still thick from anesthesia, from the trauma. Clearly she was forcing herself to speak, showing great concern. Still, the symptoms were common enough, not at all unusual for a head-trauma victim.

"I don't think your father was involved. No one said anything to me about a male victim being at the scene. Don't worry. Try to get some rest. You took a real—"

"No. My father . . . the police . . . my father—"

The nurse had finished her brief check. There were a lot

of other patients left to go. The work load left no time for chat.

"Try to rest. You were in a serious accident."

The RN remained in the doorway for a moment longer than her schedule permitted. The patient was so distraught that the nurse paused to offer more reassurances, telling her not to worry about her father for the time being, reciting the line about how she could see her mother later. There wasn't much else she could do to ease the patient's agitated state. Strong tranquilizers can't be given to head-injury patients so soon after surgery and the nurse couldn't stay any longer to offer personal comfort. So she just made a mental note to add a few extra stops to this room on top of the usual schedule of every fifteen minutes that the patients in critical recovery normally get at Holy Cross.

And then she was gone. In the back of her mind she was already reviewing the history on the next patient.

Even though Natasha lay helpless, unable to take any physical action, old mental skills that she had honed with years of practice went to work automatically. She struggled to focus her mind, to force herself to remember everything and glue it all into place. She ran through the memories as if through a piece of film, staring hard at the mental images just as she had learned to do years ago, back when some inner wisdom had told her that the very first resource of those who refuse to be willing victims is to remember. Remember everything. Remember with a vengeance.

Part of her wondered fearfully where her father was at that very moment. Was he nearby, trying to get into the hospital? Would she even know him if he appeared in the room? Without her contact lenses, she couldn't see as far as the door frame; shapes were blurred so badly at that distance, she wouldn't even know if the person coming in was wearing a hospital uniform.

Natasha had no idea how much longer she might survive, but enough of her memory had returned so that she knew without a doubt that there was somebody out there with a very strong motivation to kill her before she could remember all of the details. And before she could get someone to listen to her. So as each minute dragged by, she labored to retrieve every scrap of memory and set it in proper order among the others. To remember.

It had been just after five o'clock on the afternoon on which the crimes began, when her best friend, Patty, pulled the white Ford Festiva to a stop in front of Natasha's house and parked with the engine idling. The July sun was still high over the horizon. It wouldn't be dark for over three hours.

"Sure you don't want me to come in, Tasha? Your dad's car is here."

"No," Tasha replied, getting out and closing the door. She leaned back into the open window. "I was supposed to do some laundry before we went to stay at Jennifer's last night. And I have to mow the lawn before we go back out. Besides"—Natasha teased her with a grin—"these are the same clothes we had on yesterday. You're not going to Magic Mountain in that outfit, are you?" They been friends for a long time; it was never hard for Tasha to get a rise out of Patty. And Tasha knew just how far she could get away with pushing her.

"Hey, I don't have to go change right this *second*." Patty scowled, annoyed. But she glanced at Robert Peernock's car and made no move to turn off the engine.

"Go on." Natasha smiled wanly. "I'll call in a couple of hours. My Fiat's still dead, so if Mom won't let me use her car when she gets home from work, you can come back." She noticed that Patty didn't look pleased. "Hey—okay?"

Patty sighed and met Tasha's eyes with a resigned smile. "Yeah, okay. But I'm *sure* your mom will just fork over her keys after the way you trashed her car before. Look, it's not like I'm afraid to come in if you want me to.''

"I know, I know. I'll call you." Natasha pushed away from the window. "Remember to call Eric and Jeff and make sure they're still going to meet us." She waved and Patty nodded, then drove off.

The front door was locked. This caught her by surprise. She had to pause for a few moments and fish around for her key. The house was usually unlocked when anybody was home, and right now both of her father's cars were in the driveway. He hadn't lived with the family for the last four years, spending nearly all his time at his girlfriend's condominium thirty miles away. But although Tasha had been hoping to get her chores done before her mother came home from work, it was clear that she wasn't going to be alone there today.

Her father was somewhere inside the house.

She got the door open, stepped in, closed it behind her. It had been a long time since she had come home to find him there. For years now, if some errand required him to be at the house, he had always made it a point to be gone before her mother got home. That policy suited Natasha fine; she didn't need to listen to the fighting. Now she paused on the tile section inside the doorway and listened for just a moment. The house was totally quiet. It seemed empty.

Tasha hoped she was going to be in luck.

She didn't realize she'd been holding her breath until she heard herself sigh heavily as Robert Peernock appeared from the backyard and opened the sliding glass door to come inside. She had a straight view to the back of the house while he stepped in. Their eyes met through the glass. If she stayed in his line of vision they would have to talk, but if she didn't talk he might take it as an insult. So she broke off the gaze and headed down the hallway to her bedroom just as he stepped inside and shut the sliding door behind him. Tasha tried not to hurry. She knew that if she rushed, it might provoke him.

The words would pepper her like bullets. What are you running from? What did you do this time? So she hurried, the way she had learned to do: keeping her moves casual but quick.

The escape was good. A few seconds later she was in her room, hoping for the sound of the front door closing and for his car to start up in the driveway. She wondered, why was he here so late, anyway? For the past month or so he had been coming around much more than usual, nearly every day, picking up personal items, paper files, clothing, tools. And whenever she happened to come in while he was there, he never failed to berate her about something: her friends, her schooling, her style of dressing, the cost of utilities in the house. Name it.

"The same old yelling story," she called it. There was no use fighting it. Instead she became skilled at avoidance.

Tasha puttered around the room, killing time. She changed into more casual shoes to mow the lawn in and decided not to put on fresh clothing until her chores were done. And still there was no sound of him leaving. Finally she ran out of ways to kill time and gave up in exasperation. She couldn't hang up the rest of the day by hiding, so she decided to just go on out. Carry out her business as quietly as she could. Work on her invisibility.

She didn't see him when she walked back down the hallway and went into the kitchen, so she relaxed a little and began making herself something to eat. It was just a snack before going out. Her plans for the evening didn't include having dinner at home. She hadn't started eating yet when Robert walked into the kitchen from the family room. At first everything seemed normal enough. He leaned against the door frame and watched her for a moment. Then he casually asked if she had any plans for the evening.

But she wasn't about to open that can of worms if she didn't have to. She told him she wasn't sure.

He asked if Patty was coming over. Robert knew they were inseparable. Patty had lived there for several weeks recently while she was having trouble at home. She stayed until it got worse there than it was at her place and her own home didn't look so bad anymore. But Robert hadn't taken a liking to her and Tasha knew he wouldn't be thrilled to hear that they were planning on staying out late with friends tonight. So she played dumb on that one too.

Tasha tried to focus on making her simple meal, trying to get the message across to him that there wasn't any point in talking to her, but doing it gently enough to avoid setting him off. It didn't do any good. He just kept hanging in the doorway. His questions turned to the topic of her mother. When was she due home today? Was she working late? Did she have plans tonight?

Tasha played dumb to all of it. But maybe she ignored her father a little too hard this time. Perhaps that's why the irritation in his voice changed so abruptly to raw anger. He suddenly dropped his questions, began pacing back and forth in the doorway, berating her for the high utility costs as he waved an electricity bill at her. He reminded her that even though he didn't live there he still paid a lot of the bills and that as long as she stayed in *his* home she was on *orders* to turn off the television, *every* time she left the room.

Throughout the tirade she glanced at him often enough to avoid making him feel he was being ignored. She had learned how to do it so that she hardly even saw him. Her concentration kept focused on getting the food ready, moving very evenly, deliberately. An invisible blanket softened the blows of his verbal attack.

Finally he played himself out and walked away from her in disgust. He returned to the backyard patio, sliding the glass door closed behind him as he went.

But he left the TV on in the family room. Tasha shook her head with a grim smile. So much for his concern about energy.

She began to hurry, trying to get the food ready while he was still outside. Maybe the chores could wait until tomorrow, if he wasn't going to leave her in peace. The food was almost ready. In a few minutes she could get it down and be gone. She could always walk to Patty's place; it wasn't that far. She could shower there if she had to, even borrow some clothes if there wasn't time to change before Robert came back inside.

But she was hungry, so she didn't walk out right away. She didn't want to give up on the idea of finishing her meal before she left.

She was just beginning to eat when Robert came back inside. At the same time, the sound of the sliding glass door somehow brought the blaring television in the next room back to her attention. It was galling to be yelled at so stupidly over some miserly energy policy that he didn't even follow himself.

The urge to fight back rose quickly inside her. She had just graduated from high school and felt the power of her independence, her beauty, her strong spirit. She might have kept her mouth shut if she had taken a moment to think about it, but the words leapt out into the air, fueled by years of resentment and this new feeling of strength that was just beginning to enter her life.

"What was that you said about the TV?" she called to him as he passed the kitchen door.

"What?" He stopped, turned back, stood glaring in the doorway. "What did you say?"

But she knew he had heard her. His voice tone gave it away. His expression.

Still, the need to recapture something of her assaulted dignity was strong inside her.

"The television," she continued. "I didn't turn it on. So who did?"

His eyes turned to steel. The corners of his mouth turned up slightly. But it wasn't a smile; it was smug, dangerous. Without words, the expression said, *You've played into my hands.*

Tasha wasn't really seeing him, even though her eyes looked directly at him. She felt offended down into the marrow of her bones by this father/stranger whom she saw as only coming over in the last four years when he felt like making trouble, grumbling around the place like some guy just waiting for anybody to knock the chip off of his shoulder. She was sick of the years spent standing silent under the onslaught of his same old yelling story. She had raised the invisible blanket again.

And so she just had to add one more line:

"Because you would never turn the TV on, and then walk out of the room for half a minute. Would you? Who's wasting the electricity now?"

She knew he would hit the ceiling at that one. She expected him to scream and yell and threaten her. She even knew that there was a good chance he would strike her, maybe knock her to the floor as he had in the past.

So she wasn't really all that surprised when, without a word, he leapt the distance between them and grabbed her with both hands around her throat. As he clamped her windpipe closed, her hands went instinctively to his wrists and held on tight. He didn't say a word as he pounced on her and she couldn't do anything more than gasp for what little air still managed to bleed in through her constricted throat.

Tasha's adrenaline spurted through her. It made their movements seem to snap into slow motion, as if the duo had lapsed into a deadly graveyard waltz. He drove her with his weight, forcing her to back up as he spun her around in the opposite direction and slowly walked her out of the kitchen.

Robert was six feet tall and weighed over 180. She struggled, but it was useless. At five feet eight inches and 130 pounds, even though Tasha's slim frame was built on long legs and firm muscles toned from her love of outdoors and physical activities, even though Tasha had grown up a tomboy and was never seriously accused of being a wimp by anybody, she had neither the physical nor psychological strength to mount any real defense against a sudden and brutal attack from her father.

He directed all the power of his rage into clamping her throat closed while he drove her steadily into the next room. Now, for the very first time since he had given her swimming lessons so many years ago, for the first time since Tasha was a doting toddler obedient to Daddy's every word, for the first time since those days, years before, when Robert was still the flattered father who loved his beautiful young daughter, the two moved once again in perfect sync.

They became a father-daughter dance team as they staggered onward together. Tasha's feet were barely on the ground as she struggled, twisted, writhed, in his grip. Dancing on air.

Moments later they ended their last waltz as she fell backward and Robert landed atop her on the floor of the family room. But even with Tasha flat on the floor and helpless in his grip, his hands kept biting into the soft flesh of her neck.

Up to that moment Tasha hadn't felt that afraid, not really. She became calm. If normal and natural fear was blasting through her insides at the realization that she was under deadly attack, years of conditioning had calloused the part of her where she ought to have felt it. Her instinct for self-preservation took over and prior family experience rushed in to go to work. She had weathered a lot of his violent storms in the past and had usually come through them without having to go to the hospital.

She knew the trick: Don't resist. Take whatever blows he

has to deliver and let his rage burn off before you get seriously hurt. Ever since she had foolishly stepped between Robert and Claire during that big family fight back when she was thirteen, ending up with a shattered arm and three weeks of traction for her foolishness, Tasha had learned well the lesson of dealing with her father's rage.

Let him lead; he feeds on open defiance. Keep him as quiet as you can and wait for your chance to escape.

But now the impact of the floor against her back and the weight of his body on top of hers brought Tasha's true emotions home. She instantly filled with a high-octane mixture of fear and outrage that struggled to explode out of her. She felt the cries building inside, hammering to get out. But the only point of self-control left to her was the need to avoid giving him the slightest satisfaction at terrorizing her. She strangled her own sobs down in her throat even harder than Robert was strangling her with the pressure of his thumbs. Keeping her eyes hard, she held the cries deep inside until, without warning—

Robert stopped the attack. It ended as suddenly as it had begun. He remained on top of her, panting slightly, staring down into her face. Tasha began to hope that it was finally over, that she had played him correctly and let him satisfy his rage and his need to assert domination before she had to endure a more serious form of violence.

"Are you okay?" he asked matter-of-factly, as if she had just fallen off a bicycle.

Tasha glared up at him as he pulled his hands from her throat. All her fear had already given way to indignant outrage. "I'll live," she answered as harshly as she could, voice still husky from the shock to her vocal cords.

She rubbed her throat and avoided looking into his eyes. She wasn't afraid to meet his gaze but didn't want to absorb any more of his energy than she had to.

Enraged thoughts flashed through her at lightning speed.

This was it, she thought to herself. She was out of this dump, permanently. After all, she'd only remained living in her mother's house because Robert had been separated from Claire for the last few years, supposedly giving Tasha a chance to grow up in some amount of peace. But if he was going to start showing up around the place again, acting this way whenever he wanted to, she was absolutely getting out. Now that she was eighteen nobody could force her to stay there anymore.

Meanwhile Robert kept staring down at her and regarding her curiously, as if wondering exactly what his next move should be. When he finally spoke all trace of his rage was gone.

"You have to understand, Natasha, I just can't go on like this anymore." He spoke softly, making an appeal for her to respect his deep need to strangle her. He shook his head sadly, full of pain. "Not the way my life is."

He sat back, still straddling her. But he didn't get up. He just shook his head again, deeply depressed about the way his life felt to him.

Natasha inhaled hard, pulling enough air into her chest to manage a reply. She forced the words out of her throbbing throat. "Well, you don't have to worry about it anymore. I'm moving out. Patty and I are getting our own place. I was going to tell Mom anyway. I'm never coming back here. I won't be a part of your life anymore."

Maybe her reply caught him off-guard; his response threw her a curve.

"Do you need any money?"

He remained on top of her, holding her flat on her back with his weight.

She glared up at him. So, she thought with disgust, now he was offering her a bribe.

"I don't want any money from you." She was used to his abrupt changes of tone, but from now on all of that would only exist in the past. Natasha knew in her heart that she would never willingly remain in this house now.

That turned out to be true. She would never live in that house again. But there was a much different reason for it, as she was only moments away from learning.

CHAPTER

3

Robert looked back down at Natasha for the last time before he rose. He seemed to have made his decision.

"I have something that will make you feel better," he said. He walked away, leaving her sitting stunned on the floor while he stepped out the front door of the house.

Tasha fought to regain her wind and her self-control. The fear was growing sharper inside her now. Whatever her father had to make her "feel better," she didn't want any part of it. It was abundantly clear that she had made a mistake in remaining in the house while he was still in the backyard. She didn't want to repeat it by waiting around to see what was coming next. But her thoughts ricocheted around without producing any answers while she labored to force a plan.

She couldn't go out the front without running into him. She could head for the back door, but the backyard was bordered by a steep hill and a wire fence blocking off an open field.

Both routes at the sides of the house would only lead from the back to the front, returning her to where he already was.

The garage door opened only a few feet from the front door, leading her back to Robert once again.

Of course if she really turned up the volume on the situation, broke the lifelong family taboo about exposing their troubles to the neighbors, she could run screaming into the street and hope that some neighbor would get involved on her behalf before Robert could hunt her down and hurt her badly. But after years of living in this area, the male neighbors mostly avoided Robert Peernock and the female neighbors rarely even came to the house if they saw Robert's car in the driveway.

What if nobody stepped in to help? What if nobody happened to be around to do anything at all, not even call the police?

Then he would have her. He would be very angry as he hauled her back into the house. Alone.

Her desperate attempts to form a plan never went any farther. She heard a car door slam just outside the front entranceway and before she could form the hope that he might drive off, she felt footsteps vibrate the floor behind her as Robert returned to the family room.

Everything began happening quickly. Before she could turn around she felt a burst of brute physical power seize her. It instantly took control. Her wrists were roughly grabbed from behind and held in back of her the way police will hold a suspect's arms; there is little muscle strength available for struggling in that position. Panic flooded her, gave her extra power to yank against the grip while she squirmed and fought as well as she could from her position on the floor.

Though she did everything possible to battle the much bigger man standing over her pinning her arms back, the conversation of wills was carried on without a single word. Nothing but gasping sounds came from both members of the father/daughter team. Their last dance together had turned to primal chaos.

In seconds Tasha felt steel bands snap tightly around her wrists, first one and quickly the other. She was able to twist around just far enough to get a glimpse of a pair of handcuffs. But in the next instant she felt her head forcibly twisted back to the front; she realized the handcuffs weren't the only things that her father had brought back inside to make her feel better. A flash of blue canvas flicked in front of her eyes and she felt her father's hands on top of her head. Some sort of rough fabric was pulled over her face. His hands were forcing it down over her eyes, her mouth, all the way down to the base of her neck.

Everything went dark. The hood had no eyeholes, only one small hole for her nose and another for her mouth. As she continued to fight him, kicking out with her feet in the last defensive moves left to her, a little bit of light sometimes bled in as the air holes moved around just enough to tease her with a glimpse outside. But each glimpse lasted only for a flashing instant before the darkness returned.

She tried to throw herself onto her side and rub the hood off her head by scraping her face on the carpet, but her father yanked her up into a seated position. She felt something like a hangman's noose dig into the base of her throat, searing the flesh.

Any further resistance was impossible.

But once she gave up her fight the tightness around her neck loosened slightly. She felt his fingers fumbling behind her at the back of the hood and realized that what had felt like a noose was actually some kind of lacing tied at the base of the canvas, woven through the fabric like shoelaces. Even as the pressure eased and allowed her to breathe without choking, she could feel the tiny loops of the laces digging into the flesh at the base of her throat and at the sides of her neck. She had no choice but to remain still. If she moved her head very much it pulled the hood tighter against her throat, cutting off her air.

Now, as she found herself handcuffed and hooded and pinned to the floor, Tasha could clearly feel the bite of her fear. The long-standing protection that had always been afforded to her by the invisible insulation blanket around her feelings was of no use. With her skin, with her flesh, and with the marrow of her bones she felt all too clearly the piercing cold terror blasting through her.

And some part of her that didn't give a damn about handling the situation carefully just had to know whether or not she was watching her life in this world come to an end. She blurted out the words before she could stop herself.

"Are you going to kill me?"

"Yes." The answer landed like a blow from a blunt instrument. No more explanations about how Robert's life couldn't go on this way anymore, no more pleading for her to understand. Just yes, Natasha, one of the things Daddy had brought you to help you feel better after being choked and dragged into this room and thrown on the floor is to assure you that your fears are correct. He is going to kill you.

The hood's mouth hole wasn't much bigger than a dime, just large enough for the next surprise. She felt a rigid plastic tube press against her lips as it was jammed through the hood. Tasha started to cry out in reflex, but as soon as her lips parted the stiff tube was shoved down into her mouth. She had to concentrate to fight back the gag reflex, fearing that if she vomited she would surely choke to death right there on the floor of the family room.

She didn't know how it was being held in place, but she couldn't spit the tube back out. Tasha wasn't able to form words anymore even if she tried. The tube had focused all her efforts on breathing.

The next sound seemed out of place, surprisingly harmless in the midst of this horror show. The squeaky pump of a spray bottle reminded her of cleaning windows in the summertime, or cleaning the glass doors leading out to the patio where her father had been when she failed to get out of the house on time. Cleaning the patio doors wasn't one of the chores Tasha was supposed to do that afternoon, but it didn't matter anymore. The other chores weren't going to get done either.

She could hear it easily, right in front of her. But it wasn't pumping window cleaner; Tasha tasted alcohol dribbling through the tube and into her mouth. She thought it must be some kind of hard liquor, but she didn't drink hard liquor and couldn't tell what kind it was. The taste was strong, harsh. She coughed and tried to spit it back out, gagging it back onto the fabric of the hood.

"Swallow it, Natasha. This is the best way. Just swallow it."

He pushed her down onto her back again and held the tube firmly in place as the harmless little pumping sound continued. Squirt, squirt, squirt, the alcohol ran down the tube and into her mouth, slowly enough for her to swallow, not so fast that it would run out and leave evidence on the carpet.

"Just swallow it," he kept repeating, trying to persuade her that accepting the alcohol he was force-feeding her was the best way.

He didn't specify if it was the best way for her or for him, but by openly assuring her that she was about to die he was showing entirely new behavior from Tasha's past experience. She tried to think of anything at all that he might do to get himself out of the trouble he would be in if anyone ever learned what he had done here today, but she realized it would be impossible for him to explain it. In just these few minutes, things had already gone too far for explanations.

She thought again of his matter-of-fact tone of voice when he'd answered her trembling question by confirming that, yes, he was going to kill her all right. Try as she might, Natasha couldn't think of a single reason to disbelieve him. Not during the next two or three minutes while he continued to force the alcohol into her, and not when he decided to go to the next stage of his plan of activities to make her feel better and dragged her to her feet, forcing her to stumble blindly down the hallway. When she felt him turn her to the

right, Tasha knew that they had entered her mother's bedroom. The one with the pleasant mess scattered around on
the dresser, testimony to Claire as a working mother with
little time for cleaning off a dresser no one else was supposed
to see anyway. The photo of Natasha's beautiful smiling face
sat in its elaborate wooden frame, reflected in the mirror next
to the little ceramic Doberman puppy and the tiny man made
of silver wire, swinging forever back and forth on his bal-
ancing bar.

Natasha imagined herself reflected in the mirror as he
shoved her down into a seated position on the bed. Her
cuffed hands braced her from tipping over backward. Her
fingers could feel the familiar touch of her mother's bedspread. It was the only thing familiar to her in this haunted-
house nightmare of distorted sensations.

Her father pumped a little more alcohol into the tube, but
this time the pumping didn't last long. Robert Peernock was
a list maker, an itemizer of objects and activities; at this point
he still had plenty of items yet to check off on his list of
objects and activities designed to make Natasha feel better
after being strangled.

His hands left her body. Briefly, the hope ricocheted
through her that he would leave the room, maybe leave the
house. But the hope never had time to fully form. All he did
was lean over and turn the radio on. An FM station was
preset to play classical music, the way Claire liked it. Robert
left it tuned to that station. Now Tasha's encounter with her
father in her mother's bedroom had some refined musical
accompaniment.

He got up, but he still didn't leave her. A moment later
Tasha heard her mother's closet door open. She tried to quell
the panic, struggling to think clearly. What could her father
be looking for inside her mother's closet? The answer came
flashing back: of course. The closet wasn't only her mother's.

Though Robert had moved out years before, he still kept

a large presence of himself in the house. His files, office records, tools, clothing, and personal objects were scattered everywhere like voodoo tokens guarding the house from another man's intrusion. The bedroom may have been used only by Claire now, but as a wave of nausea twisted Natasha's insides she remembered that Robert had things in the closet too.

He had guns in the closet: a shotgun, a revolver. He kept plenty of ammunition in the closet. And as he emerged he didn't keep her guessing about what it was he had been rummaging around to find. She heard it, right next to her ear: click-click, snap . . . click-click, snap . . . that would be the revolver, the black six-shooter with the wooden handle.

Her father was holding the barrel of the gun at her head and pulling the double-action hammer back, rotating the bullet chamber, pulling the trigger. She didn't know if the gun had any bullets in it right now or not. But she knew there were bullets in the closet. Plenty of them.

Up to this point Robert had been a man of few words, but now he apparently felt it was time to speak again.

"Natasha . . ."

Click-click . . . snap.

"If you don't cooperate with me . . ."

Click-click . . . snap.

"I'm going to—"

Click-click . . .

"Blow your brains out."

Snap.

Tasha couldn't answer; the tube was still in her mouth. But she did the next best thing. She sat quietly and offered no resistance. Robert didn't like resistance. Things had been great between them when she was still a little girl and accepted his authority unquestioningly. She had always told her friends that he didn't begin to hate her until she developed into a willful young woman—and started putting up resistance.

And now her plan worked, in a way. He didn't begin beating her. He just went to the next item on whatever checklist he was working from and took steps to make sure she wouldn't be offering any resistance, whether she felt inclined to or not.

He pushed her onto her side, knocking the tube out of her mouth. He pulled her feet up onto the mattress and quickly tied her feet together with rope. She couldn't see the rope but she could feel the bristles against the skin of her ankles.

And now it would seem that the next item on Robert's list was to hog-tie Natasha like an animal being prepared for slaughter. A moment later she felt her father roll her over onto her stomach and yank her feet behind her, all the way up to her wrists. Then he tied the rope that was binding her ankles to the chain between the handcuffs.

And still Robert was at no loss for ideas. Tasha felt the stiff tube jammed through the mouth hole once more and again forced between her lips, far back into her mouth. She heard the friendly little pumping sound, tasted the harsh liquor as it began to dribble into her mouth. By now she knew better than to try to spit the alcohol out. He was in no mood for resistance.

"Swallow it, Natasha," Robert commanded, no doubt feeling sure that here at last was a teenager a parent could deal with. "Swallow it. It's the easiest way."

She had to swallow some of it now, but still she tried subtly to let some of it leak out around the edges of the tube and onto the fabric of the hood. At first Robert didn't notice, he was busy giving her further orders.

"You need to cooperate, Natasha. It's very important."

Click-click . . . snap.

"You and your friends like to get high? Well, I'm going

to get you drunk. In fact, I'm going to get you and your mother both drunk.''

Click-click . . . snap.

''Then she's going to sign some papers. And if you're a good girl, Natasha, and if your mother does *exactly* like she's told, then I'm going to finally be able to get out of your life forever. You'd like that, wouldn't you? Hey, don't spit that out! Swallow it!''

Click-click . . .

''Or I'll blow your brains out right *now*.''

Snap.

Tasha began to swallow the alcohol. All of it. There was no more resistance left in her.

CHAPTER

4

It was 6:00 P.M. on the day the crimes began when Tina Nussbaum left for the evening. She didn't know that Claire Peernock's daughter was already bound and gagged inside Claire's bedroom, but as Claire's boss at a property management firm in West Los Angeles, she knew that Claire was staying behind at the office to catch up on some late work. That was nothing unusual. Claire always tried to book as much overtime as she could; Tina had known that about her when she hired her as a secretary five months earlier. Since that time, Claire had often been the last to leave at night, but she never seemed to abuse the overtime privilege. Once the work was caught up for the day, she always locked up and went home.

They had become friends of a sort, and over time Claire had gradually confided her marriage difficulties to Tina. Speaking in her soft voice and delicate French accent, Claire told how she had nearly gone through with the divorce before Christmas, but Robert had urged some kind of a six-month "cooling-off period" for reasons of his own.

The whole thing about a cooling-off period or any kind of possible reconciliation seemed odd to Tina, since Claire made no secret of the fact that Robert had been living with his girlfriend throughout that time and that he kept his youngest daughter with him whenever she didn't have to stay at Claire's to attend her grade school across the street from the house. Claire seemed relieved that this coming weekend the girl was to return to her home and get ready for the new school term on Monday.

Tina knew the deadline on the temporary hold in Claire's divorce action was only nine days away. Then Claire could begin to officially disentangle her life from a man she described as causing her so much fear and unhappiness.

It was good to see Claire determined to get her house in order. Claire had an easy laugh and a playful sense of humor. She never showed any outward signs of depression over her situation, but Tina could guess at the amount of pain it would take to cause her friend to work so many long hours. The overtime was Claire's only way of creating a financial cushion thick enough to make sure that once her divorce began, she wouldn't have to fear being unable to provide for her children.

So Tina left feeling relieved to know Claire was finally about to get away from the clutches of a man who seemed to have caused her so much hurt and given her such reason to fear him.

Of course, she had only heard Claire's side of the story. Tina was a fair-minded person, so as she walked out to her car she reminded herself that there was no way of knowing for sure if Robert was really as dangerous as all that.

Once Robert finally got Tasha to accept the alcohol as it flowed down the tube, he seemed to tire of the game. After another few sprays, she felt him walk away. Then everything got quiet. She didn't hear Robert close the bedroom door as he walked out, but it felt somehow as if he had. She lay helpless on the bed, hearing only the delicate music on her mother's bedside radio and the hammering of her own pulse in her ears.

By that point the amount of alcohol he had forced down her wasn't all that much, so she could still think fairly well despite the liquor and the emotional shock of the attack. But as she began to try to weigh out the situation, it was clear to her that she was no longer physically able to help herself; the hood was tight around her neck and she was still hog-tied. Even if she could somehow make it over to the bedroom window, there was no way to climb out and certainly no way to run. The room had a phone, but she couldn't move toward it without making noise. It would be impossible to dial. Even if she reached someone, he would surely hear her speak. Wouldn't he kill her instantly?

She was going to have to hope for some kind of outside help.

Tasha lay quietly while her thoughts screamed through her. She tried to guess how much time had gone by, knowing that it had probably been between 5:30 and 6:00 when the attack began. Perhaps another half hour had passed since then. Her mother could be home from work at any time after six o'clock, but she almost always worked overtime whenever she had the chance. That meant Claire could come walking into the house in a matter of minutes or a matter of hours.

But even if she came home right away, Robert's idea about forcing them to get drunk and coerce Claire to sign some papers didn't make much sense. Claire didn't drink to any degree. If Robert actually thought he was going to get her to sit down and knock back a few stiff ones, he was badly mistaken. To get alcohol into Claire he would have to more or less repeat the situation with Natasha, taking her by surprise. He would either have to do it as soon as she walked into the house, or, by posing as being there late in the evening on some errand, maneuver her into some position for a surprise attack. Tasha knew Robert would never get Claire to drink with him voluntarily. And certainly she would never sign anything simply on his demand, not without putting up strong resistance.

So if Claire came home alone, as she almost always did, what defense would she have against a surprise attack from the man she still trusted enough to allow him open access to her home?

The classical music pieces on the radio seemed to go on forever, making it hard to gauge how much time was passing. By the time one would end she didn't have any idea how long it had played. Sometimes another would come on without the announcer ever saying a word and it would play for an entirely different length of time.

But she was sure he hadn't left the house. He could never risk having his daughter found there like that by Claire or Patty or anyone else. No, he was somewhere nearby. And whatever he was doing in some other part of the house right now, she had no doubt he would be back.

Eventually the edge of the mattress sank down again under his weight. Fingertips played at the base of her neck as he untied the hood, pulling it back up over her face and off her head.

Then Robert's face was there, right in front of hers. She met his eyes, searching for some connection that might tell her there was an end to this in sight. But she found nothing, no hint of compassion, no trace of doubt about what he was doing. He had launched into some kind of plan and showed no hesitation. The expression told her she could forget any hope that he might falter or reverse the course he was following now.

"I can't feel my hands anymore," she said softly.

He regarded her for a moment, wondering, perhaps, if she was going to try anything funny. But then, Robert had control now.

He released the handcuffs and untied the rope that held her feet back against the cuff chain. Keeping her ankles tied together, he lowered her feet to the floor and pulled her arms around to the front, then fastened the cuffs again. But they weren't as tight this time. They didn't need to be. He had control to spare.

He held up a small glass full of amber-colored liquor. "Drink up," he ordered, businesslike, a stern bartender suggesting some original concoction.

Tasha held the glass and sipped without fighting, but she had trouble getting it down. It was the same stuff that had dribbled down the tube, and the strong liquid kept gagging her. She turned her head for a second, trying to shake off the taste. The blue canvas hood caught her eye as it lay on the bedspread. She could see the plastic tube still wedged into the mask's small mouth hole and saw for the first time that the tube was red in color. Teeth marks covered the mouth side of the tube. She realized that she must have chewed it nervously while Robert was out of the room.

But Robert pulled her gaze away from the face mask, taking her by the chin and holding the glass of liquor in his outstretched hand. "Come on, just cooperate. Drink it."

She got about half of the glassful down before she began to choke on it. This time Robert didn't push her to drink more.

"That's okay." He pulled the glass away, apparently satisfied that things were going as planned. But before he set the glass aside he produced a small oval-shaped white pill and put it between her lips. "Swallow it," he ordered, offering her one final sip of the liquor to wash it down. The fresh burst of fear that washed over Tasha quickly dissolved into resignation. If he was going to poison her now, there wasn't anything she could do to stop him. It might be better than the gun, anyway. She wondered if he could have gotten his hands on cyanide. Didn't cyanide have some special kind of taste to it? But whatever taste the pill might have was covered over by the alcohol. In another second the pill was swallowed down.

Robert set the glass down on the nightstand. When he moved out of her line of vision she got a quick glimpse of the spray bottle resting there as he set the glass down next to it.

A moment later he picked up the hood, pulling the leather strips so that the bottom of the hood was wide open. He moved closer to her with it. She didn't bother lifting her cuffed hands to stop him; in seconds it was back over her head. And then everything was dark again. She felt the thin leather laces dig into her flesh as they were pulled tightly against her throat. He pushed her back over onto her side and walked out of the room, leaving Tasha to count her heartbeats by the throbbing in her throat. If he had indeed given her some kind of a drug, she felt no effect so far. The fear coursing through her must have beaten back any sense of being under the influence.

But if the pill was really some kind of poison, she wondered whether she would feel anything before it killed her. She lay quietly, searching her senses for any poisonous reaction. Minutes began to crawl by. Five . . . ten . . . fifteen. Time thickened.

She became aware of Robert nearby again, felt him pour more alcohol into the tube. It was easier to swallow, now. Soon he was gone once more.

The silence inside her became warmer as the music on the radio drifted up and down. It reminded her of some faraway boat bobbing along on the ocean, way off on the horizon. Natasha drifted with the boat, floating toward some destination she couldn't begin to imagine, letting the current carry her along, helpless to do anything to alter its course. At some point an announcer on the radio gave the time: eight o'clock. Still, nothing happened. Nothing changed.

Until Robert's voice stabbed her.

"Don't make any noise!" he hissed. The sharp jolt shot through her electrically. She was instantly awake, her heart slamming, every sense wide open. Her father was there, right over the bed. He had come out of nowhere.

Her hearing had been sharpened by the blindness forced upon her. She picked up the difference in his voice right away. The volume was soft but his tone was harsh, desperate. She realized that something must have gone wrong with his plan. Something had entered into the situation that he'd never counted on.

Then her heart leapt into overdrive. Of course! Patty was there, it had to be her. Tasha's breath began to heave in her chest like that of a sprinter pushing for the finish line. It *must* be Patricia. Instant gratitude flowed through her for whatever wisdom had kept her from revealing her plans for the evening when Robert asked about them.

And now her best friend was there to pick her up! Patty must have gotten tired of waiting for her to call and just decided to come on over. Help from the outside: her only hope had just become Robert's worst nightmare.

Tasha heard her father duck back out of the bedroom and close the door. Her thoughts spun like wheels on slippery ice as she tried to think of how to use this chance. If she screamed now, would anyone outside the house hear her through the face mask, through the closed bedroom door, through the closed front door of the house? How long could she scream before Robert would be on her like a wolf bringing down a rabbit?

Besides, what if Patty was alone? Surely the front door was locked, just as it had been when Tasha came home. So what was Patty supposed to do, kick her way in like a SWAT team? What could she do against Robert, armed and waiting inside for her? Even if Tasha screamed and Patty ran for help, how long would *that* take? And in the meantime, what would Robert do to her in his panic and in his rage?

She couldn't scream.

Maybe Patty would just figure out that something was wrong and call somebody. Tasha fought to remember: did Patty know where Claire worked? Could she reach Claire even if she wanted to? A warning call to her mother at work might bring a call to the neighbors, maybe even the police.

Then she remembered—Patty could get in the house whether it was locked or not.

When the two lived there they had both used a method of jimmying the lock on the window next to the front door whenever they forgot the keys. If Patricia got curious enough about things, if she started to wonder if maybe Tasha had fallen and hit her head in the shower or God knows what, then she could be in the house almost as fast as anyone else could open the door with a key.

Tasha felt her blood run cold. Her heart sank as the question beat its way into her thoughts: Where was Robert right now? Was he cowering on the other side of that window, just in case his daughter's best friend should get curious and decide to come on in, ruin his plans? And if Patty started in the window, what fate was waiting for her at this moment on the other side?

Tasha began to concentrate with all her might, to reach out mentally through an act of sheer willpower. She pictured her friend as clearly as she could, while she beamed the simple message to her: *Get away. Get help from somewhere. Get away. Get help from* anywhere.

She sent silent images of wrongness, feelings of danger. She wrapped them in a powerful mental plea and beamed it out with the energy of desperation to the one friend in the world she was closest to at this point in her life.

Bad trouble, Patricia.

The very worst kind of trouble.

Patty knew that Eric and Jeff weren't going to hang out in her backseat all night waiting for her to figure out what was the deal with Tash. But it was her car, after all, and this neighborhood had some *vicious* hills for foot traffic. No, Patty knew that the guys were going to have to get a lot more pissed off before they actually got out and started walking. Besides, hitchhiking to Magic Mountain would be a complete drag. So Patty figured she could give this thing another couple of minutes.

Because so far it was totally weird.

She had been calling the house over and over, beginning shortly after arriving home that afternoon. There had never been any answer, just that new answering machine Tasha's dad had installed at the house three or four weeks before. It was bad enough having to leave messages on a machine with *his* voice answering the phone when he didn't even live there, but not to get any answer from her friend, hour after hour—it gave her a creepy feeling that had grown stronger all afternoon.

The feeling had started when she'd happened to pick up her senior yearbook after getting home that day. She had reread Tasha's note to her on one of the pages inside. It talked about their friendship, their plans to take a trip to Lake Tahoe together. And for some reason she didn't fully understand, Patty picked up the phone and began calling over to Tasha's house, even though they had just spent the day together and had already made plans for the evening.

She just felt this need to hear Natasha's voice.

When the machine picked up her first phone call she wasn't too concerned, even though it was bizarre to have a phone machine there when she knew perfectly well that Claire had refused to have one in the house for so long. Patty hoped that maybe Natasha was just out in the yard mowing the lawn and that her father had already left. That would be fine with her. Still, she had felt the need to hear her friend's voice *right then,* not two hours later, so she kept calling and calling, leaving one message after another. As the time kept passing she didn't like the way that the feeling kept building up inside of her, even though she couldn't explain it. Finally she went and got the two guys and headed on over without waiting for Tasha to give them the go-ahead.

But she had been knocking on the door for several minutes, getting no answer. Both of Mr. Peernock's cars were still parked there just as they had been when Patty dropped off Tasha that afternoon. Darkness had closed in by now; she could see light from the TV screen coming through the curtain covering the front window.

Claire's car wasn't there. So, Patty thought, hadn't she come home yet or what? Natasha was pretty reliable, especially when it came to going out and having fun together. If something had come up, she would have called.

She went around to Tasha's bedroom window and knocked on it. Could her friend have fallen asleep?

"Hey, Tash, are you in there?" Patty called up at the window. No answer. Not a sound. There was something even stranger; the curtains were closed. Tasha never liked the curtains to be closed, and unless someone reminded her to shut them she tended just to leave them open. But now they were pulled tightly shut. And the TV was on inside. And nobody was answering the door.

Patty went back to the front, thinking that the whole situation was getting extreme. Mr. Peernock's Cadillac was parked there all the time, it was true, but it was usually just covered up and sort of stored there. His regular car, the one he drove mostly, was hardly ever there at night. This wasn't even his place anymore, really.

At that point she noticed that the grass hadn't been touched, although Tasha had made it clear that one of her chores was to cut the lawn before she went out that night. So what was the deal? Tasha had to keep up with the chores if she wanted to get any cooperation out of her mom. No, it wasn't like she would just blow it off or anything.

Finally she was back at the front door, knocking one last time. Was there a movement inside the house? Did she see a shadow pass across the window curtain, or was it some reflection from the TV screen?

She could always go through the window. It was a small section of lower window, not high off the porch level. Patty got down on her knees. She reached for the latch . . . and the little hairs on the back of her neck stood up straight.

A cold feeling washed through her, a funny kind of cold. It gave her gooseflesh as a little shudder shook her.

Patricia stopped short.

Natasha's best friend will never be able to prove that she was stopped by telepathy and not by sheer common sense. After all, on the practical side she knew better than to just barge into the house when Mr. Peernock was there. Back when Patty was staying there, he had made it clear that he didn't like any of Tasha's friends. And he wasn't supposed to know that the lock on his door was a joke to these two resourceful girls. She knew that even if Tasha was stuck in there with him, maybe being put on restriction for something or other, Patty wouldn't exactly be a welcome intruder. No, if Tash was going to make it out of the house, she'd already had plenty of chances.

And yet something made Patty turn away. Today she confirms that she can see it in terms of unspoken communication between two friends whose invisible link was strong. Whatever kept her on the safe side of the window that night—

She turned back.

Everything went quiet inside the house. Tasha tried to listen carefully, but the silence thickened again. Soon, with no disturbance to puncture the buzz of her thoughts, deprived senses began to focus on inner images alternating between hope and despair. She felt no doubt that Robert's burst of panic had come from Patty's arrival there, so while she lay physically helpless in the darkness and focused on pumping out messages of warning to her friend, she had listened with dread for the sounds of commotion. Now each minute of silence that passed gave her the growing feeling that somehow she had reached Patty and kept her away.

But would her friend actually call the police? It seemed clear that Patty was safe now, but how strong would a psychic message have to be to make Patty start some kind of huge ruckus with the neighbors or with the cops? With a sinking sensation Tasha realized that wasn't going to happen. And while she reasoned her way to that inevitable conclusion, a deep sense of dread began to creep through her.

It took another fifteen or twenty minutes for Robert to come back into the room after Patty left. But Natasha didn't ask what had happened. That would give away too much. No, she thought, let him wonder who else might be coming. Uncertainty was the only retaliation she could throw at him. Let him sweat.

For his part, Robert wasn't offering information either. With the tube again wedged into Natasha's mouth, he held her down on her back and poured another few swallows of alcohol into her. She heard no pumping sound this time; the stuff flowed faster, but still slowly enough for her to swallow most of it.

And then she heard him walk away. He disappeared back into whatever part of the house he was waiting in for Claire's return, back to whatever he was doing to keep himself busy in the meantime.

Now there was nothing to mark the passing of time except the long, unfamiliar selections of classical music and a soft-voiced announcer who tastefully avoided bothering the listener with idle chatter. The music on the radio began to blur into fuzzy collections of nattering instrumental lines, anonymous and hypnotic. Tasha lay still on the bed, inside the blackness forced upon her by the hood.

Time passed. More than a few minutes, less than a few

hours. Buzz time. Dream time. Tasha wasn't really conscious of any particular effect from the alcohol or the drug. But then there wasn't much to measure it by, bound and hooded and lying there as she was in total darkness.

The dogs. Niko and Queenie. Why were the dogs barking? Tasha struggled to come alert, forced her eyes open. But when they finally opened she still couldn't see anything.

Niko and Queenie were really going at it, going *crazy*. They hardly ever barked like that, never made that kind of noise at ordinary dog-bark things like cars going by, like strangers coming to the door. What had happened? Tasha couldn't think.

She cleared her mind enough to realize that the dogs weren't in the house. If they had been, the barking would have been much louder. Someone must have put them in the backyard. Was her mother home? She fought to clear her mind, but thoughts felt thick and heavy.

Then Tasha felt the fabric against her face, and she remembered. She wasn't aware of the handcuffs as the dogs brought her back to earth, but when she tried to roll over she felt the restraints against her wrists.

The dogs were frantic. They must be at the glass doors in back, jumping up against the panes, landing on top of each other the way they would do when something really set them off. It didn't happen often. Since they couldn't see the street or the sidewalk from the backyard, they were usually quiet unless something was going on inside the house that disturbed them. It would take a lot to get them this worked up, though. She had only seen it happen a few other times.

Like when her father tried to hurt her or her mother.

Something hit the floor in the next room with a huge bang. The family room. The impact vibrated through the wooden floors of the house, barely muffled by the carpeting on the floor. The sound went through Tasha as if she had just been slammed in the stomach. The dogs were going ballistic. She realized that whatever was setting them off must be right in their line of sight, visible through the glass doors. Niko and Queenie were watching whatever had made that sound. They were seeing, at this very moment, what she could only imagine.

And there it went again. A heavy thud shuddered the floorboards, as it would whenever Tasha and her sister were roughhousing in the family room, turning cartwheels. Falling down. Landing heavily on the floor.

As Tasha lay alone in her mother's bedroom, feeling her mother's bedspread against her skin, she stared into the black nothing that was given to her eyes by the homemade canvas hood. It was still held tight over her head with long leather strips laced through the bottom and pulled tight against her throat. But her mind's eye could almost make the switch, *almost* leave the hooded face mask and enter the eyes of the dogs and be with them there in the backyard, bouncing up and down two or three feet off the ground as the two white frantic furballs bellowed and snarled and clawed at the glass, watching these things that were making such heavy noises in the family room. Witnessing.

The floor banged again and the heavy thud was only a few feet away, just on the other side of the wall from where Natasha lay barely inside her own body. While her physical self remained helpless in the darkness, her awareness hung in the air halfway between her bound form and the eyes of the loyal pets she so desperately wanted to enter into and look out of, whose knowledge she wanted to share as they watched something taking place so close by that if it weren't for the hood she might see it through her own eyes. If it weren't for the handcuffs she might reach out with her own fingers. If it weren't for the thin wall separating the bedroom from the family room, her fingers might even brush momentarily against something as it went by, heading toward the floor again, toward the impact with the carpet covering the wooden floorboards, sending out the jarring thump that Tasha could feel traveling through the monster house.

Because the dogs knew. The dogs never made those kinds of noises unless something was dead wrong.

CHAPTER

5

Another thick pall of silence fell back over the house. Natasha's drained state overcame her at last. Lying silent in the darkness, pumped with alcohol and some mysterious drug, she couldn't measure how much time passed between intervals while she drifted in and out of real consciousness. During that time she had no further awareness of her father entering the room.

Much later, she roused herself enough to focus on the radio when the music paused. The announcer began to say something. She concentrated on the words, laboring to hear them clearly. When a brief time check was announced, her awareness seized upon it: eleven o'clock. For a moment she felt steadied by the knowledge, oriented as to time and place. She realized that her captivity had already gone on for six hours.

Although Niko and Queenie left her with no doubts that her mother had come home and that the thudding sounds in the next room, vibrating the floor and the walls, had been caused by a struggle between her parents, she had never actually heard their voices. There had been no screams, no shouting, no cries for help. She wondered fearfully what could have happened to her mother to keep her silent under such an attack.

But the answer came back to her as quickly as she formed the question; Tasha hadn't yelled or screamed either. Something about the shock of a sudden and brutal attack had stunned her into silence. Had the same thing happened to her

mother? After all, that simple question Tasha had posed
when she asked her father if he was going to kill her had
been spoken so softly that if others had been here in the next
room, they wouldn't have heard it either. Or had there been
some kind of brief shouting match before the dogs went into
action, had the alcohol numbed her to it?

There wasn't a sound anywhere in the house now. She
realized things must be very bad. Her mother would never
have remained in the house for so long after returning home
without entering her own room, not if she had been able to
move about freely. And she would never have remained in
the house at all after being attacked by Robert with the kind
of violence that had reverberated through the floors.

But if Claire ran outside, Robert would have to drag her
back in. If he wasn't able to catch her, then he would have
had to hurry in and take Natasha out before anyone could
discover her there. Her mother would have sent help to check
the house if she had been able to do it.

So had Robert presented Claire with the "papers" he mentioned? Had Claire scorned them? Of course Claire would
scorn signing anything on demand, with the divorce action
set to resume in just a few days. Had she spun on her heels
and started for her bedroom, thinking she was simply walking away from Robert? Worse yet, had she been threatened,
told that even now their daughter was bound and helpless on
Robert and Claire's former marital bed?

Tasha knew that would have sent Claire into an instant
rage. Her mother wouldn't have paused for an instant, not
even long enough to shriek her outrage at Robert as she
darted down the hallway to yank open the door and free her
captive girl.

And Robert would have had to stop her on the spot. Jump
her. If she had any idea that her daughter was in the house
suffering at Robert's hand, he would have to quickly render
her defenseless. He would have to do anything necessary to

make her unable to put up the resistance he loathed. Perhaps a full-fist blow to the side of her face, right below the temple, as he straddled her on the floor? The dogs would have a clear view there. They would go berserk at witnessing this attack upon the woman of the house by a man who was far less familiar to them. The sounds of such an attack would travel instantly all through the house, vibrating the floors, the walls, like rambunctious girls on rainy days turning cartwheels and landing on the floor.

The mind can only absorb so much horror and helplessness. Numbness filters in to protect it from the jagged edges of situations too awful to sustain.

The thick black blur descended on Tasha once more. She no longer knew if she was drifting in wakefulness or sleep as the time wheel turned unmarked. Only vague sensations found their way as far as her preconsciousness when she would shift position on the bed, try to lift her arms only to discover the handcuffs again, try to open her eyes only to encounter the hood once more. She never heard another announcement of time on the radio. If one was broadcast, it went by unnoticed.

Tasha had steadily pushed her sluggish brain through a process of elimination until it worked its way up to the realization that her mother had to be there still, somewhere inside the house.

But where was she now? Tasha floated away on the question.

Black velvet hands reached down out of the black velvet sky. She could clearly feel one hand travel under her knees as the other reached across the back of her shoulders, behind her arms.

''As a groom would carry a bride across a threshold'' is the way that both the prosecution and the defense would later refer to it, while attorneys jousted through their intense legal combat inside the courtroom where the search for truth is symbolized by a blindfolded young woman.

As a bride would be carried by a groom across the threshold, she felt herself lifted off the bed, carried out of the room, down the hallway. She was awake now and recognized the groom's body. She could tell that it was her father, built solidly, familiar to her in every respect, in his touch, his smell.

Not a word was spoken. Tasha was past asking questions that she knew would get no answers, or worse, that would get answers she had no more strength to hear.

They had traveled only a few steps before she felt her father bend over and lay her on the floor. They hadn't turned any more corners, so she knew that she was being placed in the family room. She recognized the feel of the carpet on the floor where she and her sister had once been boisterous girls playing in the house whether they were supposed to or not.

After a brief pause she was again picked up by the same strong arms. She felt herself borne a few more paces, turned sideways to slip through a door, carried down a couple of steps. She recognized the sensation of being in the garage. The outside air was relatively cold, the way it gets deep in the night up in the high desert, even in the middle of summer.

After a few more paces she was placed in a car and left there. The door was closed and everything became silent for a moment. She was almost in a sitting position, slumped to the right against the passenger-side door, her bound feet in front of her. She pushed her feet outward slightly, felt the back of the front seat, and realized she was in the back of her father's Cadillac. Her cuffed hands could reach down and stroke the smooth leather seats; it was the only car in the family with leather seats.

The Cadillac was roomy, even in the back. A backseat with room for three full-sized adults to ride America's roads

in luxurious comfort, if they are sitting up. It even had room
for two adults to slump sideways, hooded, bound hand and
foot, and packed in so well that the tops of their heads
wouldn't be visible to passing police cars. Or to curious pe-
destrians out for an early morning stroll. Or to the odd possibility of flirtatious single women idling in the next lane at
a stoplight somewhere and making eyes at the driver, a soon-
to-be-single married man deeply involved in the process of
simplifying his life.

Tasha could hear deep, regular breathing coming from
someone lying on the backseat next to her. With her hands
still cuffed in front of her, she was just able to reach over
and nudge the person. There was no response. But once her
fingers brushed the hair, the skin, she recognized the touch
of the woman she had spent her life with. And then the sound
of the deep, regular breathing registered clearly in her mind.
As a little girl growing up, she had listened to her mother
breathing during a hundred naps, had roused her mother on
countless wake-up-Mommy mornings. The sound of
breathing that had serenaded her even before she entered this
world needed no explanation.

The driver's door opened and someone got in. Tasha never
doubted it was her father. She had heard no other voices,
sensed no other presence in the house, when her father carried her to the car. But much later, when the Confusers would
come, she would be forced to admit that she hadn't been
able to see the driver. She hadn't heard the driver's voice.
She had never spoken with the driver of her father's car.

She didn't even make an attempt to speak with him, to
ask questions. Her senses told her once again that her best
chance for survival lay in passivity. Her father hadn't been
in a mood, all night long, to tolerate even the smallest resistance. So Tasha played possum and lay still in the darkness
of the backseat, inside the blackness of the hooded face
mask.

Now she felt the car begin to move as the driver she was sure was her father, but could never afterward prove to have been her father, drove the two family women away. They left behind once and for all this attractive house in this comfortable, upscale neighborhood that none of them would ever live in again. He rode alone up front like a chauffeur.

She guessed that they traveled for fifteen or twenty minutes, but by now she had endured hours of isolation, blinded and bound, terrorized and drugged. Her senses were struggling to make sense of the scrambled information coming to them, so that she couldn't be certain if the car was stopping from time to time at intersections or if it had moved onto the highway. As they rode she kept listening for the sound of her mother's breathing, hoping to hear some indication that Claire was waking up. But the breathing remained even and very deep. Even as Tasha fought the sleepy numbness and the sheer fatigue of a night of pain and fear, it was clear that her mother was not going to be able to help either of them.

Sometime later, just before Tasha was pulled entirely away from awareness by the hum of the tires on the road, she felt the car come to a stop. And still nothing was said from the driver's seat. She heard the driver's door open and immediately noticed the nearby sound of big trucks going by, moving very fast. She realized they must be near the highway. For a while she and Claire were left alone in the backseat while the driver whom she would never prove conclusively to be her father tended to other business. She heard and felt the trunk of her father's car being opened. There was a pause. Soon after, a metallic clanking sound began from the rear area of the car.

How strange it was, in the cold predawn air, to hear this purposeful, busy activity behind the car and to lie helpless beside her unconscious mother and feel these vibrations coming from the rear area, to hear some odd business taking place down near the gas tank and back near the Cadillac's rear towing hitch. It was the strong kind of towing hitch, easily capable of pulling a car such as Robert Peernock's much smaller Datsun F-10.

Tasha heard the rear passenger door open. She felt Claire being lifted out and heard her being quickly placed back inside the car, this time in the driver's seat. In moments she felt herself lifted up and carried to the front passenger seat. Then the tinkering sounds under the car resumed.

Tasha's thoughts raced. Desperation overtook her. Could this be a last chance to try for an escape? But she knew she couldn't run, couldn't walk. She had no way of knowing if anyone would hear a scream for help. There would be no time for a second one. If she made any attempt it had to be fast and it had to be final. She struggled to her left and felt the steering wheel. Her fingers traced down the steering shaft. Her fingertips brushed the key, a single key still in the ignition, taunting her with the possibility of freedom like smells of spring wafting through the bars of a prison cell.

A train passed by. Like the nearby traffic, the train sounded close, but not right next to the car. Wherever the Cadillac was parked, there was enough distance involved that the people in the trucks and the people on the train were most likely speeding by without ever knowing that two women lay trapped in that big black car over there at the side of the road, in desperate need of someone to call the police. If a phone call was made quickly enough there still might be a few minutes, a couple of final moments, if somebody noticed and became concerned and decided to risk getting involved.

But it is at this point, just as she was about to make her move, that her memory of the crimes ends. The memory gap is as sharp, as final, as the last foot of film rolling off the spool with no more images to display, flapping around on the gears of the projector. Even though the human brain records every sensation relayed to it by every nerve ending in the body, access to memory is sometimes mercifully denied.

Teams of experts later offered bits and pieces of crime-scene facts and expert opinion as to the events of the night, the speeding crash, the fire in the trunk, and the burning rope wick.

Using forensic medicine's reconstruction of the methods by which invisible killers do their hidden work, investigators can take a physician's detailed descriptions of wounds and reveal the manner in which those wounds were inflicted. Logic and science shine unrelenting lights, sweeping across endless midnight countryside. And with the power of these illuminations, the force of simple logic can then direct its own beam of light down gloomy valleys, flashing into hill-side caves and offering glimpses of the games played by monsters in the dark.

The attacker seized her and set upon her like a wild animal. The tire iron slammed into her face. That first blow could have easily torn away the canvas face mask, revealing Tas-ha's attacker to her as he hovered and raised the steel bar to strike again.

Natasha knows that she was struck with the tire iron first, because she had no sense of her mother being attacked once they left the house. She knows that she was still wearing the tightly laced hood and the handcuffs when the attack began, because she cannot remember them being removed while she was still conscious. And although her injuries looked essen-tially like her mother's when the authorities found them later that morning, there is one crucial fact that explains the thin margin of difference between her injuries and her mother's fatal wounds. This difference was just enough to grant Tasha the barest shot at survival.

Her mother's head injuries were inflicted, the coroner and

his investigator said, with the edge of a metal bar wielded by someone standing directly over her as she lay on her back. Someone struck her, standing in a face-to-face position, swinging from the upper right to the lower left, using full arm blows. Claire's injuries were all concentrated in one small area of her head, because she was already out cold as her attack began. She endured it in an utterly helpless state.

Natasha was almost, but not quite, as helpless. Her wounds later showed that she was also struck while lying more or less on her back, by a face-to-face attacker swinging the metal bar with full-strength blows. But since Tasha was initially conscious as her attack began, she was able to do one thing that her mother could not. And the slightly different pattern of her injuries offered proof of it.

She could thrash her head from side to side, in the only defensive motion left to her. This way her injuries were dispersed over a wider area of her head. The puncturing and crushing effect on the bones of the skull was narrowly avoided. Although Natasha cannot remember, may never remember those first blows raining down on her in complete surprise as she lay blind to her attacker, the wide pattern of marks indicates that some part of her was conscious and functioning. Some part of her was able to continue trying to roll and thrash her head away from the blows she could not even see coming.

Police investigators know that her feet flailed helplessly against the bottom of the dash, pulling against the rope that bound them, because there were no defensive wounds on her legs. She was never able to use them to shield any part of herself from the tire iron. Likewise investigators surmised that her cuffed hands were probably held out of the way by her attacker because her arms also lacked any defensive wounds.

One of the first impacts tore away the flesh around her left eye, the assailant striking with the downward motion in a typical right-handed fashion. This would shut down her vision on that side, of course, as the bones of the eye cavity and the upper sinus shattered and fragmented. Shock would slow her perception of time into near-frozen motion at that point. Sounds would probably go dead. Yet the reason the investigators know that she could still move is that, incredible as it sounds, Tasha still did not give in. She began the long, slow process of turning her head again, shielding her shattered bones and her torn flesh from having to take another strike over wounds already made. Her feet were still bound and flailing in the passenger footwell, her cuffed hands still held out of the way by her attacker, but the last muscle control left to her was directed full out on the motion of tilting her head far enough, soon enough, to take the next impact on an uninjured part of her. And so as the bar struck at the top of her forehead, it ripped away flesh but it landed on bone that was still sound enough to hold up and to protect the brain from rupture.

Even as the last of her consciousness left her, Tasha still refused to give in. Perhaps she even found command of her voice for one flickering instant, forcing a short scream of protest through her throat. Why else would a blow land squarely across her lips? It shattered those perfect teeth that had flashed through so many smiling pictures over her eighteen years.

A pretty girl's face is no match for steel. The last blows were directed against a head that could no longer try to swing out of the way. The last blows took possession of her in the darkness and they chewed her without mercy.

Later, both women must have seemed dead to their attacker while the car was readied for its solo drive toward the dead-end wall. But Tasha retained the thinnest little lifeline to the world as their bodies and the interior of the car were doused with gasoline, as the gasoline-soaked wick was lit under the car near the bottom of the gas tank, as the small fire was started in the trunk, as the accelerator linkage was pulled tightly toward the Cadillac's front fire wall so that the gas pedal stuck flat to the floor while the car was dropped into gear.

When the mother and daughter began their brief, high-speed journey, all indications are that Claire was already gone, even as the Cadillac's wheels began to roll for the last time.

The prosecution would eventually offer two possible theories of the way the car left the road and avoided the dead-end wall. One is that the crown of the road, designed to promote rain runoff, was angled just enough to slowly tilt the car to the right as it traveled, gaining speed. The slope slowly ran the car off the side of the road and into the telephone pole before it could reach the dead-end wall at the much faster impact speed that was intended.

The second theory is that the long leather strip found later across Claire's face had been used to tie her upright to the steering wheel, mimicking a driving position. And so even in death, Claire made one final move to protect her daughter. As the car gathered speed, she slumped to the right, which turned the wheel and sent the car off the road. This second theory explains why Claire never hit the steering wheel or the windshield. It explains why she was found on the floor, jammed up under the dashboard. Since she had already slumped over onto the seat when the car hit, she flew under the steering wheel entirely.

If this second theory is true, then it was Claire who took the car off the road in time to avoid the explosion that would have resulted at higher speed as the tank-puncturing sharp steel bar, with its point only half an inch from the thin metal of the gas tank, punctured it upon impact and spewed gasoline to be ignited by the rope wick. Even in death Claire offered this fragile safety net to her brutalized young daughter. If this theory is accurate, and there is no evidence to show that it is not, then it was truly Claire Peernock who saved her daughter's life.

But Natasha had a few challenges left to overcome before she could hope to leave behind her ordeal of captivity and brutality.

It would not be nearly enough simply to survive the high-speed crash designed to explode the gas tank and turn the Cadillac into a roaring inferno, simultaneously a murder weapon and funeral pyre.

Hardest of all, she would have to fight to have her story believed, while she herself struggled to regain her emotional and psychological balance after suffering the ultimate betrayals at her father's hands.

This is why her battle did not end out on a lonely road that night.

That's only where it began.

II

Around the Tree and Back into the Hole

The rabbit comes out of the hole,
runs around the tree . . .
and jumps back into the hole.

*—Boy Scout method for remembering
how to tie a knot that only grows
tighter under stress*

CHAPTER

6

Claire Laurence married Robert Peernock on April 16, 1967, when she was a newly arrived French-Canadian from Quebec. Soon after, as a twenty-four-year-old bride living in Hollywood, California, Claire Peernock described her life to friends as being full, with a promise of future happiness.

A former family friend who was a guest at the pool party where Claire and Robert first met describes Claire as having been immediately swept off her feet by Robert. The sparks between them were apparent to onlookers. Nobody expressed any surprise when Claire and Robert soon became constant companions and later husband and wife.

Claire confided to friends that Robert fawned over her with a level of attention far more intense than anything she had ever known. She was completely captivated by the relentless sweetness in his treatment of her, by the pleasure he took in being with her. She would do anything he wanted. This pleased him more.

Their first child was born a little more than two years later, in June of 1969. They agreed to name the girl Natasha. Both parents doted on their baby girl, but Robert immediately made her his princess, fawning over her at every opportunity. With video cameras not yet on the market, Claire filled photo albums with snapshots of Robert cuddling Natasha, playing all kinds of games with her. Whenever Robert had the chance, he applied his hobby of making home tape recordings to the pursuit of capturing every sound his daughter made.

Natasha's early childhood photos show a beautiful flaxen-haired child with a glowing, confident smile and bright, intelligent eyes. She was unquestionably Daddy's little girl.

For the first ten years of the marriage, Robert moved up the corporate ladder as a technician with expertise in computers and a gift for complex problems in circuitry. He eventually rose to the rank of vice-president at Network Electronics Corporation, where his specialty was in testing explosive devices for their subsidiary, the Ordnance Technology Group. Robert's technical skills were above reproach. He had a firm grasp of the complex problems in explosive circuitry and his ability to guide currents through countless connections was a gift, cited in numerous job reports.

In the early years of their marriage, Claire admired his ability to identify a problem at home or at work and focus on it relentlessly until a solution was found. Claire was proud and secure; she knew there would always be room in the job market for a skilled troubleshooter.

Robert Peernock could shoot trouble like nobody's business.

THE BIRTH OF A WHISTLEBLOWER

Robert John Peernock turned fifty a couple of months before the night of his wife's murder and his daughter's brutal near-death beating. Up to that point, he had, in a number of ways, led an enviable life. During the rise of his career he had continually displayed qualities that society expects from its captains of industry. He amassed undisputed professional skill with complex and powerful computer control systems. He later supervised the testing of sophisticated electronic detonators for pyrotechnic devices. Strongly self-guided, he took additional courses of study throughout his career, developing an exemplary level of technical expertise. His determination to achieve excellence in his work and his powers of concentration gave him abilities with circuitry that reached levels shared only by a select group of electronic engineers around the country.

Whatever fears Peernock nurtured of professional or personal defeat were kept hidden. He consistently showed a relish for conflict once he decided that there was a reason to target someone or something for battle.

The dark path that eventually led him to a seat at the criminal defense table facing charges of murder, attempted murder, solicitation of murder, kidnapping, and arson is a long one. The journey had begun many years before.

Part of that journey is now a matter of record, filed in the early 1980s when Robert Peernock came before the United States District Court to sue the State of California and a host of his superiors at California's Department of Water Resources. The complaint reads like a textbook primer on standard conflict situations between whistleblowers and the corruption they seek to expose.

The main plot of the Peernock struggle begins with his employment as an inspector for the DWR at about age thirty-five. Peernock swears that shortly after being hired he was told by a superior that instead of actually doing his appointed job of serving as a watchdog against malfeasance by contractors and suppliers to DWR, Peernock's *true* responsibility was to sign off on inferior work done by DWR contractors whether the work met with specifications or not. Further, he was ordered to then dream up excuses for the contractors to reap further rewards by helping them submit change-orders for the repair of work that had been improperly done to begin with, thereby creating a double-dipping situation for the contractors, using taxpayer funds.

He tells of being warned that if he didn't play along, not only would he be forced out of his job at DWR, but that the

DWR had Mafia ties and he would be endangering himself severely by attempting to oppose the cover-up scheme.

After repeated threats were lodged against him he finally went to the man who had hired him at DWR and complained that if he did as he was told, equipment would not meet minimum safety requirements and it would take years to correct all the problems, at the cost to California of millions of dollars. Worst of all, the inherent safety problems could create fatal hazards for DWR workers.

He says his superior admitted that all of this was common practice and a known problem, but that if Peernock was strong enough to try to force contractors to meet specifications, his boss would see to it that Peernock received full backing of the DWR via the division chief. When Peernock acted upon that advice, the supplier answering to Peernock's inspections eventually furnished a huge computer control system to DWR called the WINDGAP 68-35, "by far the best control system" received by DWR up to that time. It required no additional fix-it costs.

But instead of drawing praise, Peernock was informed by various employees that he was going to be harassed out of his job for daring to see to it that the taxpayers got a good deal.

He had bucked the system. And he had made enemies.

He was stripped of his inspector's authority and the contractors were told that they were free to ignore him, with the result that more inferior control systems were supplied to DWR in the subsequent months and years. Since these systems failed to meet specifications, there were further billings for huge amounts by the same contractors to bring them up to specifications that they should have met in the first place. Now the double dipping was continuing right under Peernock's nose and he had absolutely no ability to stop it.

Peernock started making more noise. And more enemies. The following story taken from Peernock's Second Amended

Complaint CV-023124 LEW (Tx) in U.S. District Court describes his version of what was going on with the Department of Water and Power and some of its officers. Peernock claimed DWR supervisors began flying down from headquarters in Sacramento to warn that he was creating too many waves and he would be well advised to give it up.

When he spurned the warnings, bribe offers replaced them. If he cooperated and kept quiet, Peernock could join in the system and participate in the rip-off.

If he didn't play along, he was advised that even though his reputation for competence was too strong to make a case for firing him, the company would build a set of false charges against him by alleging personality problems. Management people at DWR would encourage their contractors to write letters of complaint so that they could harass him out of the company one way or the other.

Peernock claimed that he was told all state-department management people "dance together" in Sacramento. By refusing, Peernock was in ever-increasing danger of having to take the consequences. He told of receiving threatening calls at home and claimed that he was assured by higher-ups that he would never be promoted because of his actions in writing internal memos to inform on contractor rip-offs. His automobile was subject to constant sabotage, the brake lines cut repeatedly.

Nevertheless he sent several letters to upper-level politicians, keeping his identity secret to avoid still more violent reprisal. He alleges that his bosses realized he was the complainant and responded by paying the contractor $50,000 to write numerous letters saying that Peernock had all kinds of personality problems which were the true root of his complaints.

Finally, when a major overflow of water occurred at one of the state's biggest pumping plants, costing the taxpayers millions of dollars in damages, rumors floated around that

Peernock had shut down the system himself by way of protest. But he replied that the event occurred because a company involved failed to comply with required safety features. The disaster, he said, actually proved his claims.

One thing was clear. Somebody wasn't dealing in the whole truth.

Phone threats escalated at Peernock's home. Employees began to confront him at work, trying to start arguments. Although he stands six feet and then weighed about 185 pounds, they repeatedly tried to tempt him into fights.

The odds continued to stack against him.

Peernock felt partially vindicated when an audit report was issued by the auditor general's office confirming that state contract procedures were not up to par, but the report never went any farther. Soon his fears about the extent of the corruption grew larger. Peernock claimed the Auditor General was forced out over what Peernock says were false charges leveled in retaliation for confirming Peernock's accusations. The new Auditor in that office offered Peernock no satisfaction in the pursuit of what Peernock described as a huge network of bribe takers and crooked office holders.

The stakes rose again. Now Peernock was confronted by a field engineer and warned that one of their former engineers, who had also threatened to disclose conflict of interest in the awarding of state contracts, had been found with his head blown off by a shotgun. A "suicide." Peernock was assured that the same thing could happen to him.

By this point the hostility against him at work was open and widespread. More sabotage dogged him. Lug nuts were loosened on his car wheels. Sometimes the lug nuts were removed altogether. The brakes and warning-light lines were again cut. Peernock was told that he was like Serpico and that his campaign against this endless system of crooks and thieves was merely an attempt to "hold back the incoming tide."

His mentor at DWR was removed and replaced with a hand-picked enemy who immediately subjected Peernock to all sorts of administrative harassment at work, attempting to force his voluntary resignation. One company officer even claimed to know, but refused to reveal, who was doing the sabotage.

The California Department of Water and Power had closed ranks against Robert John Peernock.

Peernock changed tactics. He formed a union and got himself elected shop steward, using his position there in an attempt to bring further leverage against the DWR and the crooked contractors. But other employees were not so eager to unite "against the tide," especially after Peernock was injured when a large car mysteriously ran into his at a stop sign. The driver fled on foot and was never caught. Peernock was not only knocked out by the impact, he suffered the further indignity of being robbed at the scene before he regained consciousness.

Coincidentally, there was an open whiskey bottle in the other car.

And now for the first time the DWR conflict moved outside the state contract system. He insists that reports of the accident were falsified by the police, who now seemed to have been pulled into the fray against him. He protests that their behavior in covering up this attempt upon his life makes it clear that the cops themselves are under the control of a crooked administration. Further, he continues to this day to assure all who will listen that the state administration can and will use the police as a taxpayer-paid private army of reprisal, attacking and destroying anyone who dares to buck the system.

Thus, from the late 1970s through to the very morning of his wife's murder on July 22, 1987, Robert was constantly involved in a long series of lawsuits in state and federal courts in his ongoing attempt to sweep all of the corrupt officials off the state payroll. He presented bits and pieces of evidence to support his claims, but never enough to trigger the federal investigation that he desired. His history through-out those ten years is a bogglingly complex tissue of accusations and allegations against individuals and businesses, against co-workers, bosses, private contractors, and state agencies. Although the lawsuits occupy thousands upon thousands of pages of transcripts in courthouses all over California, Robert never presented any of the courts with a smoking gun sufficient to generate the kind of sweeping reform action he desired.

But it is the arrest report for the only crime Robert Peernock was ever convicted of prior to the destruction of his family that clearly lays out the series of events that finally stuck in his gut. It all took place after he turned forty-two, seven years after his whistleblower struggles began. The arrest report tells how Peernock was at the job site discussing a company calisthenics program with one of the men whom he supervised when Peernock lost his temper and attacked the man.

He grabbed the man around the neck.

When the man tried to retreat, the police report notes that Peernock struck him with a fist to the side of the head and face, on the side of the head opposite to that where Claire Peernock's fist-sized bruise would be found years later.

This attack resulted in his eventual conviction on a misdemeanor count of battery. But that's not what stung him so badly, eating at him inside like a slow acid drip until the obsession began to bleed throughout his thoughts. This is:

The charge landed on the desk of Deputy District Attorney Myron Jenkins in the Newhall branch of the Los Angeles District Attorney's Office. In fact, the charge was already there when Jenkins inherited his job early in the new year, but Jenkins signed off on it as he routinely did with the dozens of others that came across his desk. This allowed the case to go to trial. But first, as a matter of common practice, Jenkins notified Peernock's attorney to offer a plea bargain deal that included a simple hundred-dollar fine and probation for disturbing the peace.

The arrangement would have allowed Peernock to save the taxpayers the expense of a trial. It also offered minimal impact to Peernock's record.

But he rejected the hundred-dollar plea bargain offer and insisted on the trial. So one of Myron Jenkins's staff attorneys was assigned to prosecute the case for the DA's office.

Peernock was convicted.

Unbowed, he appealed the conviction. He insisted that both the charge and his conviction had been engineered by Deputy District Attorney Myron Jenkins as retaliation against Peernock for his efforts against the corrupt state system. This theory entails the proposition that the Los Angeles District Attorney's Office, the largest law office in the world with over a thousand prosecutors in its service, operates at the behest of the state government to frame and convict anyone who dares to come forward and speak out against organized corruption in state government. Robert Peernock has no trouble visualizing and describing the countless connections on this giant circuit board of corruption.

In his appeal, he claimed that the victim's story had been, in Peernock's words, "impeached by his own testimony." But the court noted that Peernock himself had only two witnesses, and that their testimony broke down completely. It was filled with inconsistencies and recountings of events they could not possibly have been in a position to witness.

By contrast, the victim's story was borne out by the hard physical evidence as well as the witnesses for the victim. So the Court of Appeal refused Peernock's assertion of self-defense, given that Peernock's victim was eight years older, four inches shorter, nearly seventy pounds lighter, and was in poor physical condition.

Peernock also argued in his appeal that he had not been permitted to outline his long list of grievances against the DWR at the trial. But the court ruled that even if that story was true, it would do nothing to explain his innocence with respect to the battery charge.

He was left to try to frame an appeal by presenting accusations of bias on the part of the trial court as being part of a plot against him by "the state, his supervisory employees, the sheriff's office, the office of the district attorney, the prosecutor, and the trial judge."

In the end the three appellate judges found that these claims were also unsupported and that his trial had been a fair one. His request for a new trial was denied.

If Robert had accepted the small defeat of the hundred-dollar fine, he could have walked away. But the obsession had nailed him. The sting burned deeply. He could not, *was not,* going to let it go. He could see how it was all connected. As it happened, one of the connections turned out to be true, in a turn of coincidence that Peernock would never see as being anything other than a further example of conspiracy among the lawyers trying to hound him into prison. At the time of Peernock's battery trial Myron Jenkins was slightly acquainted with a law clerk over in the public defender's office in the suburb of Newhall.

The law clerk's name was Victoria Doom. She hoped one day to become a sole practitioner, but for now, she and Myron Jenkins were on opposite sides of the fence in a relatively small judicial district. Their business sometimes brought them into contact, but Victoria Doom had no way of knowing how much she and Jenkins would one day have in common via the strange legal history of Robert John Peernock.

Claire tried to ride out the situation for the first few years after Robert's whistleblowing campaign began. In an age where elaborate rip-off schemes on the part of government contractors are constantly coming to light on major news programs like *60 Minutes,* his campaign, to her, initially seemed to have the ring of truth.

She hoped that Robert's plan might actually succeed, that he could sue the state agencies and the managers involved until the kickback scheme was brought to light. Her husband talked long and often about the need to save taxpayers' money, how deeply and bitterly he resented the waste of good tax revenues on the complex scheme of bribes involving a staggering number of state officials.

But their problems at home only grew, aggravated by his devotion to his work. By the time Claire and Robert's second daughter was born in 1977, he was spending less and less time with his family. The distance between him and Claire was growing relentlessly.

His fixation on his cause célèbre grew because in rare instances a few of Robert's countless letters, complaints, and lawsuits were actually starting to get results. He claimed that these victories proved that his overall premise of massive corruption was the truth, but his opponents grumbled that he was simply learning how to overwhelm the legal system by bombarding it with self-filed lawsuits. Nevertheless, concessions were sometimes made at work, with bosses agreeing to alter procedures to Robert's specifications.

Ground had been given. Robert began to feel that he was finally proving his point in a way that the state and eventually the feds would not be able to ignore. He stepped up his efforts, filing more complaints accusing fellow inspectors of taking bribes and filing more grievances against his bosses for allegedly condoning such behavior.

Natasha recalls that it was at this time, in the late 1970s and early 1980s, that her position as Daddy's little girl was lost. She was developing a will of her own, no longer the malleable child she once had been. And so the rift between

Robert and most everyone else now included his former princess child.

Natasha found herself replaced in his affections by her new little sister, who was still a toddler young enough to be completely controlled by Robert whenever he had time to spend with her.

Claire Peernock was spending most of her time at home alone, or in violent arguments with Robert when he was at the house.

Natasha says that by then, because of Robert's repeated outbursts against Claire and because of the violence Natasha witnessed him repeatedly inflict on her mother, she had already concluded that her father was evil.

Claire simply worried that no concession, no settlement, would ever be enough as Robert's campaign against the state dragged on. She knew that for Robert, intellectual battle with organizations was easier than emotional rapport on a one-to-one basis. She confided to friends that she feared he had found his true niche.

Maybe he had. He could see the connections of the conspiracy, countless connections laid out on a circuit board the size of a state of thirty million taxpayers. And the taxpayers weren't going to take a beating while Peernock was on the prowl. As the 1980s dawned, Robert began keeping detailed notes of complex strategies, taping conversations with fellow workers. He hired attorneys and won cash settlements. No victory was ever enough to suit him; he stuffed the settlement cash in bank accounts and kept right on shooting trouble.

Despite the limited formal schooling that caused him sometimes to falter at spelling and grammar when he operated outside his technical arena, Robert nevertheless grew so adept at legal tactics through his constant use of lawyers that he was eventually able to save money by running lawsuits himself. This freed up funds to file more motions to take on still more of his growing list of opponents. He found corruption everywhere. In some cases Robert offered documentation; in others he only had his gift for visualizing circuits, connections. The judges were on the take, the state water agencies were on the take, the private contractors hired to do the work were on the take, the cops were on the take. The most populous state in the nation was riddled with corruption, bleeding its citizenry dry, and nobody was yelling except Robert Peernock.

Robert's cause on behalf of the taxpayer might have been tolerable to Claire, taken by itself, but his obsession gradually took control of him. He seemed to resent her unwillingness to hang in there with him on what he perceived as the battle of his life.

The battle wore on his health. He had terrible trouble trying to sleep. He became touchy. *Very* touchy. Robert started coming home angrier and angrier, constantly protesting outrageous retaliations that the state was taking against him for trying to derail their fat scheme of corruption at the public expense.

He was indignant that no one appreciated his public-spirited efforts, not even his wife, whom he wanted at his side in this monumental struggle. His nerves were often frazzled after a long day battling corrupt officials; Claire had shown family friends her bruises to demonstrate how dangerous it was to anger him when his tensions were high.

He filed several claims alleging injuries from physical attacks, supposed attempts on his life by co-workers who were in actuality operatives of the Department of Water Resources, eager to silence his relentless gadfly activities. He finally succeeded in having a disability pension awarded for a back injury that he claimed to have suffered when fellow workers deliberately caused heavy equipment to fall on him. In this way Robert secured an income that would be guaranteed even if he never found work again owing to the state-wide blackballing that he now claimed had been set up against him. But he took small satisfaction in the pension. It was little enough thanks for his civic-minded work on the public behalf.

In recent years the problems between Claire and Robert had grown like cancer. Claire had no more patience for Robert's campaign against the state and Robert felt utterly betrayed by her refusal to support his efforts. The hostility infected their communication on every level, down to conversations about the most mundane things in their daily lives.

By 1983, the pain and anger inside the marriage was repeatedly spreading outside the relationship. Claire intervened as often as she could to keep Robert from taking his outrage out on Natasha when the headstrong girl would be foolish enough to defy her father. In May of 1983 Claire and Robert were having one of their typical arguments in the kitchen area when the confrontation turned violent. Natasha tells how she saw Robert grab Claire and begin to manhandle her. Natasha leapt in front of her mother and demanded that Robert leave her alone. The next thing she knew, Robert had thrown her bodily against the kitchen wall.

She slid to the floor with a searing pain running down her side.

Robert drove her to the emergency room. On the way he made sure that Natasha understood that she was to tell the doctors that she had slipped and fallen while playing in the house.

She spent the next twenty-one days in traction for a shattered collarbone.

Claire came to visit her and told her daughter that she agreed with Robert; Natasha should keep up a good front for the hospital staff. Claire was afraid of what Robert might do once he was alone with them again. Natasha did not have the strength to speak out against her father publicly, alone.

She did, however, give a different story to everyone who asked at the hospital, hoping that someone would notice that the lies didn't add up. Either nobody put it all together or no one bothered to come forward with their suspicions. The violence in the Peernock home was still a secret and would remain a secret for another four years.

Shortly afterward, Claire made one tentative visit to a lawyer to see about getting a divorce from this man she had come to fear, but she later told friends that Robert had threatened to kill her if she went through with it. She claimed that he'd promised to hunt her down if she fled with the children. After years of watching Robert's skill in dealing with investigators and with the courts, Claire had no doubt that he could find her anywhere she might go.

Her first tentative attempts to flee the marriage were abandoned.

But permanent damage to the marriage had been done. Robert later claimed that it was about this time that he and Claire "announced" their separation to friends and acquaintances. What little socializing Robert did, he now did on his own.

At one of the parties that he attended as a single, he met a pretty divorced woman named Sonia Siegel. Robert had no constraints against pursuing another woman and Claire had no interest in him whatsoever, so Sonia became the object of his affections. By the next year Robert was sleeping at Sonia's place nearly every night, even though he continued to keep all of his belongings at his family house.

That suited Claire and Natasha just fine. Claire was glad to have the place to herself, and Natasha says she finally felt safe at home for the first time in years. Claire found a good secretarial job and began considering the possibility of a real life on her own. A fresh start.

By the time the traditional marriage had ended, the checks were rolling in every month on his real estate holdings, even though Robert was no longer employed. Settlements on a few of his many lawsuits left Robert enough spare cash to have stuffed well over a quarter of a million dollars into a series of bank accounts. And to have paid Claire's house mortgage down to a few thousand dollars. And to own several other houses as income properties.

Despite the fact that he had moved out and set up house with his girlfriend, Sonia, he still visited Claire and Natasha weekly, delivering small sums of money for living expenses to augment Claire's salary as a secretary. He wanted Claire's emotional support in return.

But darker problems arose. He began to voice strong suspicions that the company Claire worked for was also involved in the government's scheme of selling construction contracts. Robert began to wonder aloud, over and over, whether someone there had managed to pay Claire off to get her to cooperate in the scheme. Robert feared Claire had personal reasons to punish him, to pay him back for moving out and finding a girlfriend who believed in him the way Claire wouldn't. Or if not, he feared that at the very least Claire was, in her naiveté, being manipulated by her company and slowly turned against him.

By the end of 1986 Claire Peernock finally came to the end. Nobody knows exactly what triggered her determination, whether it was a particularly bad fight that the daughters were not around to witness, or just the accumulated weight of years spent trapped inside an empty marriage. But something finally drove her to action.

And so in early November of 1986, despite her sweet nature and despite her patience and despite her years of inability to break away from the hold of a man she remembered loving dearly, her time as an enabler of her husband's violence toward his family was over at last.

Claire Peernock left the house to hunt down a divorce lawyer.

She could have picked from a number of attorneys to consult about a possible divorce action. Saugus is a small town in the high desert outside Los Angeles, but it's plenty big enough to offer an array of choices to anybody shopping for a lawyer. Claire can no longer reveal why she chose the little law office in a single-story mall on Soledad Canyon Road. It may have been a referral from a friend. Or maybe she just wanted to discuss the private, painful issues with another woman—seeking the first female lawyer she came across.

Or perhaps Claire just needed all the psychic energy she could muster. She was about to confront this forceful man with the knowledge that she wanted to divide their property and claim her half of the small fortune he had amassed through a relentless campaign she had not supported. And for that reason she may have taken strength from the very sound of the name out on the shingle:

VICTORIA W. DOOM—ATTORNEY AT LAW.

Certainly as Claire kept her appointment for the initial consultation, she had no way of knowing she was taking a step that would shatter the attorney's law practice and bring her to the brink of financial ruin, in addition to placing Victoria Doom's name on a killer's hit list.

And so on November 13, a few days after the initial consultation, Claire returned some financial papers to Victoria Doom's office for use in determining property settlements. She paid a retainer.

The divorce was finally under way.

Two days after that, on November 15, in an unexplainable twist of premonition, Claire took out a State Farm life insurance policy on herself for $10,000, payable to her daughter Natasha. She called her longtime friend Louise, who had been at the pool party where Claire and Robert met twenty years before, and told her she was finally initiating a divorce. She expressed her fears that Robert might try to kill her, but vowed that she was resolved to make the leap she had dreaded for so long. She never mentioned her new life insurance policy to Louise. But whether it was a specific pre-

monition or just a general sense of dread that caused her to
buy the policy, she could never have imagined how ironic
the eventual use of that policy's funds would turn out to be.

For the time being, despite Claire's best intentions that
day, her actions did not set her on the road to freedom; they
put her on a high-speed collision course toward a dead-end
wall.

And they changed Victoria Doom's life forever.

CHAPTER

7

Sometime after 8:00 A.M. on the same morning that Claire's life ended on the dead-end road, Patty was dressed and ready for a round of job applications, fully prepared to drag Tasha out of bed if she had to. As she drove through the cool morning air she felt determined to straighten out whatever had gone wrong with their plans for the night before and then get on with the day they had planned.

Yesterday afternoon both young women had agreed that even after going to Magic Mountain and staying out late they would get up early and look for work together this morning. The six weeks since graduation had been a lot of fun for both of them, but neither had the funds to take an entire summer off.

Patty knew that Tasha was interested in seeing what kind of a future she could make for herself in the design world. Tasha had already persuaded Claire to hit her father up for a couple of thousand dollars toward the fashion-design college she was enrolled in for the fall. Claire chipped in some more herself, but Tasha was going to have to work in order to get together her book money and commuting expenses. So whatever had gone wrong the night before, Patty approached her friend's house feeling sure that Tasha would be ready now despite the early hour. Nevertheless she was still in the grip of the uneasy feeling that had followed her home last night.

When Patty pulled her car a stop in front of the Peernock residence, what she saw there didn't do anything to make her feel better. Both of Mr. Peernock's cars were gone, but Claire's car was still in the driveway. She wondered who could have taken his big Cadillac. The Peernocks were not a married couple who exchanged cars. She couldn't remember having seen Tasha or her mother ever drive the Cadillac; Mr. Peernock would have had a fit at the thought of either of them taking off in his pride and joy.

When Patty got out of her car she noticed that the front left tire on Claire's car had gone flat. For a moment she wondered if this could explain things. Would Mr. Peernock drive off in his Cadillac in that case, leaving his Datsun for Claire to use? But that still didn't seem right. These were two people who avoided talking to each other unless they had to; they could hardly be civil. No, if Claire's car was out of commission, she would have had to call a friend for help.

And so at least one of Robert Peernock's cars should still be in the driveway.

The lawn hadn't been mowed, but that didn't tell Patty much. Tasha had always been a night owl who stayed up late, sleeping in whenever her schedule would allow it. Even if Tasha had come back home after whatever had taken place the night before, Patty knew her friend wouldn't get up early to do yard work before going out to hunt for a job. That would be a little too much reality for a midsummer day.

Patty hesitated at the front door. Now that Mr. Peernock was gone, if either of the women was at home the door ought to be unlocked. Claire and Tasha never locked it during the daytime if anyone was there. Patty put her ear to the door—there wasn't a sound. But when she reached out and tried the handle, it wouldn't move.

Now the same bad feeling from the night before came over her again. More than any of the strange facts or unusual circumstances, it was this feeling that convinced her of trouble. The feeling was clearer than it had been last night, as if by sitting in the back of her mind through the hours since then it had somehow penetrated her rational defenses and probed deeper into her inner fears.

As during the night before, something told her to leave this place. And, again she felt the hairs stand up on the back of her neck. But her need to find out what was going on with Tasha had grown strong. So she turned to the front window, which looked so solid but which the girls had learned to pop open with ease. She got down on her knees, ready to get inside the house and look for clues. Patricia was resolved not to leave the neighborhood until she found out what had happened to her best friend.

She was about to get her wish.

Just as she'd begun to pull the window open a woman's voice yelled out her name. Even before Patty turned around, the tone of the voice plugged right into the creepy feeling that had settled into her spine.

"Patty! Get away from there, right now! Get away!"

She looked around to see Danielle, one of the neighbor women and a longtime friend of Claire and Tasha's. Danielle was running toward her. Patty stood slowly, taking in the woman's expression as she reached the sidewalk near the house and stopped there pointedly, without setting a foot on the property.

"Come away from there! Come on! Right now!"

Patty's heart began to pound as she hurried out to meet the woman, who appeared distraught and near panic. She immediately threw her arm around Patty and turned her away from the house, walking her up the street toward her own place.

"What's going on?" Patty began, but the neighbor leapt on the question as she rushed Patty along the sidewalk.

"Just wait. Wait till we get back inside!"

A few seconds later they were in her house, the door shut

and locked. Danielle spun from the door with tears streaming down her face.

A sick feeling of dread began to pound inside Patty.

"Patty," she began, "Claire . . . she's . . . the police came by early this morning and . . ."

"What is it?" Patty asked, the fear rising in her throat. "What happened?"

"There was . . . an accident last night and she and Natasha were in Robert's Cadillac and there was a car wreck. Claire's gone. She was killed. And Tasha's in the hospital."

"What?" Patty blurted. "Which hospital? How bad is it? How is she? I want to go see her!" Her mind was already full of the images that had haunted her all night long, images that now lurched into much sharper focus.

"We don't know about Natasha yet," she answered. "But it's serious. She's in intensive care right now. They won't let anyone visit her."

"I'm going down there." Patty started for the door. But the neighbor held her back.

"You can't see her. They promised to call us as soon as they know anything, but—"

"Wait a minute!" Patty shouted abruptly, disbelief suddenly overpowering her shock. "Claire and Tasha *together*? They never go anywhere together. Come on, this is a bunch of— You know how independent Tasha is! And in her father's Cadillac?"

"I know. I've never seen Claire drive that car, or Tasha either. But now they're—"

"No *way*! I don't believe it! Claire never drives at night. Her eyes are, you know, she's got that thing like in her retina and so she can't see at night—"

"I know, but—"

"And besides, she hates driving anyway. She drives with two feet, one on the brake and one on the gas—"

"I know, but—"

"And she's so safe, she drives the speed limit and follows the laws to the point that it's *ridiculous,* I mean it takes forever to get anywhere with her, I always tease her about it and—and besides," she added, finally taking a breath, "Claire would never take Robert's car."

Patty finished her loud objections softly. Almost in a whisper.

"He'd kill her."

The first and last time that Claire was ever seen by Accident Investigator Mark Warschaw was on the morning of the crimes. She had already died. He tried to speak briefly to Natasha before they loaded her gurney into the ambulance, but she was too badly injured to be of much help. All she could do was mumble a few words in response to his question about the identity of the other passenger. He hadn't told Natasha that the other passenger, the one Natasha named as Patty, had died. Warschaw had been an accident investigator for the Valley Traffic Division for over eight years and had been at thousands of accident sites; he could see that Natasha was fighting for her life. He would just have to hope that the paramedics could get her stabilized and give the doctors a chance to save her.

Hours later, just before noon, Warschaw stopped by the hospital to check on Natasha and learned that she had passed the crisis point but was still in the intensive care unit. He was pleased to receive permission to talk to her for a few minutes; the hours since the accident had only produced more mystery.

Warschaw had been cautioned that she wasn't responding to questions well. She was fading in and out, giving erratic statements. With his first glance he could tell that he wasn't going to be able to press her at all. She lay semiconscious, pin-cushioned with lines fed by IV bags. The doctors were still assessing her head wounds and working to stabilize her condition before putting her under anesthesia and beginning to operate. Warschaw moved in close to her bedside and quietly introduced himself, but she seemed barely aware of his presence.

Warschaw didn't know if her condition was the result of medications or just the product of her severe head injuries. But with a possible homicide investigation developing, he had to learn anything he could. Especially if she didn't make it through surgery. This was, he realized, probably the only person in the world who might tell him the truth about what had happened; whoever had inflicted the blows had plenty of cause to lie.

Warschaw began his questions. He worked slowly and gently, but his interview subject faded in and out of consciousness as he tried to coax her forward. The quality of most of her responses was hardly better than the fragmented monologue that Paramedic Clyde Piephoff had heard from her as he and his crew loaded her into the ambulance.

But gradually, one tiny step after another, she managed to give out one or two meaningful words at a time through her broken teeth until a rough story came out in bits and pieces. Natasha gave the last name of her companion Patty, but wasn't sure of the spelling. She recalled dimly that they had left Patty's house on the day the crimes began, estimating at about 7:30 or 8:00 P.M. when they went to Natasha's house. She said that they then left Natasha's at about 10:30 P.M. and went to meet "some guys."

She murmured that this was the last thing she could remember before waking up at the hospital.

Warschaw wasn't sure if Natasha meant that she and Patty had intended to meet some guys or if they already had met them, but he had seen many victims of head injuries. No one had to tell him that severe blows to the head can scramble memories, thoughts, perceptions. The young woman seemed to be giving her best recollection of the night before, but she clearly wasn't going to be of much help for now. Mark Warschaw didn't know who this Patty person might be, but he knew that the Los Angeles Coroner's Office had already identified the dead woman as Natasha's mother.

At that point the X rays came back from the lab, showing multiple skull fractures. There was no time to question her further; interview subject Natasha Peernock was going to have to face surgery right away to avoid possible brain hemorrhage.

With nothing else left to do, Mark Warschaw silently wished her luck and left her side for the last time. He had, as always, a long list of accidents in need of investigation.

"Patty, I'm *telling* you, the police found them together. This morning at about four o'clock. It was some kind of terrible wreck. Claire died instantly."

Patty turned slowly toward the empty Peernock house. She looked in that direction for a long moment. "Something's wrong about all this."

"I know there is," Danielle replied. "But you can't go near that house again. Promise me you'll stay away from there. I mean it!"

"Okay. Okay, I'll stay away. Listen, what did Mr. Peernock say about this? I *know* he was there last night."

"That's why you have to stay away from the house."

"What do you mean?"

There was a pause. Patricia felt the dread seeping into her, but she still had no way of knowing that it was the same feeling of dread Natasha had tried to beam out to her from captivity hours before.

Patty asked again. "What do you mean that's why I have to stay away?"

"It's because of him. . . . They haven't found him yet."

• • •

It was about two hours later, at 10:00 A.M. on the morning
of the crimes. Over on the other side of the Hollywood Hills,
Claire's boss, Tina Nussbaum, had become concerned about
Claire's absence from work. Claire was never late without
calling, but no one at the office had heard anything from her.
Tina called Claire's number and was surprised when an answering machine picked up. There was a man's voice on it.

The recording puzzled her. Claire had recently remarked
to Tina that she disliked the whole idea of answering machines in a person's home. She said she would never have
one. Only three weeks before, when Tina had last had occasion to call Claire at home, there had been no machine.
Now Tina was being mechanically greeted by a man who
didn't even live there. Tina knew Claire lived apart from her
husband and that they were not on good terms. She couldn't
picture Claire asking her husband to install an answering
machine in her house and then put his voice on it.

She mentally reviewed the intimacies Claire had confided
to her about her family life. She recalled Claire talking about
Robert being upset because he didn't like the young man
Natasha was dating. It seemed that he didn't like Natasha's
friends. In Claire's opinion, he didn't appear to like Natasha
herself, and he kept as much distance from her as from
Claire.

Tina recalled that Claire had been deeply anxious to proceed with their divorce.

For all these reasons, she sensed that something was dan-
gerously wrong about the situation at the Peernock home.
She asked one of her other employees to call the police and
ask them to check out her suspicions.

Claire had expressed concerns about Robert's tendency toward violence too many times for Tina to be able to shrug
off her failure to report for work.

CHAPTER

8

At the same moment that Tina Nussbaum was making her call to Claire's house and listening with consternation to Robert Peernock's voice on the answering machine, Robert Peernock himself was not a happy man.

He had just left Foothill Savings and Loan, where he had tried to cash out his account for its full amount of $51,929.09. However, they kept little cash on hand as a matter of policy at Foothill. Instead, the manager issued Peernock a voucher slip for the nearby Bank of America, where Foothill Savings had an arrangement for their customers to obtain cash.

But when he took the receipt to the Bank of America branch, their shipment of cash hadn't arrived yet for the day's business. Despite Peernock's firm objections, the branch manager informed Robert that there was nothing else to be done. They did not have enough cash yet that day to cover a note for nearly $52,000.

Instead the manager gave Peernock $9,000, which was practically all the currency that the branch had on hand. He informed Peernock that he would have to deposit the rest of the voucher in a savings account there at Bank of America and return on the following day after the bank had the chance to get ready for such a large cash withdrawal. The only other choice the branch could offer was a cashier's check for the balance of nearly $43,000, so that Peernock could take this registered and traceable document to some other financial institution and cash it there.

Peernock decided just to take the $9,000 at that moment and return for the balance, in cash, the following day.

He called Sonia Siegel from the bank shortly afterward to tell her where he was. Sonia tried to swallow her concerns about why he had stayed out all night. Instead she just reminded him that they had an appointment with a plumber at her place at noon; Robert had said he wanted to be there. He assured her that he would be home in time to meet the plumber, and hung up.

Whatever Sonia's instincts may have been telling her at that point, she later recalled that Robert never mentioned a thing about a car wreck, an injured daughter, or a dead wife.

Although Robert Peernock has said that he "announced" his separation from Claire sometime in 1982, five years before her death, he continued to live in the same house with her until late 1983 or early 1984. At the time he met Sonia he was about forty-six, robust in stature and vain enough about his appearance to keep his hair permed in tight curls and his weak chin concealed by a virile-looking seaman's beard. His intense personality and piercing eyes captured Sonia's interest as soon as they met.

Sonia was barely forty years old, but looked and acted younger. Her pretty face was framed by thick, dark tresses and her breathy voice conveyed images of femininity and vulnerability that have always had universal appeal to the sort of men who like to feel that they are stronger than the women in their lives.

Whether Robert was actually stronger than Sonia or not, he came along at a time when she was single again and nearly finished with rearing her children from a prior marriage. She owned her own condo in a nice area of town and had financial means to live without being employed full-time.

For Sonia, surely the prospect of a new relationship with an attractive, dynamic man who had "announced" his separation from his wife and who was looking to move out of his marital home had a strong appeal. The two began to see each other regularly. It couldn't have hurt Sonia's opinion of the relationship's potential to know that Robert also owned half of his family's house plus three other investment properties plus a large bank account stuffed with cash. Many women in Los Angeles would consider such a man a catch; pretty Sonia Siegel was the one who caught him.

She invited Robert to move in with her and soon became utterly devoted to him. Sonia describes herself as having been very much in love with Robert. She considered the relationship one where both partners planned to spend their lives together. She tells no tales of emotional abuse at Robert's hands. She makes no complaints that he beat her or her children or that he ever caused her to fear for their safety.

In fact, only a few weeks earlier her teenage son had accompanied Tasha to her senior prom, leaving Tasha to marvel afterward that the young man described Robert as being a loving father figure. Tasha has no explanation for the young man's point of view; it is always hard to accept a description of someone when it is radically different from your own. But she remembers being thirteen years old and assuring everyone at the hospital that her arm was shattered as the result of taking a bad fall after slipping on a sock. At the time she knew better than to tell a story about her father that she would later have to live with, once she was back home with him. Alone.

Whatever actually took place in the privacy of Robert and Sonia's home lives, they remained together under her roof for nearly four years. Whenever he could, Robert kept his youngest daughter with him there. If the girl had to be back at Claire's house to attend school and if she wanted Robert to be there with her, Sonia knew that Robert would stay the night at Claire's house but sleep in Claire's bed alone. On those nights Claire slept in her daughter's room.

Sonia was aware that although Claire was also a very attractive woman, if Claire had a sex life anymore it wasn't with Robert. It hadn't been for a long time.

In fact, Sonia can't recall a single instance when Robert spent the night at his wife's house from the time he moved in with Sonia, except for those few times that he stayed over just to be with his little girl.

So it had come as a real surprise to Sonia when she received the phone call from Robert just after the previous midnight, telling her that he was still at Claire's house.

It was even stranger when the night passed without Robert showing up back at her place. It was stranger still when the plumber arrived shortly after noon that day and had to start the work without Robert's presence. The plumber was still working when the phone rang again, but when Sonia answered she learned that it wasn't Robert calling to assure her that he was on the way.

It was Detective Arthur Castro from the Foothill police station, looking for Robert. Sonia told him Robert wasn't there and asked what the problem was. Castro asked her to have Robert call him as soon as possible. He told Sonia that there had been an automobile accident involving Robert's daughter, Natasha, and Robert's Cadillac. Nothing was said about Claire, but Sonia thought back to Robert's call from Claire's house at midnight and asked if Claire had been involved. He told her that there had been another, unidentified female involved in the situation but to just please have Robert call the station right away.

For the rest of the day Sonia made frantic phone calls to Claire's house, leaving message after message for Robert on the phone machine that Claire had insisted she would never want in her home, the same machine Robert had just recently installed in his youngest daughter's bedroom.

It was nearly six that evening before Robert returned to Sonia's place and got the news about Natasha being in the hospital. He expressed shock, but he didn't call the police as they had requested. He said that he refused to talk to the authorities until he could get to the hospital to check on his daughter.

The trip to the hospital would be about a thirty-minute drive. He came back a couple of hours later, telling Sonia that he had attempted to see Natasha but the hospital wasn't allowing any visitors. He claimed to have walked around the hospital trying to think up an alternate plan, but that after a while he decided to give up and returned to Sonia's.

Sonia couldn't believe what she was hearing.

"What do you *mean* they won't let you see her?" she challenged him. "She's your daughter! And you don't even know how badly she's hurt. You go back there right now, tell them you're her father and you aren't going to leave until they take you to her!"

Robert wasn't going to get any peace until he did as she insisted, so he left for a second time.

He finally returned after ten. "Okay," he told her, "I got to her this time. But she couldn't talk to me."

Then he gave her the shocking news. "She's in a coma. Her head's all wrapped in bandages. The nurse says there's a good chance that there'll be brain damage."

Sonia sympathized, but she was glad that at least Robert had done the right thing in asserting himself to the hospital staff and demanding his father's right to see his terribly injured daughter, especially since Robert had made it plain that Natasha had terrible head wounds. He said he knew that for a fact. To Sonia it was incomprehensible, a hospital telling a father he couldn't see his own daughter after such a trauma.

What possible reason could they have had for such inhumane behavior?

Sonia went to bed that night burdened by the horrible image of Robert's eldest daughter as he had described seeing her in the hospital upon his second visit that evening, with her head wrapped in bandages, deep in a coma, suffering terrible brain damage. Perhaps even the loss of all her memory.

Tasha lay in her room with her eyes wide open, trying not to move her head as the waves of pain swept through her. The doctors avoided giving her any medication except mild pain relievers. Heavy painkillers were still too dangerous to use, given the need to assess her level of consciousness and determine whether she would have postsurgery complications. She could only lie quietly, trying not to move or even roll her head from side to side. There were no bandages to protect her freshly sutured wounds from contact with the sheets; the jagged rips had to be left open to the air for maximum healing.

Tasha tried to get the message across to every nurse and doctor who entered her room that she needed protection outside her door. But medical staffers know that head injury patients often display signs of inappropriate concern and heightened emotion. There is no way to cater to all the irrational demands such patients can make.

And so the stabs of throbbing pain battled with Tasha's fears for domination of her thoughts, while she struggled to remember every detail of her last night in the family home. She tried to bring up a clear picture of Claire and to think what might have happened to her mother. But she just didn't know yet—at least she didn't know up in the front of her mind where images are clear and where words can be formed to express them.

But she knew. Deep down, way back in the shadows, she knew in those places where dreams and nightmares come from, where memories of the past and hopes for the future and fears about all kinds of dangerous things all mingle together.

She knew down in the part of her memory where she was

still a little girl wandering alone and lost, stranded among overpowering primal forces, trembling at the warnings that ricocheted inside her while she strained to hear the sources of deadly sounds circling ever closer.

She knew down there where she stored impressions of a tiny child trapped in a life of violence that could spring unexpectedly out of any situation, no matter how harmless things might seem on the surface.

She knew what had happened to her mother with that same part of her that had been born almost as soon as Tasha was born, the protective part that kept her true self back in the shadows, blanketing her feelings, hiding her intentions. That part of her understood with instinctive clarity that the scent of fear or the stab of memory could lure more of the badness down upon her.

This old inner protector had been activated the night before, with the first biting grip of her father's fingers in the flesh of her throat. It had completely taken over her memory with the first blow of cold steel. Even now, when she was alone in the hospital, it would not release full memory to her and would not show her the depth of her fears. Her old inner protector still detected danger close by, lurking unseen.

Was it a troubled sleep for Robert John Peernock at Sonia's condo that night? He had been awake all the previous night and all that day. Depending on whose story you believe, he had either been working nervously in the backyard on his spray-painting project while fretting about why on earth his wife and daughter would steal his pride-and-joy Cadillac to go careening through the boondocks on a drunken wild ride (even though the two women never partied together and Claire had never been seen drinking by longtime friends or co-workers, and despite the fact that she was known to hate driving at night because of her eyes), or else he'd been up all night busily torturing his wife and daughter and setting up their murder in a flaming car wreck using his pyrotechnic expertise with demonic skill and then hurriedly hiding the evidence and cleaning up the house during the wee hours while waiting for the bank doors to open later that morning.

Either way, a man's got to get a little rest.

But did he sleep well, or was he haunted by the image of his daughter in the hospital, as he described seeing her to Sonia, lying in a coma brain-damaged, her head swathed in bandages? Did he toss and turn, fearing for the unknown fate of his estranged wife?

By 7:30 the next morning, Sonia says that Robert was up. At 8:00 A.M. the police at Foothill Division confirm that Supervising Detective Ferrand spoke with a male caller who identified himself as Robert Peernock. He told Ferrand he was under the impression that Natasha Peernock had been in some kind of a traffic accident and was at Holy Cross Hospital. He wanted to know if the police had the identity of the other female in the car yet.

Ferrand answered that they didn't, but that while Natasha was certainly in critical condition, she was expected to live. Ferrand assured Peernock he was not a suspect, but since he was the registered owner of the car and the father of the survivor, the police would very much like to have Robert come in and talk to them.

Ferrand does not recall Peernock saying anything at all about Natasha and Claire stealing his Cadillac on that night, or about their speeding away in the darkness with Claire waving that large bottle of whiskey that was later found next to her body with her fingerprints all over it.

Peernock claimed to have a ten o'clock appointment that morning to see his daughter, but he offered to come in on his way to Holy Cross Hospital. Detective Ferrand gave him directions to the station and Robert hung up, promising to be there by nine.

• • •

At 9:00 A.M. on July 23, while Robert Peernock was supposed to be walking into the station to speak with the police, Tasha lay wide awake after a sleepless night. The morning light streamed through the window but without her contacts, every blurry shape that walked through the door of her room threatened to be her father, coming back to finish the job and silence the witness. Wherever he was at that moment, she had no doubt that he would come looking for her at some point. As her mind cleared with every passing hour, Tasha realized that her father had to try to kill her again. He had to do it soon, to crush out the story that smoldered inside her like a rope wick dipped in gasoline.

At 9:00 A.M. of July 23, Robert Peernock was not at the Foothill police station as scheduled.

But records later proved that at 9:01 A.M. he passed through the checkout line at Sav-On Drugs, where he purchased some inexpensive luggage.

At 9:02 A.M. the Foothill police, who had not had the chance to interview Robert as they had hoped to do, were instead talking to Natasha's friend Patty. She gave the first version that made sense out of the events leading up to the car wreck. Patty assured the police that she had not been with Natasha that night, as the police had already guessed, but she confirmed that the two young women had indeed planned to go out together. She described dropping off her friend late that afternoon and about their plans to go to Magic Mountain. She described calling the house and getting no live answer on the phone, the odd experience of hearing Robert Peernock's voice on an answering machine and leaving message after message for Tasha until her concern rose to the point where she decided to drive over there with the guys. She described getting no answer at the door despite all of the family cars being parked there, despite the TV she could hear inside.

Lieutenant Ferrand thanked her, grateful for the first decent lead they had obtained so far. He immediately arranged for a detective to go back to the hospital later in the day and see if Natasha Peernock's memory had cleared, to learn if she would tell a story remotely connected to the one he had just heard.

As soon as Robert bought his new luggage at Sav-On, he hurried to the bank and withdrew another $30,000 in cash from his new savings account, taking $10,000 of it in hundred-dollar bills. He left the other $11,000 on deposit and tried to give the new account manager a PO box for the account address. When the bank officer insisted that their policy was to use only actual street addresses, Robert gave Claire's home as the official address for the account, not Sonia Siegel's condo where he had lived full-time for nearly four years. He emphasized several times that he didn't want any of the statements mailed to Claire's place, but it wasn't to be sent to Sonia's either; it was all to be sent to his PO box.

Robert listed his profession simply as "self-employed," which was essentially true. He was currently living off the cash settlements from his various lawsuits, some of which he was still pursuing, plus $36,000 per year in rent receipts generated by his income properties. Those houses were now owned solely by Robert, having become eligible for being paid off free and clear by the mortgage insurance that was triggered the moment Claire Peernock breathed her last on the seat of Robert's car.

Under the terms of Robert and Claire's "Agreement" he was not allowed to transfer or dispose of any joint assets before that August 1 deadline, after which each of them would sail away into separate sunsets in a civilized divorce and a fifty-fifty split of assets. Nevertheless he was raiding their assets within hours of her death even though nobody had reached him yet to tell him about it.

Later that same July 23 morning, as police sat wondering if Robert Peernock was going to make the appointment for which he was now very tardy, Peernock was on the other side of the city at Los Angeles International Airport scurrying toward the departure gate. He arrived just in time to board his nonstop flight for Las Vegas, Nevada.

Home of the high rollers.

CHAPTER

9

The blurry figure rushed toward Natasha's bedside.

She braced herself—but this time no attack followed. No blows rained down on her, no shots were fired. Instead, as the approaching shape grew clearer, the sight was far from being anything Tasha had feared. It was Patricia, who immediately leaned over her and touched her arm tenderly and spoke in her familiar Valley-girl voice, trembling with pain at the sight of Tasha's injuries.

Patty stood and tried to believe the information her eyes were taking in. If the nurse had not told her that this was her friend, she never would have known. The face was ripped and gouged as if Tasha had been chewed by an animal. Her lips were several times their normal size. Strangest of all, it looked to Patty as if Tasha was staring at her in shock and in fear, although both Tasha's eyes were so swollen, it was impossible to be sure.

But relief was flooding through Natasha. Here at last was someone who felt to her as if they were from the same planet, who spoke a language that sounded like her own. She had never dreamed that the touch of fingers on her arm could be so wonderful or that any voice could be so reassuring. Now Tasha could finally open her emotions and let the tears come.

She could tell her story to one who would believe.

There would be others who would not. But for the moment a small measure of safety had stepped into this nightmare. Invisible lines of communication opened and began to carry energy between the two young women, reaching young Natasha on levels far deeper than the surgeon's scalpel had been able to touch.

At the same time another invisible line was beginning to appear between Tasha and a man she had never even met. He didn't know it yet and neither did she, but his energy had already begun to link up with hers, spinning her story in another direction.

As soon as the accident investigators radioed from the scene that there was a fatality and evidence of possible foul play, Supervising Detective Ferrand had looked up the name of the next detective in the homicide rotation who was in line for an assignment. This was how the job of lead investigator on the Peernock case fell to Detective Steve Fisk.

Steve Fisk had joined the Air Force fresh out of high school, a born-and-raised California boy. Upon his discharge at the age of twenty-one, he had gone straight into the Los Angeles Police Department, following the footsteps of his father, a career officer who had risen through the ranks to the level of deputy chief. By the time Fisk got the Peernock case, he had lived another twenty-one years and spent his married life raising his four children not far from where he grew up himself.

Fisk tends to take a personal interest in the destruction that murderers wreak upon his community. A big, burly cop with reddish-brown hair and a thick mustache, he has a soft-spoken demeanor that disarms suspects who expect harsh treatment. But in the next instant he can flash a razor blade of anger through his eyes that makes hardened felons decide just maybe here is a cop they will want to play ball with. None of it requires yelling and screaming. Steve Fisk is the velvet hammer. Countless interview subjects have been surprised by his gentle demeanor but have gone home wondering what hit them.

At the crime scene, a single glance told him that the situation was all wrong and only an idiot would believe an ordinary auto accident had taken place here.

Fisk went to the hospital himself to pick up the purse that the paramedics had taken away with Natasha. He saw that it belonged to Claire. He soon knew Natasha's mother was dead, that the father Robert Peernock had not yet been accounted for, and that neighbors confirmed that Peernock had plenty of money. Fisk realized that if Peernock was indeed the culprit, then he had the means to vanish quickly, out of state, out of the country. And if that happened, Fisk's twenty-one years on the force made him well aware how poor his chances would be of appropriating funds to launch a pursuit across international borders.

Natasha's initial story had been taken under the worst of circumstances; she was hardly coherent. But Fisk knew that head wounds produce varying symptoms. Thoughts can clear. Memories can return.

So as Steve Fisk walked back into Holy Cross Hospital early in the afternoon of the twenty-third, less than a day and a half after the crimes, he was determined to come away knowing anything Natasha might tell him to help find out who had done this brutal thing so close to Fisk's own station, right there on his home turf.

The case became personal for Steve Fisk right away.

When the big red-haired cop in a suit and tie showed up after lunchtime, Patty allowed herself to be chased out of the room so Tasha could be interviewed again. Patty didn't know that part of the purpose of the interview was to check her own story against Tasha's memory. It wouldn't have mattered to her anyway. Let the cops do their jobs, she figured; she was on her way home to pick up a few things, including her pajamas.

Because once Patty got back to the hospital, she didn't

plan on leaving again until Natasha could get out of there
with her.

Tasha offered Steve Fisk answers much different from those
she had given immediately after the wreck. Indeed, she had
no memory of having given them. This time she spoke from
a frame of reference much more conscious and alert.

Fisk started leading her through her story, one fact at a
time, asking her to repeat things whenever her voice would
dip to inaudible levels, having her go back over certain se-
quences if he had trouble following her.

But Tasha was frustrated beyond anything she had ever
known. She could see the images clearly, could feel the emotions boiling inside her, and yet in her jumbled state it hurt
to try to think on the detailed level that Fisk was demanding.
She wanted to help all that she could, to do anything to bring
her father in off the streets, but the images that had burned
so deeply into her memory had to filter out along verbal
pathways that weren't yet fully restored. She began to feel
herself drifting off, trying to float away from the relentless
probing.

But Fisk persisted. And slowly, slowly, the basic story
came out: the argument in the kitchen, the strangulation, the
handcuffs, the face mask, the hours in the bedroom being
force-fed alcohol.

It hurt Tasha to think. It hurt worse to say the words. Still,
it was at this point, for the very first time, that she finally
broke the lifelong family taboo against speaking out about
the brutality at home. In the clearest terms she could manage,
she told about that final explosive night in the house. There
was no longer any reason to keep silent.

That first clear version of the key events on the night of the
crimes was recorded with Fisk's interview, completed and
logged at 4:00 P.M. on July 23. When he finally left the

hospital, he was on his way to seek a search warrant for the family house.

Although Tasha couldn't tell for sure if she had found someone else to believe her, by the time it was over she had triggered a full-scale homicide investigation centering on her father as the prime suspect.

On Fisk's way out, he had the head nurse make a notation that all visitors were to be monitored. Under no circumstances was her father to be allowed inside. No information was to be given over the phone about Natasha. Not to anybody. He then arranged with the LAPD to have a twenty-four-hour guard put on outside the door of the room. Whether or not Tasha had been believed, clearly someone had listened.

Thirty minutes after Steve Fisk logged his interview with Natasha, Robert Peernock checked into room 678 at Bally's Hotel in Las Vegas. He registered under the name of "James Dobbs" from Sacramento.

"James Dobbs" paid for a special two-night package, which included a giant floor show downstairs in the *JUBILEE!* Theater. The show featured the Ziegfeld Follies—not the kind of attraction that most newcomers can resist. Fortunately for "James Dobbs," he still had plenty of time to get himself situated in the room and grab some dinner before curtain time.

Dinner was brought to Tasha in her bed but she couldn't make herself take anything in. She basically ate a vegetarian diet and wouldn't have been attracted to standard hospital fare under the best of circumstances, but now her appetite was completely gone. Even though her awareness had returned and her thinking was beginning to clear, she felt broken to pieces inside. It was as if a thousand thin crystal wires had been shattered within her; they now lay in shards around her heart. To even consider trying to recuperate and somehow go on with her life made her feel as if she were staring up at an endless wall of frozen rock, looking for a way to climb it bare-handed.

Where could she even begin? There was no one from her mother's side living in this country. Claire had been the only one of thirteen children in her family who immigrated to America. The others hadn't been all that close in recent years, anyway.

Somehow the idea of recuperating with Robert's family didn't hold a lot of appeal.

And in recent years, Robert and Claire's dark homelife had kept any family friends at a distance. Since Tasha had just turned eighteen, she was no longer at an age where the state was going to help take care of her.

She had always been a dreamer, a quiet, creative personality who was long on appreciation for the abstract side of life but short on hardheaded life skills. Now she lay in bed silently playing back her memories of all the times that Claire had badgered her, speaking in her delicate French accent with the firm persistence of a mother who insisted on being heard.

"Tasha, you're going to graduate from high school in a few months. What will you do with your life?"

"You know. I'm going to fashion-design school."

"And that's very nice, but it's a hard way to make a living. What if it doesn't work?"

"I don't know. Who says it won't work?"

"You won't have anything to fall back on. You need skills of some kind. Do you want to have to rely on a man to take care of you?"

"No way. You know I'm not going to let that happen."

Claire stopped and smiled, looked at her daughter with sad eyes as she continued softly. "Natasha . . . I won't always be here, you know. And I don't ever want you to have to stay with a man just because you're afraid of how you would take care of yourself if you try to leave.''

Of course, Claire had learned through years of personal experience how important independence can be when the primary relationship in your life goes sour, turns toxic, and eventually becomes lethal.

Even though they never had the chance to resolve the argument, Tasha realized that one way or the other she was independent now.

At 9:00 P.M. that night Steve Fisk was putting in some overtime by drawing up search warrants. A case like this made the long hours easy. The idea of a man binding his beautiful girl so that he could slam her head with a blunt instrument and douse her with gasoline was enough to puncture instantly through the armor that cops are required to keep around their feelings.

Fisk also prepared a second warrant, aimed at the condo where Peernock had been living with his girlfriend, so that simultaneous searches could take place by surprise. You can never be too careful, he explained later. Who could tell what kinds of things the man could have left lying around, things that might explain exactly why Robert Peernock hadn't bothered to keep his appointment at the police station this morning, things that might offer some clue as to where Robert Peernock was hiding at that very moment?

Bally's Las Vegas proudly presents Donn Arden's *JUBILEE!* ''The Stage Experience of a Lifetime'' produced, directed, and conceived by Donn Arden!

This lavish extravaganza of gorgeous ''Singing and Dancing Ladies and Men'' boasts special appearances by ''those famous Bally's Girls,'' known the world over for their beauty.

''James Dobbs'' sat in the dark amid a packed crowd of

gamblers and pleasure seekers whose attention was fixed upon the gala review onstage. The audience was composed, presumably, of people who had come from around the world to pack the house and marvel at the feathered fannies of Bally's Dancing Ladies and the strategically emphasized bulges of Bally's Dancing Men.

People queue up early to get the good seats. Thus Robert Peernock, alias "James Dobbs," did not need to fear recognition from others in the crowd. Eyes generally remain fixed onstage throughout the show's seven acts; Peernock/Dobbs remained anonymous in the dark, but outside the bright city lay waiting.

He was, after all, a brand-new bachelor in Las Vegas, Nevada. He had a suitcase stuffed with cash and plenty of time to kill. The brightly lighted, flashing and winking, featherfannied, silicon-stuffed town spread itself out before him.

It offered absolutely no resistance at all.

CHAPTER

10

Tasha awoke with a jolt in the hospital bed. This time the nightmare was the kind that ended when she opened her eyes. The face staring down at her was not her father's but that of her friend Patricia, who had returned to the room to be with her and to stay as long as it would take.

"We're lucky they let me in here, Tash," Patty whispered. "You're not supposed to have visitors this late."

Tasha tried to think of the usual kind of sarcastic, joking reply in the spirit of conversations she and Patty used to have. She couldn't form the words. She tried simply to smile, but her lips wouldn't spread far enough.

So she just nodded slightly. Patty took that in, then nodded along with her and giggled, glancing back at the door as if they were two conspirators who had just put one over on the hospital system.

The invisible lines between them began to crackle as the energy of their friendship danced back and forth.

"Whoa. You look like the Elephant Man," Patty teased, forcing a little laugh. But Tasha didn't smile at that one, either, so Patty dropped it.

"Patty," Tasha whispered, taking Patty's arm and squeezing it weakly, "... where's my mom?"

Patty froze at the question. The nurses had made it plain to her that before they would give her full-time visiting privileges, Patty had to agree to play ball with them about how to handle that question. Patty was nineteen years old and had never had to tell someone that a family member had been murdered. And now her friend Tasha was looking up at her strangely, as if trying to read Patty's silence.

Finally Tasha added, "I keep asking them but they give me the same stuff . . . like 'You can see her later.' And I'm all, 'Yeah, but how is she?' . . . And they just keep saying . . . 'You have to see her later.' "

Patty knew that Tasha wasn't the type who trusted a lot of people; she made friends slowly. And even though Patty was by far the more gregarious, each valued the fact that she could absolutely believe what the other said to her. Absolutely.

"Well, Tash . . ." She hesitated. The pause grew longer.

And she knew right then that she couldn't tell. The nurses had warned her that Tasha's mental state was so fragile right now that the news of her mother's death might push her over the edge. They warned that if she didn't help them protect Natasha from the truth until she was strong enough to handle it, Patty could wind up being responsible for her friend's failure to recover.

That thought scared the hell out of her. Both girls had some measure of experience with lies of convenience, told to teachers to excuse late homework or to parents to get them off your back. This was Patty's first encounter with a lie of mercy.

"She's . . . in a room just down the hall, Tash. You can see her later on. I mean, she has to rest for a while. Hey"— Patty touched Tasha's arms again, wondering where else she could touch her that wouldn't hurt—"come on. Give it some time. You guys were both pretty badly torn up."

Tasha thought about it for a moment, staring into Patty's eyes. Finally she nodded. That little smile started moving through her lips again. And even though her lips were swollen to several times their normal size, this time the smile almost felt okay.

• • •

At 1:45 in the morning on the twenty-fourth, less than forty-six hours after the wreck was first discovered, Judge Michael Luros of the San Fernando Superior Court was awake and working. He signed the search warrant for Claire's house and another for Sonia's condo.

By 4:00 A.M., forty-eight hours after the report of the wreck, teams of detectives were at both locations looking for anything that might provide solid evidence of just what had taken place at the Peernock residence two nights before. Fisk and Castro led the search at the Peernock house. The first part was easy; check for the items on the warrant. Look for obvious things: a bloody shoe, a weapon of some kind.

But Fisk soon realized that more warrants would be needed, more trips would soon be made back to the Peernock house. Because even though Peernock hadn't lived there in years, he still kept an office area jammed with files and stacks of papers. Any part of it could offer clues. Any scrap could point to answers. Fisk realized with dismay that he was looking at dozens, perhaps hundreds of hours spent sifting. And in a society growing more violent every day, time is a homicide cop's most expensive luxury, the least available commodity that he has. Therefore, even as important as these paper searches might prove to be, they were likely to have to take a backseat.

For the moment Fisk needed hard evidence of exactly what could have happened to a mother and daughter whose injuries were identical, save for the fact that the daughter survived because she was able to thrash her head from side to side, just enough to protect her skull from the fatal fractures that took her mother's life.

At 8:45 A.M. on July 24, the autopsy of Claire Peernock began. Steve Fisk attended personally. If anything should be discovered that might help bring about the apprehension of the suspect, and thereby assure the survival of Natasha Peernock, he wasn't about to sit around waiting for a phone call to find out.

The result came quickly and the findings were conclusive. Death had occurred as a result of blows from a blunt instrument wielded with great force. A fist-sized bruise had been inflicted on the left side of her face at some time prior to death. A smaller bruise was on the right wrist, judged to be a defensive wound suffered either in pulling against wrist restraints or reflexively shielding her face from the blows that had killed her.

A murder warrant was issued on Robert John Peernock.

Later on in the morning of July 24, "James Dobbs" mailed a letter from Las Vegas to Foothill Savings in Los Angeles. He wrote under the name of Robert Peernock, acting under instructions he had obtained from the bank during a phone call earlier that same day. He ordered the three Peernock accounts there to be closed, two of which were trusts for his children. The three new accounts were opened with Sonia Siegel's name added to them, giving her access to his money there and allowing her to write checks on his behalf as well as to bring in deposits of any rent receipts she might collect for him from his income properties.

At this point Sonia knew nothing of Peernock's efforts on her behalf regarding his cash flow; she didn't find out until the bank told her some days later. At this point all she knew was that the man in her life had gone to the hospital to see his injured eighteen-year-old daughter the morning before and had never returned. His eleven-year-old daughter remained with her and by now was asking questions that Sonia had no idea how to answer. By the time that the Department of Social Services took custody of the girl and drove off with her later in the day, the Old Sinking Feeling was no doubt getting hard for Sonia to ignore.

• • •

"Where were you?" Tasha murmured when Patty walked back in the room. "I woke up and there was nobody here."

"Oh, some nurse came in a while ago and lost her mind because I was sleeping on the floor by your bed. So I walked down to the gift shop to get out of her way."

"Like that?" She looked at Patricia, standing there in pajamas and slippers, no makeup, hair all stringy. In for the duration. Tasha laughed weakly, trying not to open her mouth so far as to draw in air over her sensitive, broken teeth.

"So?" Patty replied breezily. "It's not like they never see anybody in pajamas around here. Besides, at least I'm not walking around in one of their stupid gowns with my butt hanging out the back."

"Maybe you should try it," Tasha said with that odd expression that Patty had realized was the closest she could come to a smile right now. "I hear it's a good way to meet guys."

Patty laughed at that. Tasha couldn't join in with her, but her eyes locked onto Patty's and Tasha could feel the laughter almost as if it were her own. It lifted the dark gray cloud off her heart for a few seconds.

In that brief moment of strength, Tasha considered telling Patricia that she had realized her mother must be dead. There was no more reason to cover it up. After all, she had barely survived, but was still being allowed visits from a friend, so why wouldn't she be able to see her own mother—if Claire were alive too? It made no sense. The you can-see-her-later line rang hollow.

There was no other conclusion left. Robert had gotten her mother. Tasha almost spoke up, but she swallowed the impulse. She decided it would be better just to leave it alone.

The gray cloud hanging over her thickened. It wrapped around her like a wet wool blanket, squeezing out all the light.

On July 25, 1987, the *Los Angeles Times* used fourteen inches of type to reveal that the autopsy had been conclusive—the cause of Claire Peernock's death was homicide—and that detectives believed that whoever arranged the crash had tried to make it look as if Claire had been drinking and had wrecked the car. The police established that Claire Peernock had been known to dislike driving on the freeway at night and that no one close to her could find a reason for her to be in a remote section of town at that hour.

Police Lieutenant Bernard Conine explained that the car had been rigged to explode, but that the clumsy explosive apparatus had failed. He also revealed that the dead woman's estranged husband, an expert pyrotechnic engineer, was the prime suspect in the crime and was being sought for questioning.

Victoria Doom, Claire's former divorce attorney, saw the article. The headline read MURDER PLOT SUSPECTED IN FATAL CRASH IN SUN VALLEY. But she only glanced at it, so she never spotted the name of the victim, a woman she had met once, seven and a half months before. Three more days would pass before the attorney began her journey of self-doubt about the advice she had given Claire back in December.

At 12:32 P.M. on the twenty-fifth, Robert Peernock registered at the Stardust Hotel in Las Vegas. This time he signed the registration card as "Robert Thomas" from Amarillo, Texas. "James Dobbs" had apparently vanished into the Twilight Zone earlier that day, leaving "Robert Thomas" to occupy room 2323 and give an expected checkout date of two days later.

The following day "Robert Thomas" would come down and pay cash for the room, starting a pattern of visits that he would repeat every few days to settle his bill, always in cash. It was a pattern he would keep up for weeks to come.

At noon on July 27, Steve Fisk again went to see Natasha at Holy Cross Hospital. By now the investigation had taken on an even greater urgency. The crime scene was cooling and the possibility of Peernock's escape was heating up.

"Try, Natasha."

"I can't."

"You can't try?"

"It hurts to think. I can't think anymore."

"Please, just a few more questions. He's still out there. You want us to catch him, don't you?"

"Yes."

"All right, then. What kind of gun was it?"

"A little one."

"A pistol?"

"A pistol. My head hurts. It hurts to think."

"What color was it?"

"It was a *gun*!"

"Right, but was it silver or dark blue or—"

"Black. A black pistol. The bullets go around in a thing."

"A revolver?"

"I don't know. This hurts."

"Just a little more. Did you see bullets?"

"It was a *gun*!"

"Yes. But in a revolver you can see the tips of the bullets. In an automatic they're all inside the—"

"No, it's a revolver. A black one. With a wooden handle."

At 5:30 P.M. that July 27 evening Detective Castro waited at Foothill Station for the arrival of Sonia Siegel as he had arranged with her. He planned to have her tailed once she left the station, in order to see if she was in contact with

Peernock. But that wouldn't happen. Sonia Siegel failed to show up.

It was dark outside the hospital-room window. The television played softly in the background. Patty wandered out to stretch her legs. Tasha stirred as the sound of familiar music suddenly came out of the TV. She struggled to focus on the screen, but the images were a blur. Still, as the show came on, she realized that this was an episode of *St. Elsewhere,* a television drama that she had taken an interest in a few years before. The stories on the show appealed to her. And the doctors and nurses seemed more interesting than the real ones she'd met as a thirteen-year-old while lying in traction in the hospital after her father had thrown her against the kitchen wall.

And now as the episode began she quickly felt drawn into the pleasant sense of escape, while the familiar world of the show took over. She knew the characters well enough to identify them by voice, even though she couldn't see them on the screen.

In this episode one of the doctors was nearly killed. The camera entered his mind as he went through a near-death experience. The few images that Natasha could make out, combined with the voices on the sound track, caught her up in a fascinating experience. It all seemed so glorious: rising up over your body, looking down upon the scene while others fought to save your life, then floating up and away into a long tunnel that opened out into a huge ball of light at the gateway to a fantastic new world.

The spell was broken as a realization hit her. Floating? Ball of light? New world?

She had missed the *whole thing*. For the first time since she'd woken up in the hospital, Natasha felt herself getting mad. She had already tasted the shock and the grief, the confusion and the fear.

But this? Here she had come so close to having her head caved in with a claw hammer or some damn thing and the doctors had told her how she'd almost died and how at first they hadn't even been sure they could save her, and now *this*?

Nothing. Nothing at all. No floating. No tunnel. No ball of light. And certainly no sage advice from spirit guides sent to escort her onto the next plane of existence. No, if that had happened she would have remembered it for sure.

Whether it was sheer coincidence or whether it had somehow been intended that she come across this particular TV episode right now, something had finally happened that allowed her to get a small taste, a first little inkling, of something deep down underneath all of the trauma.

She was beginning to feel the first sharp nibbles of her outrage.

At 2:30 P.M. the following afternoon, Lead Investigator Steve Fisk arranged for a high-level COBRA tailing unit to be placed on Sonia Siegel in the hope of locating information on the whereabouts of Robert Peernock, who was now officially listed as the primary suspect in a designated homicide case. Fisk sympathized with Siegel's dilemma regarding the suspicions directed at her boyfriend, but this business of her not showing up for a vital interview while a suspect was at large was not going to stand.

Then he called Dr. King at Holy Cross Hospital and obtained confirmation that Natasha's wounds had definitely been caused by a blunt weapon, not by any sort of impact in an auto accident.

He arranged with U.S. Customs to be alert for any attempt by Peernock to leave the country.

He called the lab for fingerprint information and learned that while Claire Peernock's prints had been found on the whiskey bottle, they were not on the steering wheel of the car she was supposed to have been driving.

Even though she hadn't been wearing gloves.

Meanwhile, Natasha had no way of knowing how deeply she had impressed him with her story, and how strongly Fisk's instincts were being confirmed as the evidence began pouring in.

"No, really, I think some of the swelling's going down. Right here around your eyes," Patty assured Tasha as she stroked her freshly cleaned hair.

"You're just getting used to looking at the Elephant Man," Tasha muttered.

It was supposed to have been a joking reply, but Patty noticed that most of Tasha's comments were tending to land like lead sinkers, even when she was trying to show some humor. Her empathy for Tasha's feelings gave a glimpse inside her friend; the darkness there frightened her. Patty understood why it should be that way, but it scared her all the same.

CHAPTER

11

Victoria Doom has a youthful, animated voice and speaks in clipped, precise tones. Her conversation is focused with a good lawyer's clarity of thought and is sprinkled with a broad base of facts, metaphors, and references.

But she still falters when she discusses Claire Peernock. She replays that one meeting with Claire over and over in her mind, questioning the strong advice she gave at the initial consultation, wondering if there is anything else she might have told Claire that could somehow have changed the outcome of a single night that ended in slaughter.

So while Victoria the attorney can verbally slug it out toe-to-toe with tough opposing attorneys from high-priced downtown law firms, while she can match wits with jaded judges behind closed doors in chambers, Victoria the woman has since given up her Saugus law practice and moved far away. Now she lives with her husband, a retired Air Force colonel, on a large parcel of rural land with a menagerie of exotic animals. Years after that single meeting with Claire, Victoria the woman is sure that she blew it somehow. But hindsight doesn't help her to isolate whatever she might have done to magically reach into a troubled relationship and hand Claire some bit of advice that might have kept her from disaster.

Giving a wife strong advice had never been a problem for the attorney, until she met Claire Peernock.

"When Claire came in to see me, there wasn't anything exceptional about it. I have a standard procedure that I run through at the office for everybody who comes in for a divorce. I tell them about the process, how long it's going to take, what needs to be done. I answer their questions and, you know, I try to give them a backbone if that's necessary. I try to make them behave themselves if that's necessary. I hand out Kleenex.

"She was concerned about her share of community property. It seems that her husband was one of those men who like to control the purse strings and keep the little wife in the dark about the finances. She wanted to keep the house they were living in, reasonable child support and spousal support, and whatever else she might be entitled to under the California law. She didn't sound money hungry.

"Robert was served in early December of 1986 with a petition for dissolution and order to show cause, to set temporary child support and temporary use of the property, with a hearing date set for that coming January eight."

At this point in Victoria's story, there is a shift in her voice. The confident tones leave her as she steps away from her recital of the facts and evaluates herself. Victoria had indeed given Claire some strong advice. But the attorney leaves the woman to finish the thought in a slightly softened voice, a much more hesitant delivery.

"And unfortunately . . . you know . . . when it came to Claire, I missed the mark. Totally.

"That was the first and last time I ever saw her."

In fact, when Victoria had last heard from Claire Peernock, she thought the matter had been dropped. Claire had left a phone message at her office advising that Robert had shown surprising resistance to the idea of getting divorced. He wanted a few months to try to work things out. If the relationship wasn't going to survive, he wanted at least to make a venture into some kind of business using their jointly held properties. Robert even voluntarily signed an "Agreement" assuring Claire of continued support payments through August of 1987. And if, by that time, he and Claire had not arrived at an arrangement that suited them both and gave her reason to reconsider her demands, Claire could reactivate her divorce proceedings. By the time Claire left the message telling Victoria this, it was Christmas Eve of 1986. She had already signed the ''Agreement.''

On the same day that she received Claire's message, Victoria wrote back and acknowledged that the divorce would be stalled as requested. She advised Claire very strongly not to sign any more documents without at least letting Victoria read them over for her. Then she closed the letter with the expressed hope that once August arrived, if divorce was still necessary, Robert and Claire would be able to proceed with an uncontested dissolution.

She knew it is rare that a husband and wife can divorce and divide a small fortune without hotly contesting each other's position. But having met Claire only once and having been told that she had already decided to take this course, Victoria decided to accept her portrayal of the home situation as being one that would be resolved in a civilized fashion.

She put Claire's legal file back in the cabinet and made a note on the calendar to check with her on the first of August. As an attorney this was all she could do for Claire at that time. She made no further attempt to contact her.

Seven months later, less than a week before Victoria was scheduled to call Claire and see whether she intended to go forward with the divorce action on the August 1 deadline, the first step on Victoria's journey of self-doubt began. It was three days after the first newspaper article appeared regarding the crimes.

On July 28, a man walked into her office and identified himself as Claire Peernock's brother, Maurice. He had just arrived from Claire's homeland of Quebec. Speaking in a thick French-Canadian accent, he told how he had found Victoria's letter to Claire inside the Peernock house, along with

some other papers. The letter guided him to her; he didn't
know who else to call upon for legal advice. Maurice assumed that Victoria already realized Claire had been beaten
to death, that Natasha had been brutalized, and that police
were searching for Robert. He asked Victoria to meet with
him to discuss what should be done about Claire's estate and
the protection of the children.

Victoria stood in stunned silence and tried to absorb the
news. In the nearly five years since she had become a sole practitioner, she had never been confronted with such blunt evidence of the deep rages inside the divorces she was hired to
handle.

Maurice also informed her that he had just come from a
brief visit with Natasha in the hospital. The young woman
was going to survive and was expected to recover, physically
at least. Although her sister would be taken into foster care
in order to be able to stay in America, Natasha was going to
need somebody to look after her interests, to help her deal
with the family belongings, sort the property, protect the estate.

Maurice told her regretfully that he did not have the means to
remain in California long enough to look after so many complex legal details, and an eighteen-year-old was not qualified to
walk that minefield by herself. He added that since Victoria had
been Claire's attorney, Claire must have trusted her. On that basis, he appealed to Victoria for help.

Even as she stood weaving, trying to absorb the shock of
Claire's death, her mind raced. She asked herself how she
could possibly accept this man's request for help. This was
a situation that called for an experienced probate attorney,
but she had virtually no experience in probate law; her background was primarily family law and criminal law.

She protested to Maurice that if she took this case for Natasha, Victoria would be throwing herself into a crash course of

home study to bone up on procedure. Was anything like that going to be good enough for Natasha's interests?

Maurice countered that for him to go to some stranger and ask for help would be nothing more than a roll of the dice with regard to any assurance that Natasha would be treated fairly. No, he repeated, if Claire had trusted Victoria, then so would he. And the ability to trust the attorney meant far more to him than matters of procedure.

Victoria felt the room closing in as she made a few silent calculations. This case was a load of grief that she definitely did not need. She had a good reputation and never needed to advertise for business; most of her clients were referred by other clients. The prior year had marked the first time that she had earned $100,000 in her own practice since passing the California bar exam. But if the complexities of this case required her to do so much background study that she had to neglect her other cases, she might wind up having to farm everything else out to other lawyers. Stepping outside of her expertise could easily turn out to be a walk into quicksand. She knew that the courts weren't going to cut her any breaks just because she was venturing into a field of law that was new to her. And whatever law firm she wound up opposing in court would be even less likely to do so.

Besides, as Claire's former divorce attorney, she had no ethical obligation to become a probate lawyer for some young woman she had never even met. There were risks in every direction and no reason to get involved, except for the simple dignity of this man's request for honest help from a woman he did not know but whom he had decided to trust because his sister had.

Victoria had her own marriage to think about. A case like this was surely going to follow her home at night. So far, her husband, Richard, had been understanding with her every time she brought home yet another abandoned animal to add to the growing zoo at their little ranch, but now, if she actually did this thing, she would have to rely on him more than ever. He would have to assume even more responsibility than he already had for the care and feeding of those animals, just so she could spend her free time studying the Probate Code and applicable case law.

No, it was clear. There was just not enough reason to take the risk. This simple request from this frightened man far away from his homeland threatened to impact on every area of her life. It offered no other appeal than the fact that someone respected her and had made an emphatic request for her help.

She took the case.

Later that day, long after Maurice had left to go back to the hospital, promising to bring Natasha in as soon as she had recovered enough to make the trip, a stunning realization hit her—she had the physical proof of a motive for Claire's murder.

She was keeping it right there, in her office files.

Claire had sent it to her months ago for safekeeping, almost as if she was telling Victoria that she wanted her to have such proof just in case something like this should ever happen. It was the original "Agreement" that Claire and Robert Peernock had signed, and it outlined all the reasons why Robert's last chance to keep a major portion of their estate for himself was going to expire on August 1, four days away.

Victoria rushed to the file and flipped through the papers until she found it. Typed neatly with Claire's secretarial skill, it was carefully worded and showed that Claire had clearly put a great deal of thought into the terms she outlined here. The document was dated and signed by both Claire and Robert. As Victoria began to read it, she had to sit down. She felt the blood drain from her face as she went down the list.

AGREEMENT BETWEEN
ROBERT & CLAIRE PEERNOCK

I understand that Claire Peernock has filed for divorce and that our first court appearance is scheduled for January 8, 1987.

Because I am in the process of developing a new company, I have asked Claire Peernock to postpone such proceedings until August, 1987. She has accepted under the following stipulations:

1. I will not, during this period of time, transfer, encumber, hypothecate, conceal, or in any way dispose of any property, real or personal, whether community, quasicommunity, or separate, except in the usual course of business or for the necessities of life and,

I will notified [sic] Claire Peernock of any proposed extraordinary expenditures and an accounting of such will be presented on August 1, 1987, or on demand.

2. Since the only purpose of delaying this divorce is to establish my business, Claire Peernock will, of course, benefit from the fifty-fifty split of my business assets in August 1987 when proceedings resume.

3. Since Claire Peernock has accepted this seven-month delay, I will in turn, when divorce proceedings resume, cooperate fully in order to expedite and minimize expenses of dividing all assets equally. Such assets include but are not limited to said business, three (3) houses, one (1) parcel of land in Pennsylvania, all cash accounts, gold coins,

silver coins, stocks, bonds, etc. Full cooperation will also be given for division of furniture, cars, incidentals, child custody and support, and all other matters related to this divorce.

4. I have agreed to pay $2,000 to Claire Peernock, which consists mostly of back food payments (9 weeks @ $125) + different bills and penalties incurred for late charges and payments of expenses during the past two and a half months.

5. I agree to resume payment of $125 per week for food. This check will be given religiously every Sunday.

6. I agree to make payments of house mortgages on time, taxes, insurances, all utilities (including cable TV).

7. Since Claire Peernock was counting on proceeds of divorce settlement to help defray college expenses for Natasha, I agree to make available at least $2,000 for college next year. If more is needed, agreement could be reached.

8. Although we both agree to try to dispose of property (houses, land, etc.) without interference of lawyers or court, Claire Peernock reserves her option to have every transaction reviewed by her attorney, Mrs. Doom. Since I have agreed to be fair and to divide everything fifty-fifty, these legal consultations will be for her peace of mind only, therefore she has agreed to defray these minimal legal expenses.

9. I agree to not attack, strike, threaten, assault, and batter Claire Peernock and her daughters. . . .

I will continue to have some kind of father-daughter relationship with [the youngest daughter] when acceptable to all.

I will refrain from yelling at, ridiculing, or even talking to Natasha [the rest of the sentence was crossed out and initialed by Robert, as follows:] . . . *since all my comments are invariably negative.—R.J.P.*

I will not threaten to throw her out of the house when she turns eighteen ever again. [Robert wrote in the following and initialed it by hand:] *The above is not an admission of any wrongdoing but is an agreement in spirit, for future understanding. R.J.P.*

Any breach or violation of any part of this agreement will nullify such and Claire Peernock will then have the option of proceeding with the divorce immediately.

By the time Victoria got to the end of the "Agreement" she felt as if her temperature had dropped ten degrees. Items 4 through 9 offered an especially revealing glimpse inside this household; for months before Claire finally decided to break away from the marriage, Robert had been withholding monies for his family's funds for food and shelter. He hadn't even bothered to cross that part out.

But she wondered what Claire had accomplished with this

document. It did nothing more than force him to behave in ways he was already required to do under the law. Most of all, why had Robert *really* wanted the time extension? Maurice had told her that he had found no evidence of any "new company" at the house, even though Robert kept most of his files and all of his electronic supplies there.

So why would Robert beg Claire for a seven-month delay and then do nothing with it? Victoria thought back to the time when it was signed. What else had been going on then? The couple's relationship had completely soured; alienation was complete. However, Victoria's experience with the way people behave in divorce situations told her that it would be no more than human nature for Claire to have shouted in anger at Robert that she was finished, she had made up her mind to divorce him.

What, then, if he had started planning to kill Claire at the moment she revealed her divorce plans, but she had surprised him by the swiftness of her actions in seeking out a divorce attorney and in having him served with papers? In that case he could hardly have dared to go ahead with any such plan within days of being served; that would be as good as an admission of guilt. However, if he got her to give him time supposedly for things to cool off, he would have the leisure to refine a murder plan and set up an accident that would have worked perfectly if only the car hadn't veered off the road and avoided the evidence-cleansing explosion and fire.

And even now, with the survival of Natasha, in court it would only be his daughter's word against his.

Except for the matter of this "Agreement" that Victoria held in her hands. In the event of Claire's death *after* the August 1 date, any suspicions of murder would fall squarely on the husband who was being divorced. Thus the "Agreement" established a clear motive for a staged accident to take place in the week before August 1, when the "Agreement" would expire and put the divorce back on track.

Did Robert know she had this thing? If so, he would surely want to get his hands on it.

She wondered where he was at this very moment. A cold burst of fear shot through her. She had no way of knowing that it was only the first of many yet to come.

At 5:00 P.M. that evening, Steve Fisk received a phone call from some private attorney he had never heard of before named Victoria Doom. She wanted him to know that she had a document in her files that might shed a lot of light on Robert Peernock's status as a suspect.

Fisk asked her to wait for him at her office and left immediately to go pick up the file. It was bad enough wondering whether there would be another attempt on Natasha's life before Robert could be brought in. But until the whole thing had time to shake itself out Fisk didn't need to have documents floating around out there that Robert Peernock, if indeed he was guilty, might be strongly motivated to put on some private hunting list.

Fisk greeted Victoria hurriedly. The moment he ran his eyes down the page she handed to him, he agreed; a motive had been found. It was not proof, but in the right hands it was clearly a reason for murder.

Tasha struggled to focus her way out of the dark gray fog that persisted in settling over her heart whenever she got quiet for a while and didn't have enough distraction to keep her from thinking too much. She glanced around and saw that the room was empty except for a blur that turned out to be an orderly who had propped the door open while he mopped the floor. When the orderly left he picked up her untouched dinner tray.

As Tasha lay quietly she began to notice voices of people outside in the hallway. It was an odd sensation; they were again discussing her as if she weren't aware of them. The

voices drifted back inside, just enough to give her the gist
of the conversation. She closed her eyes and sorted them out,
identifying each speaker by sound. Patty and Uncle Maurice
were being lectured on Tasha's condition by one of the
nurses.

"You all don't seem to understand," the nurse was saying.
"Natasha's injuries only *start* with the physical wounds.
She's not going to just go home and pick up where she left
off. This is a young woman who will have to have *years* of
therapy along with her physical recovery." The nurse
dropped her voice to a whisper that Tasha could barely hear.

"This can destroy her mental health, don't you see that?
If what she says about her father is true, then she's probably
going to hate men, maybe for the rest of her life. You talk
about getting her out of here like you're springing her from
jail. She could well need to spend her life in a mental institution."

Tasha felt as if a hole had opened up in the floor and swallowed her, bed and all. She could tell that Patty and Maurice
were both protesting the nurse's take on the situation, but the
words blurred in her ears. Up to this point she hadn't even considered her own mental state. She had just automatically assumed that if she could get her physical health back and if she
could ever again look like something that wouldn't make children cry in the supermarket, then her only real challenge would
be to find some way to make a living.

But here she had just heard herself discussed as if she were
a bug on a microscope slide; the specimen had been pronounced flawed. She had been judged to be damaged goods,
perhaps beyond repair.

Was she? she asked herself. Tasha tried to run a quick
self-check, casting her mind's eye around inside. But it was
like sifting through the remains of a house burned to the
ground. Was anything left inside of her that could be sal-

vaged? She wondered if she could ever rebuild herself out of the rubble.

She turned inside herself completely, sorting through the scorched debris like a homeowner on her knees sifting ashes with her fingers. And as she worked, the dark gray cloud slowly settled down over her again like smoke from an arson's fire.

The cloud was a lot thicker this time.

Fisk arrived back at the station from Victoria Doom's office at 5:30 P.M., just in time to take a call from Sonia Siegel's next-door neighbor. The neighbor reported that Robert Peernock had just called him and had been pressuring him for a phone number where Sonia could be reached right away. The neighbor was aware that Sonia was at her aunt's house, but he hadn't given Robert the number. The neighbor had made some excuse about not being able to locate the number at the time. Robert had said he would call back after waiting for ten minutes while the neighbor "looked for it."

There wasn't time to set up a trace on Peernock's return call, but the report confirmed one of Steve Fisk's suspicions: either Sonia Siegel was actively helping Peernock or else Peernock was frantically attempting to induce her to cooperate.

Another piece dropped into place on the rapidly expanding game board.

CHAPTER

12

On July 28 at 8:30 P.M., Lead Investigator Steve Fisk was still at the Foothill Station, far into his overtime hours as he interviewed Louise, Claire's longtime friend. She was quick to point out that she was a friend to Claire and the girls but had never been close to Robert, whom she described as rude and obscene underneath his surface charm. Louise had broken off contact several years ago, except for private visits when Claire could come by alone, sometimes bringing Natasha and her sister along.

Louise told how in the last ten years of those visits, Claire had been slowly opening up, revealing stories of Robert's increasing violence inside the home. Occasional slaps during fits of anger had been escalating into repeated punches and choking.

Louise had begged Claire to leave Robert, but Claire had been afraid that she couldn't make enough money to keep the girls away from Robert in a custody fight. Louise watched Claire begin desperate attempts to upgrade her earning potential in preparation for making a break from Robert. Claire went to real estate school, got her license, and attended continuing education programs to bolster her skills. When the real estate market went soft, she used her clerical skills to get the highest paying jobs possible in that field and booked all the overtime that she could.

Louise hadn't heard from her since the previous November, just before Claire went to find Victoria Doom and again begin divorce proceedings, determined to make them stick

this time. Claire had told her that she was now more frightened of Robert than ever, because since she'd begun threatening once again to divorce him, he had abruptly changed;
he'd begun acting much too nice, in a conspicuously face-
tious way.

Claire told Louise she was certain he would try to kill her
before she could get out of the marriage with her daughters.

Louise had assured her that Robert wouldn't dare. Too
many people already knew about Robert's temper.

"No, Louise," Claire replied. "I think he will make it
look like an accident."

"But, Claire," Louise countered, trying to swallow her
own fears for her friend, "Natasha would know. She's seen
his violence. She's been a victim of it herself."

"But that's just it, don't you see?" Claire replied. "He
will have to go after her too. I tell you, Louise, if I don't get
out of here very soon, you are going to read about my death
in the newspaper."

Louise, as it turns out, contacted the Foothill Station, hoping that she could be of some help, immediately after her
husband called her attention to an article in the newspaper
about the Claire Peernock murder investigation.

At 9:30 P.M., Fisk requested copies of the picture of Robert
Peernock from the photo lab, wondering how many copies
he might need to facilitate Robert's arrest.

He ordered two hundred and fifty.

Then, just to be sure every stone was being turned, he
began preparing two more search warrants, one for the Peernock house and one for Sonia's condo. He worked far into
the night.

Tasha could hear the nurse clearly, right outside the door to
her room. She wondered if the woman really didn't know

that Tasha was aware of her. Or was she deliberately letting Tasha in on her opinion?

"Patricia," the woman was saying, "you aren't even supposed to be here after hours. If you interfere with our procedures again, we can take away your visiting privileges. So you just go back in and tell her that all that thick hair of hers is clotted with dried blood and it can infect the wounds on her head."

"Hey, I didn't interfere with anything!" Patty retorted, exasperated. "She's the one who said she didn't want you cutting off the rest of her hair, I'm just trying to explain that she's always been kind of funny about it. I mean, she has all this great hair and she's really proud of it and—"

"Honey, her hair has already been shaved four inches back off the hairline. What does she care if the rest goes now?"

"Look. What if she washes it? Like really clean?"

"That's what started all this! She won't let me touch it, says it hurts too much. But if those wounds get infected, it'll hurt a lot worse. Now, since you two are the great all-time buddies, maybe you should let her know that either we wash it or we *cut it off*. And I mean today!"

"Okay, okay." Patty came stomping into the room in frustration, muttering over her shoulder, "You don't have to get so hyper about everything."

She stopped, glanced back toward the doorway, then turned toward her friend and dropped her voice. "Tasha . . ."

"I heard. They're not taking the rest of my hair," Tasha protested, as if she had the strength to stop them.

"Hey, look. What if *we* wash it?"

"We?"

"Well, I will, I mean. We'll work together. Your job is to not scream."

"What if it hurts too much?"

"Then they're coming back in here and shaving your head."

". . . Get the soap."

Half an hour later they were still at it, with Patty washing and rinsing a strand at a time, working as gently as she could to avoid tugging the hair.

Tasha did her part and stayed busy with not crying out even though the pain was worse than anything she had endured since waking up in the intensive care unit. But somehow the removal of the rest of her thick hair was a loss she just couldn't accept. All day long she had slowly chewed on the knowledge that her life had exploded on every level and just about anything that had ever been familiar to her was gone. She wasn't letting anybody take anything else away from her now.

And she just didn't give a damn if her need to keep the rest of her hair sounded crazy to the staff or not.

On the morning of July 29, Fisk was back on the job extra early. He began by finishing off the search warrants, picking up where he'd had to abandon them the previous night, when gritty fatigue had built up in his eyes to the point that it became hard to see. By 6:30 A.M. he had already finished that task and also verified that the tailing unit was in place over at Sonia's condo.

By 9:30 he was at one of the police impound yards, Black & White Towing, to meet with Highway Patrol officers Ed Carlow and Walt Rose. The officers had gone over to the impound to check Peernock's car for mechanical defects. Alignment problems, for example, might explain why the car had run off the road before hitting the dead-end wall.

When the alignment theory turned out to be an empty lead, Fisk wasn't surprised. According to the profile he was building of Peernock, the guy was shaping up as being much too thorough to forget to ensure that his alignment was good, the way most people do: checking to make sure the car drives straight at high speeds. Even with no hands on the wheel.

The full-blown investigation began to roll on many different fronts and the days were speeding up for everyone involved. By noon Fisk was back at his office moving on half a dozen leads when a phone call came in from an attorney named Larry Samuels. Fisk's chronological log shows that Samuels claimed to be Robert Peernock's "domestic attorney" and that he had just received a long-distance call from Peernock himself.

Peernock told Samuels that Peernock's wife and daughter had been in a hit-and-run accident and that *Peernock had heard that his wife was implicating him.* Attorney Samuels said that Peernock wanted him to call the Foothill detectives and check on the status of the investigation. Peernock had arranged to call Samuels back in two days.

Samuels was informed that so far there was no arrest warrant on Peernock, which was true. But he was also told to make sure Robert Peernock understood that the police very much wanted to talk to him.

Samuels promised to relay the information.

Throughout the day of July 29, the scene at Sonia's house was one of deepening fear and chaos. Robert was making sporadic attempts to reach her. Sonia was aware that she was being followed by the authorities; whatever she had told the police didn't seem to have satisfied them. She began making frantic attempts to locate attorneys who could and would be of help to the most important man in her life, the man she had shared her home with for years and who claimed to be at war with corrupt forces in the government establishment.

To Sonia, it seemed that she and Robert were both under attack from nearly every direction.

• • •

Tasha had a strange dream only a few days after they'd put her in the hospital. She dreamed that her old boyfriend had come home on emergency leave from the Navy. He walked into the room and told her that he had tried to get leave to see her earlier, but the Navy refused until his mother got on the horn and raised a fuss. Now here he was, with his hair all short and everything. Tasha was glad it was only a dream; she would have been mortified if he could really see her puffed up and torn and discolored, feeling like some kind of circus freak. Like the Elephant Man.

In the dream the guy really was sweet. He told her that he still loved her, whether he actually did or not, and he told her that he wanted to marry her right away, just as soon as he had finished with his advanced training following boot camp. Then they could go away to his first assignment together.

These were not the conditions of proposal and marriage that every little girl dreams about. But Natasha had never been particularly conventional, and she had recently lost her taste for the traditions associated with marriage, such as being carried over the threshold.

After this pleasant dream was finished and the guy disappeared, she dreamed about something else. When she awoke it was hard to tell where one dream had left off and the other begun.

It wasn't until later that the remarks other people were making caused her to realize that it had all been real and that she was now engaged to be married.

It would have been nice to be madly in love, she thought, head over heels in love. But nobody gets everything she wants.

At 2:45 P.M. on the twenty-ninth, Fisk arranged to have Peernock's Cadillac moved from Black & White Towing to the crime lab for a thorough analysis and fingerprinting of the interior and exterior.

He then contacted the California Highway Patrol and made sure they were available to reconstruct the accident at the scene as soon as possible.

At 4:30 that afternoon he hit Judge Luros for yet another set of search warrants on the Peernock house and on Sonia's condo. He accompanied the search officers to Sonia's place first, since the Peernock house had been sealed and there was less danger of evidence being tampered with in that location.

Later that evening he accompanied Criminologist Lawrence Joiner, who performed a luminol test on the walls of the Peernock house. Joiner verified that blood had dripped onto both sides of the hallway at heights of between two and three feet. Blood was also smeared on the light switch next to the glass doors leading out to the patio. Blood was also spotted on the vanity in the master bathroom of Claire's bedroom. All the bloodstains were verified as having occurred at the same time.

Fisk noted that some anonymous kindly neighbor had been dropping off food to the two dogs, who still padded about the backyard, frightened and confused. He contacted the Department of Animal Care and arranged for them to be taken to a shelter. He hoped that somebody could be found to adopt the dogs before their time ran out and the county had to destroy them. There had already been too much evil fallout from whatever had taken place inside this house.

It was 1:00 A.M. when Fisk and his team finally cleared the crime scene. He didn't have to be back at work for five whole hours.

CHAPTER

13

July 30 was the day Tasha was to be released from the hospital with cooperation from the police. Uncle Maurice helped to finesse the release on the pretext of a transfer to Kaiser Hospital, but the plan was to take Tasha and Patty directly to her fiancé's family home and to immediately place her under twenty-four-hour guard until Robert Peernock could be located.

Maurice came into her hospital room alone and closed the door with a grim expression. He started to tell her it was time to talk about Claire, but Tasha quietly revealed that nobody had been fooling her anyway. After an awkward pause he began again, telling her that Claire had let him know years ago that her wish was to be cremated when she died. The coroner's office was ready to release the body now. They had told Maurice that it was Natasha's legal duty as Claire's oldest child to dispose of the remains, so long as the husband wasn't coming forward to do the job. As a matter of law and as an issue of public health, Natasha had no choice but to deal with the situation right now. He sadly handed her a pretyped coroner's release form to sign. Then he gave her an authorization form allowing the mortuary to handle the cremation. She signed both, barely reading them.

Last of all, he handed her an insurance form. As the sole available surviving adult of the family, Natasha may have been required by state law to deal with Claire's remains, but she was penniless. Maurice had a large family of his own and no financial means to cover the expenses himself. Unless her mother was to be buried in a pauper's grave by the county, Natasha had no choice but to sign the insurance proceeds over to the mortuary to pay for the costs of cremation and funeral.

The policy was in the amount of $10,000, enough to cover everything. Natasha would not find out until later that it was the State Farm policy taken out by Claire two days after her visit to Victoria Doom's office. Claire's premonition had served her after all, giving her daughter the means to carry out the duty of making final arrangements for her mother.

The mortuary also wanted to know if they could expect any cooperation in handling the final arrangements from the husband of the deceased, the father of the children.

Uncle Maurice just told them that it didn't seem likely.

Robert's situation was now coming home to Sonia Siegel with a heavy impact. At 9:30 A.M. on July 30, Steve Fisk had Sonia's car impounded to go along with the items his team had taken from her condo the evening before, expanding the search for any physical evidence of Peernock's whereabouts.

That afternoon Natasha was brought out of the hospital in a wheelchair. Police guards scanned nervously in all directions as she was wheeled up to the curb and helped into the waiting car. She and Patty were then driven to her new fiancé's family home, a condominium not far from the former Peernock house. A police escort tailed them all the way, having already begun their assignment of twenty-four-hour guard duty.

Once they'd arrived, Patty was told she could sleep downstairs near the police guards while Tasha began her convalescence alone in an upstairs bedroom.

● ● ●

Back in Las Vegas, desk clerks at the Stardust Hotel noted that Robert Peernock, alias "Robert Thomas," had failed to come down and settle his tab in cash as he had previously done on the twenty-sixth, the twenty-eighth, and the twenty-ninth. They checked the hotel's computer and saw that there had been no activity for his room. No payments, no room service, no messages, no phone calls. Nothing. There was nothing the next day either. Still, at this point they didn't get too concerned.

They knew that it isn't unusual for guests there to take off on little side trips out of town. Maybe even out of state.

At 6:05 P.M. of July 30, Sonia Siegel and her aunt were tailed as they drove to a restaurant on Ventura Boulevard and had dinner. During that time Sonia was observed making a seven-minute phone call from a public telephone. The undercover stakeout officer meandered by slowly enough to overhear Sonia saying into the phone, "They were out here today," and moments later, "Maybe tomorrow."

On July 31, as the month wound down, events began heating up for everyone involved.

Early that morning Steve Fisk had a full "Suspect Wanted" bulletin distributed to law enforcement divisions and agencies. He had partial reports that Peernock might be visiting with a former co-worker at a home outside Los Angeles.

He also contacted L.A. Criminologist Bill Lewellin, a scientific investigator with additional training with the FBI, and had Peernock's large vise removed from police impound in order to compare the X-shaped marks Fisk remembered on the cutter bar under the Cadillac with the pattern of the teeth on the vise itself. The test method Lewellin used was to take a soft lead plate and clamp it in the vise to get a sample of the clamping marks, then look for similarities of pattern be-

tween those marks and the ones on the crime tool. He used
the special double-lensed comparison microscope to study
each object simultaneously and found identical features on
the two patterns.

These features went beyond the mere similarities of the
vise teeth as they came from the factory; they included the
nicks and wear marks that give each vise its own particular
"fingerprint." Lewellin found three major dings on the
clamping surface of the vise, plus a couple of smaller stria-
tions. Their size, shape, and orientation to one another
formed a metallic "fingerprint," and they were the basis of
his conclusion that the metal bar found under the Cadillac
had undoubtedly been made in Peernock's vise.

At 10:30 A.M. Fisk's men observed Sonia Siegel leave her
aunt's house and load suitcases into a blue Toyota that she
had rented the day before, after the police went out to her
place and impounded her car. She drove back to her condo.

Later that day she drove to Century City, a prestigious
business community adjacent to Beverly Hills. The COBRA
unit tailed her to an attorney's office inside the gleaming
white Twin Towers, a matching set of designer skyscrapers
housing dozens of prestigious law firms. More big-time corporate legal work gets done in Century City in a single day
than many small towns see in a year.

Sonia asked her attorney, Paul Moore, if she should be
helping Peernock by paying his bills.

"That's a personal decision," he answered. "I can't advise you on that."

"I just feel that I should be loyal," Moore remembers her
reply, "—that I've been in love with this man for a period
of years. I don't want to, you know, be his friend and because
of the circumstances just remove myself from him."

Robert Peernock, however, was not sitting back and pas-
sively relying upon his girlfriend to find out things for him.

As Tasha lay in her "safe house," she had no idea how close by he really was.

Deanna Bello shared a common wall with the condominium of Natasha's future in-laws. But Bello had no idea that Natasha had just taken temporary refuge there while she tried to get some balance back into her life.

Bello had decided to put her condo on the market and had recently hung a "For Sale" sign out on the balcony. It was a good spot for the sign, clearly visible to any potential lookie-loos who might be cruising the neighborhood in search of a good deal on a place to live. The balcony was right above the garage and faced directly onto the street.

As Deanna Bello later recalled for detectives, it was at the very end of July or the beginning of August that she was at home on her hands and knees scrubbing the wall-to-wall carpet. She had just put her small child down for a nap and while working she kept the door to the garage open to get some cross breeze. Bello was so busy scrubbing that she didn't hear the man approach her until after he had entered through the open garage door and stepped inside.

He quickly identified himself as a realtor, offering her a card with a Latino surname that she didn't really focus on. But she did notice that when he handed her the card his hand was shaking.

She also noticed that his Latino name didn't seem to fit his Anglo features.

Despite her eagerness to sell the place, this just wasn't sitting right with her. She tried to stop him, suddenly nervous about this intrusion. She was annoyed at him for presuming to enter uninvited and at herself for not having taken the sign down until her cleaning was finished. Besides, being alone there with her little boy sleeping upstairs made her feel even more vulnerable. She explained that she wasn't really ready to show the place today because the rug was wet.

But the white-skinned realtor with the Latino surname was already sweeping his eyes all around the room. "That's okay," he replied without looking at her, then proceeded to walk in uninvited. She didn't stop him as he passed, but she trailed close on his heels.

The mysterious visitor went straight for the back sliding glass door of the condo and peered out at the adjoining lawn, toward the place next door where Natasha was staying. From this vantage point he was able to see the other place over the wood fence separating the backyards.

He stood for several minutes, not doing or saying anything, just looking out the window. Bello kept herself between him and the room her child was sleeping in while an uneasy feeling grew inside her. Finally the man turned abruptly and walked toward the kitchen. Once again he focused on looking out the window, but from there Natasha's temporary home could not be seen, just a truncated view of the people living on the other side. This didn't seem to interest the realtor as much; he stayed at that window for only a few seconds. She watched him nervously and tried to think of ways to get him out of her house without appearing frightened.

He then moved to the sliding glass door. He seemed to have forgotten Bello completely and didn't bother asking the constant patter of realtor-type questions that she had come to expect from professionals who dropped by to evaluate the prospect of a sale.

The sliding glass door had a curtain on it. He moved the curtain aside in order to look out at the yard. Again, that view didn't seem to tell him what he wanted to know. He spun around and walked upstairs without bothering to ask for her permission.

She followed nervously as he walked right into her master bedroom and looked out the sliding glass, once more toward

Natasha's temporary home. He remained there about a minute.

Suddenly he turned to her and muttered something about his clients, that he would "have to get back" to her. Bello was so grateful he was leaving that his comments didn't even register.

She gladly followed as he moved down the stairs and stepped outside, where he stopped and stood for another moment in front of the garage, looking around.

As the realtor got in his car and drove away, she noticed that it was, in her words, a squarish blue car.

Robert Peernock's Datsun F-10 was small, blue, and built with a "squarish" design.

It is an interesting coincidence, as such things go, that Deanna Bello was a nurse at Holy Cross Hospital, from which Natasha had just checked out. But at this point she didn't yet know anything about her new neighbor's dance with the grim reaper, so she had no reason to go next door and mention anything about what had taken place. She was just glad the strange episode was over.

Bello would later identify Robert Peernock from a police photo lineup called a "six-pack," where his image shared the page with those of five other men. Whether or not any of them were actually employed in the real estate market, none had the Latino name on the business card that she later turned over to the police.

Steve Fisk blinked back the burn in his eyes and struggled to concentrate. You can only put in so many eighteen-hour days before they start catching up to you. But as he sat interviewing Jeanette, a longtime friend of Claire Peernock, he found that what she was telling him dissolved away the fatigue. She later repeated the story for this book.

"It was about three years ago," she said, her voice shaking slightly under the weight of the memory.

"Claire had made a left turn at a yellow light. An oncoming car ran into her and she ended up with a broken ankle. But the thing is, and she was so upset when she told me this, Robert was furious with her. Claire thought that it was not for wrecking the car, but . . . for surviving the impact."

Jeanette inhaled and continued in a softer voice, in which the pain and the anger were nevertheless plain. "She told me he seemed disappointed she didn't die. It would have made everything easy for him, don't you see? Nobody wanted to believe her, of course, when she called several of us and begged us to make sure that if she was ever killed in a traffic accident, to see to it that it was investigated. I mean, I grew up in Louisiana where human respect, basic decency, it still means something, you know? Because even those of us who knew Bob, and knew what he was like, we never wanted to believe he would actually . . ."

Lead Investigator Steve Fisk left Jeanette's place knowing it was going to be a while longer before he got any decent sleep.

He knew that the Foothill Homicide Division had received a rash of calls in the past day or two, from former neighbors of the Peernocks as well as former co-workers. They claimed to have seen Robert driving around his old neighborhood and in the area where Natasha was now staying. He was said to be driving a blue car, but there was some disagreement whether it was his Datsun F-10 or the blue Toyota Sonia had rented a few days earlier.

It was August 1 and Natasha tried not to think about anything going on outside the room. She wouldn't have been physically strong enough to endure Claire's funeral that day, even if the cops had allowed her to risk exposure there. Her father was still at large, still sending messages through various attorneys that at some unspecified point he would be getting ready to turn himself in.

She tried not to wonder where her father was. She tried not to hope that the cops downstairs were very, very good at their jobs and wouldn't be killed in an ambush by her father, because to hope for that was to admit there was a chance that they could not protect her.

She was learning that in situations like this the trick is to get small in your thinking. Avoid the big picture. Focus on moment-to-moment victories, things like getting out of bed by yourself then sneaking into the hallway so that you can practice walking to the bathroom without somebody rushing up to help you.

It took several tries, but she finally made it without anyone having to carry her. Leaning on the wall, walking slowly, she was able to keep just enough balance to walk to the bathroom by herself.

The Elephant Man with bad legs.

While Natasha was trying to make it down the hallway without falling over, Steve Fisk attended Claire's funeral in the faint hope that something would come up that could help lead him to the suspect. Claire's husband, as it turned out, failed to show up for her last rites.

"Tash," Patty ventured softly, "everybody wants me to pressure you into going for therapy. Do you even want to try it?"

"I did at the hospital."

"No, I think they mean more like a long-term type of thing."

"Come on, Trisha, you know I'm not the type to spill my guts. This whole southern California thing about everybody telling you to get therapy every time anything goes wrong . . . I mean, people go to therapists like it's shopping or something. Sometimes I get the feeling that saying 'Get into therapy' to somebody has just become like another way

for people to tell you they don't want to deal with whatever's
going on in your life. You're just supposed to go tell it to
somebody who's being paid to listen.''

"Okay." Patty sighed. "I figured your answer would be
something like that, but I just thought—''

"Hey, why don't you go out somewhere? You've been on
duty ever since this all happened. Get some sun. You're not
as allergic to daylight as I am.''

Patty smiled, relieved that Tasha seemed to know how
much strain she was under, living for days at the hospital
and now crammed into whatever spare space they could find
for her there in Natasha's temporary home.

"Maybe I could go out for just a little while.''

"Honest, it's okay. I can pee by myself and everything.''

Patty laughed. "Hey, I know that.''

"Go on, then.''

"You sure it's okay? You won't run away from home
while I'm gone?''

"I might. You'll find out when you get back.''

Patty left reluctantly, but Tasha knew her friend needed
the breather. Patty just didn't have Tasha's experience handling bizarre experiences. Growing up in the monster house,
she had become an expert.

So she lay in the quiet of the room and listened to people
padding around downstairs and talking quietly as they tried
to keep it light and not be paranoid about her father being
at large. This was about as bizarre as anything she had ever
imagined. But who else was there who could handle it along
with her? None of them had Tasha's expertise with weirdness
either.

She knew that Patty had about come to the end of her
rope, had given all that she could. It wouldn't be fair to keep
her hanging on. Uncle Maurice had made it plain that Tasha
could return to Canada with them, or join them there later
after all the probate stuff had been handled here. But even

without bothering to reason it through, Natasha knew that this wasn't the avenue she was going to take. Canada was an unknown world to her. The huge family her mother had left behind in Quebec was essentially a group of strangers.

No, Tasha had grown up right here. What little familiarity existed for her now existed here. She could feel intuitively that the answer wasn't going to lie in running off to some foreign country to live with strangers. Her fiancé was due back from his advanced training at the end of September. So if her father didn't kill her first, it would probably be a good idea to just go ahead and get married.

It really was touching that he seemed to still want her. It would have been nice to be in love. But she wondered if that was a luxury she just couldn't hold out for now, or even if something had happened to her feelings that would prevent her from ever being able to feel love again.

On August 3, early in the afternoon, Victoria Doom met Natasha Peernock for the first time. Up to that moment Natasha had only been a name listed on Claire's dissolution form under the heading "Children of the Marriage." Victoria arranged the meeting after Maurice had told her that he couldn't remain in town much longer. There were matters that would not wait.

Victoria was concerned that as long as Robert Peernock remained at large he had the ability to dissolve away any remaining assets that might give his daughters a basis on which to rebuild their lives.

She quickly sized up Natasha as the young woman entered with her uncle. Her new client's eyes were clear. The sharp gaze told Victoria that despite all the damage done to her, Natasha Peernock would be able to communicate clearly. Up to that moment she hadn't really believed that anyone could come through such an experience and not be a complete basket case. She wondered where her strength of spirit came from.

But Natasha's physical state was still a mess, ten days after the attack. While her wounds had been stitched and repaired by plastic surgery to some degree, not a whole lot of healing can take place in so little time except for some of the swelling to go down. Her new client was very quiet as the introductions and opening small talk were conducted between Maurice and Victoria. She wore a scarf tied softly over her head wounds, but angry surgical scars spilled down from her forehead and zigzagged across her face. She appeared extremely uncomfortable and more than a little self-conscious.

"I explained what we needed to do about the estate," Victoria later said, "and I also talked to her about a civil lawsuit against her father for wrongful death on behalf of the estate which would also benefit her little sister, plus a separate lawsuit on Natasha's behalf for the personal injuries her father inflicted. There wasn't anything else we could do that first day."

But these actions gave Victoria the power to begin taking steps to lock up the estate before Robert could dissipate the rest of it. If he was never caught there was a danger that he would liquidate everything somehow through an intermediary. If he was caught and then charged with the crimes, he would certainly spend much or all of it on expensive criminal lawyers. Either way his daughters would be left out in the cold completely.

Victoria realized that if she lost in court on these actions, or if some opposing law firm simply outfoxed her because she didn't absorb her crash course in probate law fast enough, then Claire had made an awful mistake in coming to her in the first place. And Victoria would have compounded Claire's mistake by not sending Maurice away to some other lawyer.

But this case had already struck a deep chord with her,

just as it had with Steve Fisk. Although neither she nor Fisk had any way of knowing it yet, similar notes had been struck within a small group of unrelated people which would motivate them to fight this situation with all their abilities and with every ounce of energy they could muster. They were the first of an expanding group of people who would have had no reason to come together except for this case, and who would all find in it some reason to reach within themselves for their strongest powers.

Membership in that group would not come cheap for any of them.

For Victoria, doubts about her advice to Claire had already begun to wear away at her, night and day. Maybe it was just as well that she had hardly been able to sleep in the days since Maurice broke the news to her; sweating out the beginnings of a legal strategy on Natasha's behalf gave her plenty to keep busy with while she paced the floor at night.

"Natasha, the crime lab called at three o'clock. There weren't any traces of opiates in the Seagram's bottle. Why were there traces in your blood?" Fisk tried not to push her. She had just come in from meeting with her attorney and looked drained.

But Robert Peernock was still out there somewhere and Fisk needed to know anything she could tell him. Anything at all.

"I don't know. It must have been that pill. It hurts to think. I have to go to sleep."

"You can sleep, but tell me. Did the alcohol taste funny? Do you think there was something crushed up in it?"

"I told you before, I don't know. Can't we do this later?"

"Yes. We can do it later. But if you can help me figure out where he got the pill from, maybe I can track down the source. If it was a drug dealer, then maybe the dealer knows something. Maybe the dealer's still in touch with him, you know?''

"I just . . . I don't know. He takes all these pills for his back. I don't know. It hurts to think."

"Okay, Natasha. Okay. Take a nap. I'll come back and see you later."

Her eyes were already closing.

But on that same afternoon Peernock was back in Las Vegas, finishing up his initial consultation visit to Dr. Edward Kopf, a local plastic surgeon.

Peernock was again "Robert Thomas," no longer the Caucasian realtor with the Latino name from Los Angeles. He gave Dr. Kopf's staff at the front desk a fake address, fake phone number and fake social security number, while making arrangements to pay in cash. He claimed to have been an employee for the last three years at a company called Har-Tec Carburetor. Dr. Kopf's staff had no reason to check "Robert Thomas" 's place of employment. But if they had, they might have learned that Har-Tec Carburetor had gone bankrupt fourteen years before.

At his consultation, "Robert Thomas" told Dr. Kopf that he needed a fresher and more dynamic appearance to go along with a new promotion. He said he hoped that the surgery could help him avoid the envy of co-workers who might tend to be jealous of his success. He didn't explain how looking better was supposed to help quell his colleagues' envy.

When Dr. Kopf asked whether "Robert Thomas" had any medical problems the doctor should know about, he replied that he had no allergies and no medical problems of any kind. As Robert Peernock, however, he had complained of sleep disturbances in the past. Peernock's condition, called sleep apnea, causes the sufferer to stop breathing spontaneously while asleep. "Robert Thomas" didn't seem inclined to worry about that, though, as he began the process of arranging major surgery in a strange town under a false name.

On August 4 there was nothing in the house for Natasha to turn to for relief as the pain tore through her like waves of flame. The hospital had warned her that it was still not advisable for her to take strong pain relievers. So she resorted to sneaking doses of Nyquil whenever no one was looking, trying to quell the fire in her head. The pain blocked out everything.

But she knew that her mother's remains were being cremated over in Long Beach that day.

On the morning of the fifth, Natasha was back at the hospital signing forms releasing her medical information to the investigators. Travel was still hard for her, but things seemed to come up every day that required her to venture out of the house, and she wanted to do anything she could to aid the investigation. Her father seemed to have vanished like a ghost. So she dragged herself out of bed once more, all the while praying for a break in the case.

The first break came that night. It was now August 5.

Officer Graham of the El Segundo police noticed that a blue Datsun F-10 had parked in a "three-day maximum" zone that was located within easy walking distance of the Los Angeles Airport terminals. It was Graham's job to spot cars parked overtime. The city of El Segundo is one of the countless municipalities that run together seamlessly to make up Los Angeles. It plays host to countless temporary autos visiting the curbsites while their owners are away on short trips. This kind of action is a big revenue source for the city.

Although Graham always passed this spot as a part of his regular route, he hadn't noticed the Datsun before. He chalked the tire just to be sure. The owner now had three business days to move or it would be towed. However, the fact that the weekend was approaching actually made it five days before the tow truck would be by.

On August 7 "Robert Thomas" came back to Dr. Kopf for a final preoperation consultation. The doctor pronounced him fit for surgery. "Mr. Thomas" pronounced himself ready for a brand-new face.

On the same day, Steve Fisk ordered L.A. Criminologist Bill Lewellin to perform a test on the flat tire taken from Claire's car. Lewellin wasn't told where the tire had come from. He simply inflated it to full pressure and submerged it in water for several minutes. It gave off no bubbles and never leaked any air. Whatever had caused the tire to go flat in Claire's driveway seemed to have been a temporary condition. There was no hole found in it anywhere and the tire stem worked perfectly.

For the next several days Natasha's nightmares mostly focused on situations with her father chasing her. But the dreams didn't reflect the actual night of the crimes and no matter how many times investigators came and asked her to go over it all one more time, the film always ran out just after she and her mother were moved from the backseat to the front of her father's Cadillac. It ran out before her cuffs and hood were removed, just after the unseen attacker stopped tinkering at the back of the car near the tow bar.

Steve Fisk began to think he was learning to go without sleep altogether, but he didn't seem to have dropped dead yet. "I'm a family man myself, with four children of my own," he said later. "Any parent knows that teenagers can drive you up the wall, make you crazy. But I've told my kids many times that there's nothing, I mean *nothing* they could do to make me stop loving them, no matter how angry I might get at their behavior. One thing just doesn't have anything to do with the other. Now, for a father to take a blunt instrument to the head and face of his own daughter . . . I just kept thinking about what an attack like that would do to a girl's self-esteem. Teenaged girls don't have nearly enough anyway, you know? For Natasha to know her father did that, and that he destroyed her mother at the same time . . .'' His voice trailed off at that point.

Knowing that such a father was loose out there kept Fisk booking the unpaid overtime when his own family would have much preferred to have him back at home.

CHAPTER

14

At 11:15 A.M. on August 10, the El Segundo police impounded the blue Datsun F-10 registered to Robert Peernock, for failure to move from the three-day zone in a timely fashion.

The best-laid plans. Despite his elaborate banking arrangements, despite the help of a girlfriend who was desperately trying to keep her faith in him and help him remain free in the belief that he was being unjustly accused, despite the aid of a talented plastic surgeon who had given him a new face, despite more than one alias in a town of strangers and a slew of bills paid in untraceable cash—

Robert John Peernock had parked overtime.

Within hours the car's license number was entered in the LAPD computer as a matter of routine, just in case there were any overdue parking tickets or any other little legal matters to clear up before it could be released to the registered owner.

It was also on August 10 that Robert Peernock, still in his alias of "Robert Thomas," went under Dr. Kopf's knife. Robert had a face-lift and eye surgery, and also received a chin implant. After surgery he requested Linda Taylor, the head of Dr. Kopf's nursing staff, to do follow-up visits by attending him in private at his hotel room. He was informed that this was not their policy. So upon completion of his successful operation he arranged to attend follow-up visits at the doctor's office in the early mornings instead of the usual time alloted for follow-up in the afternoon. In the mornings the waiting room is virtually empty, but it gets quite full as the day wears on. The staff reluctantly made this unusual exception for "Mr. Thomas," but at no time in Linda Taylor's five years with Dr. Kopf could she recall anyone else having this particular concern about needing an empty waiting room in order to come in for simple follow-up visits.

At the hotel "Mr. Thomas" explained to the curious front-desk staff that he had recently been in an auto accident and had just had corrective surgery to repair the damage.

He did not repeat his story about wanting to look fresher for his new promotion in a bankrupt company.

Back in Los Angeles, late on that same August 10 night, Natasha's head pain backed off enough that she could move around without too much discomfort if she was very careful. The police were already asking her about testifying against her father if he should be captured alive. She began to wonder where she would find the strength to publicly tell the story of that awful night of torture and murder. The old family taboo against speaking about what went on inside the house had been pounded into her for years.

But she wondered, what was any such taboo worth now? Ever since things had turned really bad at home a few years ago, she'd never felt a real part of her family. More and more as the years went by, she had come to feel like a visitor in the house. At her school. On the planet.

That, as it turned out, was going to be her source of strength. Somehow as the years had gone by, without really thinking about it, Tasha had slowly converted her feeling of isolation to a sense of uniqueness.

She had absorbed an appreciation for uniqueness in a thousand little ways. As a native southern California girl she had grown up around the beaches and knew that you can hang around there when storm fronts roll in and watch surfers paddle out to greet impossibly high waves. A few keep it up long after the amateurs come on in and run for cover. Once the winds approach gale force there will always be one or two crazy, beautiful jerks heading out to catch just one last wave, a little higher, a little more insanely powerful than the wave before. Sometimes one daredevil actually catches the killer, the monster. And instead of going under it and getting injured or drowned by its power, he miraculously manages to rocket up to the top of the crest and hang his toes out over the edge of the board and throw his fist high into the air, screaming with pure joy at his own audacity. Confronting the monster and winning.

That's when the answer hit her: there are all kinds of waves. Somewhere in her past, she had found a reservoir of strength within her isolation. She didn't know yet if it would be enough to sustain her, any more than the extremist surfers can be sure they will survive the tidal waves that they paddle out to meet. But as of tonight she knew the direction to swim in. She resolved that she would face him down in court. She would tell the story as many times as she had to. By standing away from him in every way that she could, she would work out the poison of ever having had such a man for a father.

She would start by breaking the family taboo and telling the world everything she could about what had happened behind closed doors inside the Peernock house.

By August 12, Victoria had prepared elaborate opening papers in Natasha's wrongful death suit and taken the first steps to have Natasha named administrator of the estate, all toward the end of freezing Peernock's access to whatever money the family had. Most of what she did went on without Natasha's direct involvement, since she now had power of attorney. But whether Tasha was aware of it or not, the upshot was that Victoria Doom and her secretary, Sharie, and her law clerk, Elke, were working long past their regular hours. Even as Victoria began to have to farm out other cases as she had originally feared, she and her two assistants battled to pull fuel out of Peernock's tanks and make his flight from arrest as difficult as possible. They attacked on multiple fronts in the civil-court war, slowly freezing Peernock out of the family's real estate holdings, bank accounts, and insurance proceeds.

While they labored to make it easier for Steve Fisk's task force to bring Peernock in, they did so with the strong hope that Natasha would still be alive to testify when that day came. But they had no way of knowing how much energy was being expended to see to it that Peernock's daughter never lived to take the stand.

More calls came into Fisk's office as August rolled by. Neighbors claimed to have seen Peernock driving through the Saugus area in a new white Cadillac. Fisk didn't need to ask what Robert Peernock might be looking for. The question was, had he rented the car somehow or borrowed it, and where? He knew that there ought to be some kind of paper trail, but the guy seemed to move around like a submarine.

Sonia Siegel's attorney was now fully into the fray, making sure Fisk crossed every T in dealing with her. Sonia was repeatedly picked up and interviewed by Fisk and his team, but she still refused to help. She made it plain that Robert had terrified her by describing what would happen to him if she let the police know where he was. Everybody who had dealt with Robert in the past knew about his long history of making accusations over corruption in state contracts. This was just the kind of retaliation from state forces that he had predicted for so long. And the search warrants and impoundings hadn't, up to now, done a lot to build Sonia's confidence in the police.

Fisk kept working on her, trying to show her that she had it wrong. He called the hospital for her and spoke with Dr.

Shapiro there, who confirmed that no bandages would have been placed on Natasha's head, such as Robert had told Sonia he'd seen on his daughter the night that he claimed to have gone to Holy Cross. Peernock had never visited Tasha there, Fisk assured Sonia. He hadn't even been allowed to get near her. So why would he tell Sonia that he had?

But Sonia's loyalty still couldn't be swayed.

Peernock's parents back East hadn't heard from him, so Fisk dropped that lead and ordered the COBRA tailing unit to intensify their tracking of Sonia instead. He felt sure that she was in touch with Robert somehow.

Meanwhile, Robert's Datsun came up on the computer's linkup to the El Segundo police.

Fisk was euphoric. He immediately ordered the car searched by his investigators, knowing that this could be a major break in their manhunt. Two guns were recovered from the toolbox. One was an chromed automatic pistol.

The other gun, just as Natasha had described it, was a black revolver with a wooden handle.

On August 17, Victoria Doom filed a petition for probate nominating Natasha as permanent administrator. Paper doors, stronger than steel bars, were slamming shut around whatever remained of the Peernock family assets.

Robert Peernock/Robert Thomas went back into Dr. Kopf's office every couple of days during the morning hours to check his progress. His face was healing a lot faster than Natasha's. By the seventeenth most of the stitches could be removed.

He looked like a new man.

By August 18 another attorney, Don Reynolds, called the Foothill Station. He said that he, too, had been retained by Robert Peernock, but that another gentleman named Mark

Overland would handle the case. Mr. Overland was to call two days later regarding the "surrender of the suspect."

Steve Fisk had no way of knowing it yet, but with this first wave of attorneys, Robert Peernock's cavalcade of lawers had just begun.

Records from the Stardust Hotel show that calls were made to PSA Airlines from "Robert Thomas"'s room on August 8, 9, 12, and 14. It would have taken only one call to learn that flights to L.A. depart at constant and regular intervals all day, every day. But Peernock was traveling with a suitcase full of cash and leaving no paper trail, so it cannot be proven that he flew out of town on those dates.

It can only be known for certain that, wherever he was going in those days between doctor's visits, he somehow managed to find out that his Datsun was no longer available in the El Segundo area near Los Angeles International. Because on August 19 Robert was back in Las Vegas, where he bought a used gray Mustang soft-top for $2,800.

Now he had a convertible car to go with the converted face. Nine days after his car was impounded, Robert Peernock/Robert Thomas was back on wheels and ready to roll.

The next day, August 20, Victoria Doom was busily chugging out the legal work to dam up Peernock's assets when she discovered that there might possibly be a family will outstanding. She immediately sent her clerk to the closed-up house to bring back Claire's collection of attorneys' business cards, then called the numbers on every one of them until she found a firm that had prepared a will for Claire and Robert ten years before. Such a document could tell her all kinds of things. It could also help her to permanently exclude Robert as executor and stack the deck on Natasha's behalf by placing all the family assets permanently under her name.

• • •

On August 21 Don Reynolds called the Foothill Station again and said that he still hadn't heard from Peernock, but whenever he finally did he would make arrangements for Robert to turn himself in. Reynolds didn't mention and perhaps was not aware that Robert Peernock had purchased another car, and in doing so was not exactly behaving like a man who planned on surrendering to anybody anytime soon.

It was on that same day that the "Robert Thomas" identity evaporated in the Nevada desert. Peernock/Thomas left his room at the Stardust without giving notice and vanished like life savings at a rigged roulette table. The Stardust later sent an invoice for the unpaid balance on the room tab to "Mr. Thomas" 's home address in Amarillo. It came back weeks later marked *Return to Sender—Unable to Deliver*.

Peernock called Sonia Siegel on August 22 and asked her to rendezvous with him in a supermarket parking lot. She hurried to meet him. The market was not far from her condo, where the couple had lived together for years while she waited for him to arrange his life so that they could be married. She did not yet realize that they would never be married, would never live together again. But for the time being, luck was with her; the COBRA tailing unit was off on another case at the moment, so she was able to arrive at the supermarket alone.

This was the first time Sonia had actually seen Robert face-to-face since he'd left her place a month before, after telling her he was going to visit Natasha at the hospital. In the weeks since that time she had fielded questions from his anxious younger daughter and taken her to the police station to learn that her mother was dead. She had watched the girl snapped up by the county system. She stood by as her condo was searched repeatedly by detectives, and she had been questioned over and over by the police about Robert's whereabouts. She had done Peernock's banking for him, paid his bills, dealt with the tenants at his income properties, and withstood threats from the police that if she were found to be harboring a fugitive on a warrant this severe, she might well be deemed a co-conspirator to murder. In that case she could end up spending the rest of her life in prison. For four agonizing weeks she had spent her nights and days terrified for Robert's Peernock's well-being and increasingly afraid for her own.

But Sonia put up with all of this because she believed that Robert Peernock was a fighter against corruption on state contracts and that his efforts had finally enraged shadowy individuals inside the system to the point that they had framed him for the brutal murder of his own family in order to silence him.

She believed that the man in her life was guilty of nothing more than a fierce allegiance to the taxpayers and that he had suffered horribly for it. And she was all he had left.

But she was stunned when Peernock walked up to her. His face looked entirely different. In all of the secret phone calls they had conducted over the past month from public phones scattered around the area, he had never told her anything about changing his face. She had continued to believe in him even as his behavior became more and more suspicious. And now she was confronted by the man she had planned to spend the rest of her life loving, only to find he had removed the face she had kissed so many times and had had another stitched in its place without saying a single word to her about it first.

She didn't abandon him, she didn't call the police and give them his new motel address, she didn't stop believing in him—but she got good and angry.

Sonia had just run face-first into blunt evidence that everything had changed radically in her life and that nothing would ever be the same again.

• • •

Natasha was probably asleep as Sonia met Robert in the parking lot. She doesn't remember exactly what she did on that day, but since it was daylight she figures she was asleep. She had always been a night person by nature, but ever since the night of July 21 she had taken to sitting up all night and did not go to sleep until it began to get light outside. There were a number of reasons for that: her torture by Robert had gone on all night long; she had been delivered from evil just before sunrise.

And she knew it would be harder for him to sneak up on her to finish the job if it was light outside.

Over the next few days Steve Fisk received phone calls indicating that Robert Peernock had been to his income properties to pick up rent. One of the callers, who had rented a house from Peernock two months before, reported that within the past month Peernock had come to the house with another man supposedly to repair the air conditioner. Peernock reportedly had cuts and stitches on his head. Since Fisk didn't know anything about Robert's plastic surgery, he wondered if the fugitive had been injured in some way.

As for the rest of it, Fisk couldn't believe what he was hearing. Peernock was on the lam as a fugitive on a murder warrant, playing ''maybe I'll turn myself in and maybe I won't'' through a series of attorneys while his appearance of guilt mounted with every passing day, and yet the man was driving around his old haunts collecting rent receipts. He was gambling his life on getting away with it despite the armed-and-dangerous tag that was out on him and which could easily cause some hotshot rookie to blow his head off if Peernock was apprehended under the wrong conditions.

Fisk knew the rents weren't worth all that much. If it was anybody else, he would simply dismiss him as just being stupid. But Peernock was smarter than most people, so what was the deal with the guy? Did he think he was bulletproof?

Or, Fisk wondered, did Peernock know something about evasive maneuvers that the police hadn't figured out yet? He had, after all, successfully eluded the manhunt so far and didn't seem to be putting all that much effort into it.

Fisk stepped up his efforts. He was already down to four hours sleep a night. He supposed that he could survive on three.

On August 25 he released Sonia's car back to her after it had been searched and tested for bloodstains. It had come up clean.

Later that day he served a warrant on Foothill Savings to get Robert's full financial profile there. On the same day he got his first look at Peernock's family insurance situation and discovered that Robert was the beneficiary of a $50,000 policy on Claire with Cal-Farm Insurance Company.

He didn't know yet that the insurance policy was just the tip of the iceberg, but he realized that another point had fallen into place on the motive side of the board.

On August 29, Sonia brought Robert to the office of her attorney, Paul Moore, to execute full power of attorney from Robert to Sonia. He also prepared a new will. Either Robert was aware that some sole practitioner named Victoria Doom was checking around for the original family will with the idea of sealing off Claire's property, or he had simply decided that taking care of loose paperwork was a good time-filler while evading a ''Wanted'' bulletin. Attorney Moore knew Peernock was considered a suspect in his wife's death but didn't *specifically* know that an arrest warrant was outstanding. He later said that detectives had called him on several occasions, but never *specifically* advised him that Sonia would be arrested if found to be aiding and abetting Peernock. Apparently, like a good attorney, he didn't ask.

• • •

At 11:00 A.M. on August 31, the Foothill Station received a call from attorney Mark Overland, who advised them that there were new developments; he was not representing Robert Peernock after all. Now it was clear to Steve Fisk that his last hope for a peaceful and easy surrender of the prime suspect had dissolved. He angrily resolved to get Peernock off the streets immediately. Not only had this case haunted him from day one, but the exclusive work time that Fisk had been allowed to dedicate to it had expired weeks ago. Other cases were piling up and demanding his attention, stealing time from his Peernock investigation, from his sleep pattern, from his family. Worst of all, with every passing day that Peernock remained at large, the fugitive stood the chance of slipping through the police net by virtue of the sheer overload facing the Homicide Division. Fisk asked himself how he would live with it if Natasha turned up dead and Peernock walked away from the charges facing him simply because there was no one left to testify against him.

The COBRA unit was ordered to set upon Sonia and to stay with her no matter what. Their orders were to find out once and for all if she could lead them to Robert Peernock.

It was early in the day, so Natasha was again most likely asleep if she didn't have to be somewhere; she had no way of knowing that in Steve Fisk and Victoria Doom there were now two individuals who had made it a personal struggle to protect her in every way they could find, to do their jobs so thoroughly that nobody, not even someone who had thought of all the angles, would get the chance to finish what had been started on her.

But neither the overworked lead investigator nor Natasha's beleaguered civil attorney knew that Peernock had barely opened his bag of tricks.

Victoria's eyes slammed open in the darkness and she gasped loudly as she sat up in bed. She glanced over to make sure

Richard didn't hear her, then sat for a moment panting with relief.

It was only a bad dream. Peernock wasn't really sneaking in the window, come to get the "Agreement" that made him look so suspicious. He wasn't in the house, armed and gunning for her and her husband.

She decided to go into the living room for a while. There was plenty to do. She could always think back over her plans to locate Peernock's numerous bank accounts to prevent him from being able to cash them out and flee with his daughters' funds.

She sat heavily at her desk, wiped the sleep from her eyes, and began typing notes. Back in law school Victoria had gotten her typing speed up to a hundred words a minute. The rapid clicking sounds filled the next several hours.

The COBRA unit set upon Sonia again on September 1. This time she was followed every time she left the house. Long lists of all her movements were filed at the Homicide Division, but for the next two days nothing came to light.

September 3, though, was an especially busy day. Sonia was followed to Foothill Savings and observed there for half an hour, where she now had power of attorney to handle Robert's money for him. There she complied with Robert's wishes and transferred his bank account to her name. Now Sonia had total control over Peernock's money and none of his enemies could take it from him in their attempts to frame him for this awful murder. Another blockade had just been raised against Victoria Doom's attempt to seal off Robert's access to the family funds.

But on that same September 3 day, an eerie devil wind out on the Nevada desert rose up from the sand. Whirling stronger and stronger, it blew itself all the way to Los Angeles. By the time it arrived, the swirling hot air had reanimated itself into the form of "Robert Thomas" from Amarillo, Texas.

"Robert Thomas" made a beeline for the office of Dr. John M. Goin, a plastic surgeon on Wilshire Boulevard. There he had a final follow-up check on his plastic surgery. Peernock/Thomas confided to Dr. Goin that he was worried about how he was healing. He seemed to think that one of his eyes was coming out a bit crooked. Apparently one disfigured face in the family was plenty. But Dr. Goin gave "Robert Thomas" a clean bill of health and sent him packing for Amarillo.

Robert Peernock stepped back into the hot summer sunlight outside Dr. Goin's office. This time the "Robert Thomas" identity blew back out into the desert forever. Peernock didn't need it anymore.

As Peernock headed back to his Mustang, he had no way of knowing that Natasha was at Victoria Doom's office at that moment, signing an application form for a temporary letter of administration that would give her the power of all the probate matters in the estate of her late mother. He had been a bit too busy to keep up with Victoria's actions regarding his cash flow. Another paper door slid shut around the family resources. Even though a river of cash was still escaping through Robert's transfer of family accounts into the control of his girlfriend, Victoria had just helped his determined young daughter to move another step closer to shutting down Robert's access to escape funds.

That evening the COBRA tailing unit observed Sonia making repeated stops at Gelson's Market, but she did not seem interested in groceries. Instead her activities concentrated on the pay phones there. She was observed through binoculars from a distance of about seventy-five yards, making brief phone calls and then hanging around waiting for the phone to ring.

An undercover officer went to the phone next to her and pretended to use it, eavesdropping on Sonia's next conversation. Sonia turned her back on him, but she kept talking softly. The officer clearly heard her giving banking information and making reference to an attorney. The undercover cop heard the name "Bob" and clearly heard Sonia say, "I love you," and "I miss you." A few minutes later she hung up and walked quickly back to her car. The COBRA unit tailed her as she drove back home.

It was getting dark on September 3, time for Natasha to be wide awake. The swelling was gone on her face now and the shaved portion of her head was beginning to grow back out. She planned to cut the rest of her hair soon and to just wear it all very short as it grew back. At least she could look a little closer to normal then.

She studied her face in the mirror. The deep red scars were getting lighter. If she hung out in dark rooms, she might look normal someday. The dark rooms wouldn't be a problem; she had always joked about being allergic to sunlight and now the doctors had warned her specifically to avoid it for the next couple of years to give her scars the chance to lighten up as much as possible.

She pulled a baggy black sweater over her head. Gently. Some of Patty's friends were coming over to keep them company. Tasha still didn't feel like company too much these days, but Patty was going stir crazy, so she decided to play along. It would give her something to do while she waited for bedtime to come at sunrise.

At 9:30 P.M., Fisk's detectives activated another search warrant and went through Sonia's belongings at her condo while she was away using the public phones at Gelson's Market.

They seized two 35mm films, three cassette tapes, and some of her black shoes to check the soles for the presence of blood.

At 10:40 P.M., when Sonia returned home, she parked in her space in the back of the building. Detectives Fisk and Castro approached her as she walked up to her door. Another major thread in Sonia's life came unraveled as they placed her under arrest and sent her back to the station in a West Valley patrol car.

Fisk had decided that the waiting game was not paying off; it was time to sweat Sonia as hard as necessary. The COBRA unit had convinced him that Sonia knew where Peernock was and that he was in the immediate area. Steve Fisk had determined that Sonia Siegel was not going to sleep in her bed again until she had given up her boyfriend.

He isolated Sonia in one of the tiny, windowless interrogation rooms and gave her time to take in the atmosphere. Chipped and peeling insulation tiles lined the walls. The musty air made the place feel like a particularly suffocating elevator car that only went down.

Steve Fisk began to explain the facts of life. Quietly.

"Sonia," he told the frightened woman, "I know you love him and you're trying to be loyal. You're trying to do the right thing. But this man has a murder warrant out on him. He's going to be charged with first degree when we get him. He could go to the gas chamber."

"I don't believe that he—"

"Listen to me. There's more. We know he's been armed in the past, so we have to assume he's armed now. Do you understand what that means? Every cop out there who winds up going after him will assume that they are confronting an armed murderer who was capable of whacking out his own family with some kind of steel bar."

"Robert would never do anything like—"

"Sonia it's *too late* for that! You have to let a court decide if he would or not. You're not a judge and neither am I. But Sonia, if you don't hear anything else I say to you tonight, make sure that you hear this . . ."

He leaned in closer.

"Sonia, if I have to choose between one of my detectives going home alive and Robert going to the coroner's on a slab, what do you think my choice will be?

"You *have* to give him up now, Sonia, if you really love him. It's the only decent chance he has for a peaceful arrest. Listen to me. If you tell me where he is, I promise to go pick him up myself. He'll come back alive, as long as he doesn't try to do something stupid. He'll have a chance to fight this out in court."

Fisk moved in close for the clincher, using his gentlest but most determined tone.

"Give him a chance, Sonia, if he won't give himself one. Some young hothead cop is going to get jumpy out there and kill him flat out, sooner or later. We're *never* going to just let him walk away on this, Sonia. Never."

No one who wasn't a seasoned felon could stand up under the past month she had just endured. Fisk could see that she was cracking. All she needed now was a little push.

"You'll have anonymity. We'll say we acted on a tip, that's what we'll tell the papers. Give him up, Sonia. If you *really* do love him . . ."

He brought down the velvet hammer.

"Save his life."

At 1:00 A.M. on September 4, detectives Fisk and Knapp drove to the Vagabond Motel in Woodland Hills and checked with the desk clerk. They had two possible room numbers; Sonia wasn't sure if it was 213 or 215. The clerk told them that the family in room 213 had just checked in the night before. But room 215 was occupied by a single man who had been there for over a week, registered under the name of White. One thing was strange. The man had put a California license plate number on his desk registration, but his gray Mustang had Nevada plates.

Fisk called the room on the front desk phone. A man answered cautiously. "Hey, Bob?" Fisk began cheerily. "This is Steve. Sonia told me to call you. She wants you to know that she won't be able to come over tonight."

When the man on the other end responded affirmatively, Fisk motioned out the window to his partner Officer Knapp, who was standing outside the door of room 215. Knapp began beating on the door and demanding that Peernock open up for the police. When Peernock cracked the door open to peek out, Fisk and Knapp both knocked it aside and dived through. They pulled him down immediately without a shot being fired. A couple of the plastic-surgery stitches behind one of Peernock's ears tore loose in the scuffle, but he was otherwise unharmed during the arrest.

As Fisk had promised, Sonia had saved Robert's life.

If Sonia had seen the things Fisk and Knapp pulled out of Robert's room, she might not have felt quite so loyal. In addition to $500 in his wallet, he had $25,761 in cash. He had a packed suitcase. And he had a book titled *The Australia Traveler's Survival Guide*. Since he hadn't advised her of any plans to see Australia, she might have wondered if this was another independent decision on his part.

Like the new face.

By 2:00 A.M. a saddened yet relieved Sonia Siegel was delivered back to her condo by a patrol unit after she confirmed that Robert had had no stitches on July 22 when he left but that he had when he came back from Vegas. She had to realize that he was alive and therefore he was going to be able to fight for his innocence. Things could have been worse.

She would later learn that they could be far worse.

• • •

Peernock was transported to the jail hospital for treatment of the injury to his left ear, but he refused to provide the doctor there with information needed to treat the wound.

While he was being booked, a dejected Robert Peernock said, ''You should probably just shoot me right now and save the taxpayers a lot of money.''

The jail watch commander immediately refused to book him, as required whenever any arrestee displays possible suicidal tendencies. Peernock was transferred to the Los Angeles County Jail and placed in a medical unit on suicide watch.

By now there were a whole lot of people with a strong personal interest in seeing to it that he lived to go to trial.

At 3:00 A.M. on that same September 3 morning Tasha was still awake up in her room with Patty, but she wasn't tired yet. Their friends had begun to wear down and were talking about going home, when the phone rang. Tasha picked it up in a hurry, thinking it must be a call for her at that late hour and hoping the rest of the household hadn't been disturbed by the ring.

Steve Fisk was on the other end of the line. He sounded a lot more tired than she was. Tasha knew that for a guy who shows up at work around 5:30 every morning, 3:00 A.M. is more than just a little past suppertime. But Fisk knew of her late hours and told her that he wanted to hear her voice, to hear with his own ears that she was still alive, and to hear her reaction himself when he informed her that Robert Peernock had just been arrested.

There was a pause on Tasha's end of the line. She didn't yell or scream or break down crying. Although Fisk couldn't see her, he could imagine her nodding her head silently, the way she often did just before she spoke.

''Cool,'' she said softly. And then, after another brief pause, ''Did he get hurt or anything?''

"You're worried about him getting hurt?"

"Well, it's just that . . ." After a moment she continued as quietly as ever. "It's good news anyway."

Fisk asked if she'd mind if he got to be the one to call Victoria Doom and tell her about the arrest.

"Now?"

"Gee, I thought I'd get some sleep first. Maybe I'll call her after she gets to her office. How about that?"

"Good idea."

"So anyway, now you can get some decent rest."

"It's still early."

"Uh-huh. Good night, Natasha."

"You too. Oh, and hey, I just— Thank you."

"You're welcome, Natasha. You're welcome."

She hung up the phone and told her friends the good news. They made a lot more fuss about it than she did, because they thought that the news meant that it was all over now. They had no way of knowing that for Natasha it only meant that she had been given the chance to begin the fight for the Peernock family women. Tasha had grown up in that house; prior to receiving this news of his arrest she had already spent thirty-one days of her life in various hospitals, recovering from things that her father had done to her.

She knew, perhaps better than anybody, that Robert John Peernock had absolutely no intention of taking all this lying down.

The Confusers

There's many a beast then,
in a populous city,
And many a civil monster.

—Othello, *Act IV, Scene I*

CHAPTER
15

"Ms. Doom?"

"Yes."

"This is Detective Fisk calling. Good news and bad news."

"Great. Make it a double on the good news and hold the bad news, if you don't mind."

"Well, the good news is we finally got Peernock."

"Oh! Oh, thank God! That is great. . . . That's great."

"Yeah. Arrest went pretty smooth."

"Does Natasha know?"

"Oh, yeah. Called her right away. Also got word to her little sister's foster parents."

"Okay, then. All right. . . . I guess I can't stand it after all. What's the bad news?"

"We subpoenaed his bank accounts. The ones we can find so far, anyway. There was some $240,000 in cash that we know of, but it looks like a lot of it is already gone. It's been spent since he went on the run."

"What? Like hell! That money belongs to those kids! At least half of it, anyway. And maybe more once we shake everything out. All right, that *does* it. Peernock's had his share. I'm going to find some way to lock up the rest right now until we see what's going on with all the estate and probate work."

"Um, yeah. But that wasn't the bad news."

". . . It can be worse?"

"Think so. Thing is, you can't get at the rest of the money right now. Whether any of it belongs to Natasha or not."

"Sure I can, I just— Why not?"

"He's given his girlfriend power of attorney. Everything has been put in her name. And she's used another sixty thousand dollars to hire a lawyer named Bradley Brunon, supposed to be one of the top criminal defense attorneys in the state."

Victoria hung up the phone feeling as if she had just stepped over a cliff. If this Brunon guy was really that good, then Natasha would, in effect, wind up paying for the lawyer who had managed to put her father back out on the street. Free to finish off his disobedient daughter once and for all.

Before the month was out, Victoria had synchronized her efforts with those of the police as much as possible, to avoid retracing their steps. Fisk stayed busy on the Peernock case despite the cascade of fresh, real-life murder mysteries that landed on his desk each week. This one still burned at him.

As for Robert Peernock, as soon as he was arrested he immediately began denying guilt and accusing the detectives of beating him up, stealing his money, and furthering the government's plot against him. Peernock had his story straight in such detail that Fisk knew any bit of evidence the police could uncover might be the final key needed by the prosecution. So Fisk set to work using subpoena power to gain fast access to whatever paper trail Peernock might have left behind while he was still at large.

Meanwhile Victoria was busy obtaining temporary letters of administration allowing Natasha, through Victoria's office, to protect what was left of the family estate. She was successful by the second week of September. Next, on September 20, she obtained a court order granting an injunction to completely freeze any estate money. The following day she obtained a lis pendens to prevent any of the Peernock houses from being sold by anyone until the chaos around the case could be settled. But these actions marked the end of any relatively easy law work on the case.

Robert Peernock had begun to generate copious amounts of paperwork of his own, writing from within his jail cell.

LETTER TO NATASHA

From Robert Peernock,
Booking No. 9269283, L.A. County Jail
September 29, 1987

Dear Natasha,
It is so sad what has happened. I had nothing to do with Claire's death or your injuries. . . . "

Natasha stood mute with shock as she scanned the rest of her father's letter to her. It had arrived by regular mail, addressed in his own handwriting. Despite all of the police protection and the secrecy surrounding her presence there, it had been sent directly to the home where she was hiding to recuperate.

In his letter he spoke to her just as if she had not been present for the nightmare of torture they'd shared as their final father-daughter activity. He went on to insist that Claire had driven away with Natasha around 11:30 on the evening of the crime. He lamented that the story Natasha had told the police would likely leave him to fight the gas chamber. Although he promised to defend himself ''no matter what it costs,'' he reminded her that by the time all of the lawyers involved were finished, there would nothing left of the family estate for the two girls.

Natasha's blood hammered under her struggle to believe

the impossible words in her hands. Her father claimed that he did not know the extent of her injuries because *the hospital would not allow him to see her,* and that the police would not even provide him with that small amount of personal information. He claimed that the police first told him that she had struck her head on the steering wheel, but that they were now saying that he was somehow involved. In the same paragraph, he went on to remind her that even though they had suffered their share of arguments over innocuous things such as her schoolwork and getting a job, he would not deliberately do anything to harm her.

Natasha's hands began to shake as she read these words, in her own father's handwriting, completely disowning any knowledge of a night she would remember with agonizing clarity for the rest of her life.

The worst part came next, when he spoke to her in the grave tones of a hurt and concerned father. He reminded her that he used to give her swimming lessons and bike-riding lessons and that as a little girl she had been his constant companion, riding around everywhere on his shoulders. He reminded her that he had always supported her and had done what was expected of a father. He pointed out to her that this horrendous story she had told the police was going to put him on trial for his life.

Still, he encouraged her to use his insurance to get plastic surgery (even though he had just claimed to know nothing about her condition).

He returned to his description of Victoria Doom as a money-grabbing attorney who would do nothing more than dream up excuses to drain the family finances, leaving little or nothing behind as he fought to pay for lawyers for himself and his girlfriend.

He added another paragraph reminding her of his long fight against the state and told her that in the past, state authorities had dreamed up charges against him but that he "sued the state and won." Though he hoped to win this case as well, everyone was going to come out ahead except for the Peernock family.

He told her that the police had beaten him and described the county jail as "the worst place in the world." He claimed that people inside there get beaten or killed frequently, and said that she should hurry up and get her plastic surgery because his insurance wouldn't cover it if he died while awaiting trial.

Then again—he repeated that he'd had nothing whatsoever to do with the murder or her torture and bludgeoning. "It is," he lamented, "like a nightmare, what has happened to our family."

He concluded by asking her to write to him and assuring her that he missed her very much.

It was signed tenderly, "Love, Dad."

She did not break down emotionally. The invisible wall had already slid into place inside her. She knew that it was more important than ever for her to remain calm and get the letter to the police right away. After that, it would be all the more important for her to remain alert, even in this protected environment.

Because now she knew for certain that he was never going to give up.

Letters were not the only form of writing that Robert John Peernock was doing inside his isolation cell. Working with the stub of a pencil that he sharpened by rubbing the tip back and forth over the cement floor, he filled legal tablets with notices to judges. He repeatedly voiced his fears that because he was a target of a state-orchestrated murder charge, he would never be given adequate representation from state-appointed counsel. Serving as his own attorney, he began to exercise his knowledge of the court system to file civil suits and draft his own motions. Fighting his lack of formal schooling, he pressed his high intelligence to the task of mounting his best legal resistance to the events overwhelming his life.

As he tried to stop the seizure of his funds and his household possessions, he simultaneously battled the juvenile court system's forced placement of his youngest daughter in the government's foster care.

And Peernock offered a much different picture of the night of the crimes.

He talked of a long struggle that he and his late wife had both waged in attempting to stop Natasha from using drugs. He claimed that Natasha frequently came home drunk, and that her behavior in this regard was an emulation of Claire's own drinking problem. He explained that while Claire often avoided alcohol for quite a stretch, she always fell back into her addiction sooner or later. He stated that after a couple of drinks she was completely unable to stop herself from going on an alcohol binge.

He appealed to the court system, over and over again, to allow him enough access to his funds to hire investigators. He assured the courts if they let him do that he would be able to gather plenty of information to prove his story. He claimed that on the night of the crimes, a hopelessly addicted wife had fallen back into her alcohol cravings and had gotten into an argument with Natasha, who was only slightly more sober. He explained that at this point he left the house in disgust and returned to a shelf-painting project that he was working on in the backyard.

He did not claim to know exactly what had happened after that. Either the operatives who had been sent to silence him had come into the house looking for him but encountered the two women, kidnapping them in a hastily contrived plan, or they had staked out the house and simply followed the women when Claire and Natasha took Robert's Cadillacs and drove off to some unknown destination.

Whatever had happened next, Robert sent motion after

Claire Peernock—family and friends prefer to remember her upbeat nature and playful sense of humor, not as Robert left her in the wreckage.

Tasha at the time of her confirmation. She already feared her father deeply.

Natasha Peernock—this is one of the last known photos of Tasha taken before the night of the crimes.

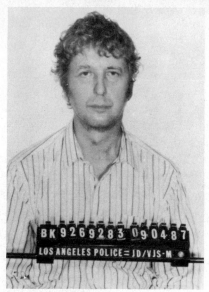

Robert Peernock complained of being brutally beaten in his arrest. Yet in the booking photo taken on the same night, Peernock shows only a few tiny dots of blood on the left side of his collar, resulting from a torn face-lift stitch behind his ear.

Robert Peernock's vise.

Close shot of the vise's gripping plate.

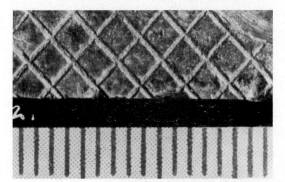

Magnified view of flaws in the vise's gripping plate.

Comparison microscope views of gripping plate's flaws shown in marks made by the soft-lead specimen on the left side compared to the marks shown on the cutter bar, on the right.

Craig Richman brought his Air Force Academy background of discipline to the case research and a radio announcer's knowledge of drama to his handling of courtroom presentation.

Victoria Doom worked for years as a legal secretary before she was able to attend law school. This is her graduation photo.

Rear view of the Cadillac shows the towing hitch.

Police Impound photo of Robert Peernock's Datsun shows the front mounts for a tow bar.

The vise found in Peernock's Datsun and the toolbox holding the guns are seen here through the rear-hatch window.

Guns and ammunition were in the toolbox. The top pistol matched the description Natasha gave the detectives.

CRIME SCENE PHOTOS: The force of the big Cadillac's impact splintered the telephone pole.

The inside of the car was relatively undamaged, given the extreme head trauma of both women.

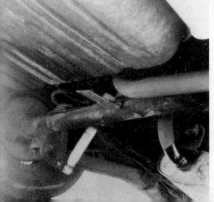

The sharpened steel-cutter bar after fire inspectors removed the rope wick and pulled it away from the gas tank.

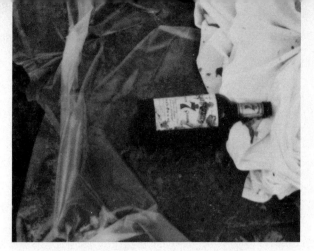

Claire's bloody fingerprints were on the liquor bottle, but not on the steering wheel. She had no gloves on.

Attorney Donald Green only could look on helplessly as Robert Peernock was dragged out of court in hysteria. Peernock did not display his teenage daughter's ability to remain composed in the face of disaster. (CREDIT: GENE BLEVINS, LOS ANGELES *DAILY NEWS*)

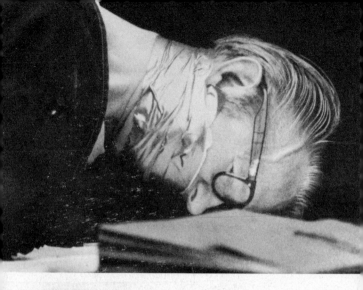

Peernock was ordered bound and gagged after repeated screaming fits during his sentencing hearing. Here he slumps to the table with his head wrapped in duct tape, while Judge Schwab sentences him to *22 years and 4 months*, to be followed by *life*, then *life without possibility of parole*. (CREDIT: GENE BLEVINS, LOS ANGELES *DAILY NEWS*)

Robert Peernock revisited five years after the crimes, at the time of his transfer out of Pelican Bay's isolation unit to the California Medical Facility. Peernock's hair had gone gray. The face-lift appeared to be holding up nicely.

motion through the court system, pleading for the chance to be allowed to show that these operatives had either caused the car wreck or, after following Claire and Natasha up until the time that the drunken Claire wrecked the car on her own, had callously taken advantage of it. Robert repeatedly claimed that in Claire's drunken state, which the coroner confirmed as a blood alcohol level nearly three times over the legal limit, she had wandered lost into an unfamiliar part of the county and finally passed out at the wheel, sending the car into the telephone pole. Either that, or that she and Natasha had been too incoherent to resist being kidnapped and were later placed inside a staged wreck. In either case, the wreck had provided the operatives with a perfect chance to affix primitive explosive devices under the car and thereby assure Peernock's rapid arrest.

He ridiculed the devices as unbelievably crude and ineffective, especially for a man known to be an expert in pyrotechnics. He pleaded for someone to notice that the devices were not merely primitive, but *were phony and could never have worked as detonators*. This alone, he asserted, should tip off an impartial observer that the crimes were not of his doing.

He also pointed out that the missing underside of the Cadillac's dashboard had caused stereo mounting brackets to be exposed, and that *these* had most likely been the source of the severe head wounds to both his wife and his daughter. The dashboard was supposedly stored in his garage, but police failed to find it. All this did was to convince Peernock that Victoria Doom had stolen it and that she'd gotten rid of it somehow in order to help the police make the case against him. He wasn't clear on why it would occur to her to get rid of a single dashboard cover out of a garage stuffed with belongings, or how doing so would help rig the case against him.

He explained his initial attempts to avoid arrest as having

been made in the hope of establishing these and other facts prior to turning himself in, to prevent the very situation he found himself struggling with now. He knew the courts would not help him prove his innocence. He had recognized the wreck as being a staged fake from the very beginning.

Authorities agreed with him that the wreck had been a staged fake.

And as Robert John Peernock himself was loudly predicting from within his tiny cell, the courts would indeed have an entirely different scenario to describe that awful night.

CHAPTER

16

By the beginning of October, before Peernock had been in custody for a month, Victoria found herself beginning to founder under the abundance of legal action being directed at her office from several different sources. She had to work in cooperation with the attorney for Natasha's sister, who was fighting Peernock's attempt to reach out from behind bars and attach custody of the child to Robert's girlfriend or to his elderly parents. At the same time she was fighting Sonia Siegel's attorney, who was attempting to dispute Victoria's attempts to regain control of the bank accounts.

Worst of all, she had been enjoined in a civil court battle on behalf of Robert Peernock by the Century City law firm that loyal Sonia had hired to defend him. The high-powered outfit was known as Dern, Mason and Floum. Through this firm Peernock was vehemently protesting having Natasha assigned as administrator of the probate actions, citing a clear conflict of interest on her part about handling "his" money. Victoria responded that Natasha was properly appointed administrator because Probate Code defines the order in which administrators are to be selected as being the surviving spouse, then the children. Since Robert had been a fugitive with a murder warrant outstanding at the time of the appointment, Natasha was clearly next in line.

Besides, Maurice had entrusted Natasha to Victoria for no other reason than that Claire Peernock had believed in her; Victoria was determined to search for every justification the

law would give her for stacking the deck on Natasha's behalf, in any way that she could, without apologies.

She would soon need that determination. Dern, Mason and
Floum was about to make her worst fears about taking the
case come to life. This multipartner firm had enough resources to assign a full roster of corporate attorneys to it,
plus all the administrative backup needed to research every
move they made.

The paperwork began to flood through the door of her solo
law practice.

As fall deepened, Tasha finally began to feel as if a tiny
rainbow of hope might be opening up on the Pacific horizon.
She could almost peer through it, gazing across the distance
from her gray-clouded present situation to sneak a keyhole
glimpse into a more colorful future.

Her fiancé had come home for a few days of leave before
rushing off to his assignment in Hawaii. All the plans were
made for her to join him there and for the young couple to
get married early in October. Steve Fisk had found enough
money in a small victim's relief fund to pay for her ticket
and also arranged for her to travel under a false name to
avoid her father's private investigators, who were rumored
still to be attempting to locate her and determine her movements. Although publicity was beginning to die down around
the case, she remained appalled at the prospect of some eager
reporter slapping her scarred face on a TV broadcast.

And so the safety of anonymity and the promise of a new
beginning in an exotic location promised to burn away the
cloud that seemed to have become a permanent resident
around her heart.

Most of the expressions of concern that greeted her in the
days following the crimes came from distant adult relatives
and former friends of the family. They arrived horrified by
the story and eager to offer support, but their commiseration

seemed in large part just good-hearted pity. For someone as independent as Tasha the sense of people feeling sorry for her was like sandpaper on a sunburn.

But her fiancé was her age, one of her old group. He looked her in the eyes as they made their marriage plans and told her that he loved her. And so even though the clouds still covered her whole world, she clutched at that image of hope. If it took a hasty marriage to cement that hope into place, she thought, then so be it.

Tasha couldn't blame Patty for leaving; her friend had stuck it out for as long as she could. As grateful as both of the young women were for having had a place to stay together while Tasha worked on her recovery, Patty had been forced more or less to squeeze herself into the leftover spaces between everybody else in the house. She'd had to remain supportive of Natasha while staying in a home to which she had no connection except the two young women's friendship.

Finally, when Patty came in late one night after a particularly long recess from her caretaker duties, she was told by the owners to conform to household conduct or leave immediately. Patty was nineteen now and even as a youngster had never been one to bow to authority easily, especially the authority of strangers. The rebellious streak was part of what had attracted the two girls to each other when they first met.

So when Patty finally left, Tasha knew she couldn't blame her. No one else had rushed to be with her as quickly as Patty had or had devoted as much energy to pulling her through those first dark days.

Tasha knew that if things had been reversed, she would have had a hard time standing as much as Patty did. Her friend had her own life and her own problems to attend to. So now Tasha tried to match her reaction to Patty's leaving with the loyalty her friend had shown her. And the only way to do that was to let her go without objecting.

But it felt like another door closing in a long hallway filled with closed doors. She thought about the hope of escape that her coming marriage offered. The thick gray cloud that had become her most consistent companion was nothing she would miss.

Thus when the ninth of October rolled around and Tasha got word that Steve Fisk had finally arrested Sonia Seigel and charged her with helping Robert dodge the police, it seemed that somehow the loose ends were tying themselves up. She had no idea whether Sonia had really taken any part in the crimes, but at least it could all get sorted out now.

She rode to the airport glad to assume the false identity, feeling it would be a sort of dress rehearsal for dropping the Peernock name altogether. A few months before, if she had considered marriage at this early age at all, she would probably have kept her own name. Now it would be a relief to shed this final tie to the man who had brutalized her so badly.

She had a vague sense of the work Victoria was doing on her behalf, but the long legal explanations were confusing. The upshot was simple enough: She was dead broke and could not work. She had no chance at getting any of whatever money might be left in the insurance policies or the remaining family estate until after all the dust had settled from the civil trials and from her father's criminal case. That could be months. More likely, Victoria had warned her, it could be years.

So when the big jet picked her up and carried her high over the ocean and beyond the huge waves thundering into the shoreline where she had stood watching the crazed loners paddling out to do battle with waves anyone else would flee, it felt almost as if her life were fastened to the tail of the airplane, being pulled through that imaginary rainbow on the horizon like thread through the eye of a needle.

It's just as well that Natasha kept distant from the action in Victoria's office; if she had known how badly her lawyer was being swamped, her sleep pattern might have been worse. Dern, Mason and Floum had been whipped into a frenzy by Robert Peernock. He peppered them with instructions from his cell, demanding that they protect his estate.

The news that his money had been frozen by Victoria Doom's legal actions sent him into a campaign of demands that his lawyers attack her with every tactic available to regain use of his money and allow him to buy the best possible defense. Bradley Brunon's $60,000 fee covered only the preliminary hearing. After that, Peernock would have to run his defense at taxpayer expense unless he could get at the family's money.

Dern, Mason and Floum responded with equal fervor, using their motions to raise questions about Victoria's basic honesty and integrity in handling the case. In opposition to her motion to exclude Peernock from his estate funds, they repeatedly referred to her as showing a lack of integrity by not cooperating with them, and of being deceptive in her manner of handling the case by showing a failure to act professionally. These terms were not just annoying insults, they were highly loaded words. If such charges could be proved, she would be liable for malpractice and face possible disbarment.

As she sat reading the latest attacks on her credibility, Victoria shook her head. It was as if Robert and his big Century City law firm were personally offended that she was fighting tooth and nail to give her client every advantage.

She knew that the accusations toward her were a silent signal to the court, pressing the judge for some sort of side action to be taken against her that, by forcing her to defend herself, would further bite into her disappearing sleep time. Dern, Mason and Floum was laying siege, burying her under paper, fighting with all the resources at its disposal. The firm was generating opposition at the rate of nearly $30,000 a month in legal fees.

Meanwhile the small retainer allowed Victoria by the court from the estate's funds would be eaten up in two months by her office overhead alone, not counting all the court's filing fees and her investigator's fees. And she could forget about any living expenses for herself. As the Peernock case rapidly became a legal black hole, she was forced to begin farming out her other cases. Her entire practice gradually centered on fighting the Peernock case, just as she had initially feared.

Still, Peernock and his lawyers hadn't yet found a way to combat the two-pronged strategy she had devised. She divided the damages in Natasha's case into two groups: anything that had rightfully belonged to Claire, and the rest of the money or property that might currently belong to Robert. She had blocked them both.

Since it was natural for Robert to want to gain access to estate money and insurance money to hire more legal help, she had no doubt that he would dissipate whatever he got his hands on, leaving even less for the girls than whatever now remained after his six-week flight. So she was determined to tie up any money that might be claimed as Robert's until the court could rule on whether he should be allowed to profit in any way from his wife's death.

By this point the case had become as personal to her as it had to Steve Fisk. She couldn't forget about the sad little "Agreement" Robert and Claire had signed, in which Claire had asked for Robert's written promise not to beat the women or to attack Natasha verbally. She remembered Claire's request that he simply pay for basic expenses without making them beg, as well as the passage that guaranteed Robert would not spend away any of the community property without Claire's permission before August 1.

But Victoria now knew that he had nevertheless gone through the bank accounts like water. He had converted both of his daughters' trust accounts to his own use on the morn-

A CHECKLIST FOR MURDER

ing immediately following the crimes. Bank records prove that he had begun the process before the police attempted for the first time to contact him with the news of the incident.

That meant that he had raided the accounts before he could have had any way of knowing Claire was dead and that the "Agreement" not to touch them could no longer be enforced.

Unless he was the one who had killed her.

And so Victoria strongly suspected that Robert might have slipped up just a tad on that little passage in the "Agreement" about not striking Claire or Natasha.

CHAPTER

17

It was late on her first night in Hawaii as Natasha tiptoed into the single men's barracks behind her fiancé. She wasn't sure why they had to sneak in, moving quietly down the hallways until they came to his shared room. She didn't know whether he had been unable to secure housing for them or was just unwilling to put forth the effort. Either way, the result was that the first few days in Honolulu involved finessing past MP's whenever they wanted to leave together, then tiptoeing back inside after hours. Most of the time she stayed alone in the room while he was at work. Her appearance kept her from wanting to go anywhere, anyway. Especially in the daylight.

But the trip had still been an adventure. Not even the muted military surroundings could hold back the thick tropical scents that floated everywhere. The varieties of palm trees put California to shame and the island's summer colors ran the spectrum. The view was hidden from her while she stayed inside, but she could feel it all out there, close by. All she had to do was bide her time and play each moment as best she could until things started to brighten up somehow. She was alive against all odds, she had successfully traveled far away from her destroyed home. Even the strangeness of seeing the island's lush natural beauty set next to the stern presence of old war monuments and menacing battleships was nothing that could faze her. Since the Peernock household had equipped her with mental compartments for storing impressions that seemed to cancel each other's message, she could handle an odd new environment and a bizarre living situation without a blink. Things had to brighten up now. The weirdness of living surreptitiously on a Navy base wasn't going to steal her sense of savoring the moment. Not for anything.

She was alive. She had escaped. The rest could be sorted out later.

On October 23, after a week or so in the barracks, the young couple sneaked away to town and met with a judge in a tiny room of some anonymous-looking official building. The service went by in a blur: a frank, no-frills ritual. Tasha didn't need the white dress and organ music. It was another step into freedom; the marriage made it possible now for the couple to seek living quarters off base.

She still had a few thousand dollars left over from her mother's small insurance policy following the cremation and burial. Part of it went to help her new husband pay for a single night of honeymoon in one of the beautiful high-rise hotels that line Honolulu's beach area. The surroundings were the best she had seen in a long time and the private room that the two shared was especially welcome after the complete lack of privacy that she had endured since the night of the crimes.

A single night in manufactured luxury allowed these two young lovers, both still in their teens, to exist inside a tiny bubble of private sweetness which they knew would end the following day. The bubble enclosed them and wrapped them in its softness just as similar bubbles have hidden lovers from the world and from their everyday lives for thousands of years, even when they know full well that the walls are hopelessly thin and cannot endure.

It made the thought of waiting for an apartment of their own a little easier as they sneaked back into the barracks on the following day.

• • •

"Hi, Vicki."

"Natasha! You're not back in town, are you?"

"No, I'm still in Hawaii."

"Good. When my secretary said you were calling, I thought you'd got some crazy idea about flying back here or something."

"No, I just—"

"Are you calling about the case? I don't think there's any news yet. Your father's just waiting to—"

"It's not about that."

"Oh. So how are you doing, then? Everything okay?"

"It's all right. I just . . ."

"You just what? Talk to me. Your voice sounds funny."

"It's just . . . sometimes we have to go out, you know, and people ask, some of them ask, about my face."

"Well, you just ignore them. Or tell them it's none of their business."

"I tried that, but you can't just offend people, and besides, that doesn't always stop them."

"Mm. I see. What does your husband suggest you tell them?"

"He can't really deal with it. I mean, he still refers to the whole thing as an 'accident.' He never even says the word *murder*."

"Oh, boy. All right, look. I know you don't want to have to explain everything to anybody who just walks up and shows some idle curiosity. So why don't you just tell them it happened in a car wreck? If they ask about your mom and dad, you can tell them you lost your parents in the same car wreck that gave you the scars. That's close enough to the truth."

"Yeah. That sounds good. What if they ask more questions?"

"Beyond that, just tell them you don't like talking about

it. Anybody who doesn't back off after that deserves to get their feelings stepped on, you know?''

They talked for a while longer, trading a little news. But Victoria hung up feeling heartsick. She wondered if her advice to Tasha about hiding the source of her scars had really meant anything to her. This case seemed to constantly call upon her to exhibit abilities she wasn't sure she had. She could only hope to have given Tasha something she could use.

''What are you doing here?''

The barracks guard didn't look familiar to Tasha. He was glaring at her with his eyes full of suspicion. She knew that plenty of the enlisted men sneaked their girlfriends in for little visits. Apparently the guard knew it too.

She was dressed in nothing more than a T-shirt and panties and she blushed under his unwavering gaze. Her mind raced, trying to size up how much of the truth she was supposed to tell this guy. The guard flicked his quick gaze around the room and drew himself up to full height, working to impress upon her that she had better not try anything funny.

''Y'know, you could get your boyfriend bagged for having you in here.''

''He's not my boyfriend,'' Tasha retorted, then made a quick mental note to keep her voice friendly as she continued, ''We're actually married.''

''Interesting,'' the guard replied, taking a good look at her long legs.

Her T-shirt felt like it had shrunk about three sizes. Why the hell hadn't she put on a bra?

''No, really.'' She smiled, trying not to shake. ''We just got married and he's at work now but we already have an apartment and as soon as he gets home we're moving in over there because this is our last day here and I'm just—''

''Your last *what*? You mean to tell me you've been living

here in *violation* of policy, *mis*using Navy property in *complete* disregard for—''

"Look. We're married."

"Uh-huh," the guard replied, not actually calling her a liar but getting his point across all the same. He ran his eyes down the clipboard in his hand. Finally he seemed to see something that relieved his suspicion a bit.

"Well, I see he's moving *out*, all right. But he's listed as being a single male until seventeen hundred hours today."

"Hey, I can't help what—" She stopped, dropped her voice, and started again. "I don't know what's on that list, but we got married last week and now we have a place to stay and he got permission from whoever. So can't we just—"

"I suppose you must have some kind of *proof,* since you're all legal and everything?"

"Well . . ." Tasha looked up at the small bag she had just finished packing. The marriage papers were in it, all right. And she had stowed it away neatly, high up on the top shelf of the tall wall unit.

"Well?" the guard asked, following her gaze.

"It's way up there. Can you get it down for me?"

The guard put the situation together fast. Only a hint of a grin flashed before he replaced it with his special interrogator's maybe-you're-a-spy scowl. "You want me to climb up there and give you a chance to run off?"

"Why would I run off? This is all our stuff. And I haven't done anything—"

"Y'know, I don't *have* to stand here and argue with you." He ran his eyes along her bare legs again. Slowly. Tasha felt the T-shirt shrink another couple of sizes.

But she thought about what it would mean to have her new husband come home and find that she had managed to get him into trouble by not handling this thing right.

"Fine." She exhaled sharply, grabbed the chair, and, pulling it under the high shelf, climbed up.

"Fine." The chair wasn't high enough. She had to brace her foot on one of the lower shelves and climb another foot or two up over the delighted guard.

"Fine." By now the T-shirt was down to about the size of a cloth necklace.

Just do it, she told herself. *Just do it just do it just do it.*

And finally she was back on the floor holding the bag. In another second she had the marriage papers stuck under the ensign's nose and felt no surprise when he hardly glanced at them.

"Well, okay," he mumbled. "I'll let it slide."

The surprise came when she noticed he was blushing just a bit. She wondered if he felt guilty about this nasty little trick or if he was just getting concerned. Would the married lady talk? Put in a complaint? Run the old paper marathon and submit it to the cap'n?

Either way, he tore his eyes off her lower half and looked her straight in the face for the first time since he'd barged through the door.

"Whoa. Your husband do that to you?"

"No. It was . . . a car wreck. Are we through yet?"

"Right. Sure." He ran his gaze over her scars one more time and whistled softly.

"Just keep away from the windows and don't make any noise until both you guys are gone."

"That's what I was doing." She stood quietly and met his gaze until he dropped it and turned for the door.

"Okay, then. Be careful." And then the door closed again and he was gone.

Be careful? she wondered. *Oh, right.* There were plenty of other guards around. And who could tell how horny some of *them* might be?

• • •

The apartment was furnished with a futon, a bed, a television, and not much else. Her insurance money had been run down to barely over two thousand dollars by the deposits and initial expenses, but she had helped to pick out the place herself. It was small, and on days when the elevators went out there was a twenty-story climb up from ground level.

But it was hers, and it was safe.

Her very first, on-your-own, dirty as you can stand it, pay for it yourself, don't let anybody inside who you don't want to, hang out and look as ugly as you feel like, make as much noise as your neighbors will tolerate, very first place.

CHAPTER

18

The unending noise inside the Los Angeles County Jail is a soundtrack from hell's lowest levels, stuck on continuous replay. A thick sour stink coats everything like a layer of nasty paint. By early November Robert Peernock was seething in his four-man cell, desperate to find a way to stop his daughter and her attorney from denying him access to his money, poisoning his attempt to mount the best possible defense.

His own money. That phrase kept coming up, over and over as he poured handwritten motions out of his cell. *His own money.* As an example of the way his civil rights were being trampled, he frequently pointed out in his motions that he was not allowed decent legal supplies and was forced to write his motions with a one-inch pencil stub, sharpened by rubbing it back and forth over the cell's concrete surface. Clerks began to say that it must have been a Magic Pencil; it sent countless pages rolling into the court clerk's office, laying out his years of struggle and introducing all who would read them to a tale of conspiracy as grand as the libretto to a jailhouse opera.

Lyle, a convicted child molester, entered L.A. County Jail around November 1. His prior conviction had been for sexually abusing his young daughter, and he was now back in jail for a repetition of the same offense.

Lyle happened to be assigned to the cell right next to Peernock's. They couldn't help but notice each other. Both were conspicuous as white men in a jail system dominated by Latinos and African-Americans.

It's a good idea to seek company behind bars if you can; the L.A. County Jail is an angry and overcrowded place. The simple act of strolling into the declared space of the wrong group can get a homemade knife jammed between your ribs. One wrong glance can touch off brawl like a match at a gas pump. So Lyle and Robert did as other Anglos do, lining up together for mealtime and recreation, following the unspoken tradition.

It was a loose affiliation. The two didn't talk much at first. Still, even before Lyle knew what charges Peernock was facing, he noticed that Peernock didn't seem to belong in jail. At the age of fifty, Robert Peernock was too well maintained to have the look of a regular customer. He was free of jail-house tattoos and the low-lidded fuck-you shuffle common to seasoned institutionals. Lyle realized that the man was a complete newcomer to the system. This meant that as a middle-aged Anglo with an education, Peernock would be dead in no time if somebody didn't pass him a few facts of life. But Lyle also knew jail life well. He knew about keeping your distance and about the value of staying to yourself. So even as they hung close physically, he kept his personal distance from Peernock. Lyle just did quiet time, leaving the strange newcomer to twist in the wind while Lyle sized him up.

Besides, Lyle had plenty to keep quiet about. Child molesters, especially the Anglos, get eaten for breakfast by the angry ''minority'' inmates who easily surpass the numbers of their lighter-skinned colleagues. Molesters don't fare much better with their own race. All of them tend to do their time peacefully and avoid undue attention.

But before long Lyle had to admit that he liked Peernock's style. Lyle recognized the man as a true jailhouse lawyer, with his cell space crammed with boxes of legal documents and bits of evidence concerning his case. Plenty of inmates try to buck the system single-handed, but after two months in captivity Peernock had focused himself on the quest for freedom like a man possessed.

Lyle was finally pulled into Peernock's corner of the world when Cowboy, one of Lyle's cell mates, sneaked into Peernock's "house" while he was asleep and stole some cash out of the money belt Peernock kept under his shirt. When Peernock awoke and discovered the theft he went ballistic. Lyle was stunned to see this fifty-year-old white man charge into Lyle's group cell and accuse the *wrong man*, demanding that the money be returned before the day's end.

After Peernock stomped back to his own cell, Lyle listened uneasily while the outraged inmate blustered out threats of reprisals for the insult. A major fight was brewing; at the best it would involve injury between these two men, at the worst a full race riot.

Lyle quickly took Peernock aside and explained, in effect, Hey, bozo, unless you're *real* tired of living, you just don't put out that kind of shit in here. To lay it out plain, you broke a strict jailhouse code by offending a man in front of his friends. Now you better go apologize and try to mend the situation before somebody gets seriously hurt. And you better hustle.

Maybe if Lyle had spent more time observing Peernock by this point, he wouldn't have bothered to suggest backing down. Peernock's outright refusal to play willing victim to the theft convinced Lyle that the next best thing would be at least to hire some protection before mixing it up across racial lines. So a Latino named Speedy was paid twenty dollars to hold back any others who might want to jump in and make it a family affair.

And that was when Peernock, who would later protest to the court that his "back condition" made it impossible for him to have carried Natasha and Claire from the house to the car, headed back into Cowboy's cell and beat the living shit out of him.

Speedy already had his twenty bucks, though, and he didn't do a thing to protect the naive newcomer who had hired him. Lyle watched the spectators getting increasingly ugly at the sight of a frenzied whitey hammering on one of their home boys. A major battle was about to erupt.

With no other recourse left, Lyle began deliberately making enough spectator noise to draw a guard and bring in the authorities in the hope of quelling the situation without taking the risk of identifying himself as a snitch.

He got his wish. The guards showed up in time to break up a brewing full-scale brawl; Peernock successfully exacted revenge for having his space violated.

And two unhappy men found themselves in the springtime of a budding jailhouse relationship. Now that the ice was broken, both reluctant residents of taxpayer accommodations began to sidle up closer.

Lyle wasn't eager to discuss his case or try to explain why he had been compelled to sexually pursue his daughter, especially after having been convicted for it once already. But in the days since his arrest he had found himself suffering a major attack of remorse over the harm he had caused in his past; he would later say that somehow the act of taking another man under his wing and showing him a few things about keeping out of harm's way while behind bars was an act of kindness that he needed to perform even more than Robert Peernock needed a jailhouse mentor. On that basis the friendship quickly grew. He became Peernock's confidant, trusted as much as anyone was going to be at this stage in Robert's life.

This is either great news or terrible news, depending on whether you side with the prosecution or the defense.

Because after a certain number of hours spent swapping the usual jailhouse b.s. and hanging out watching the stud boys shoot hoops, the new buddies' conversations slowly zeroed in on more personal territory. Finally Lyle gave out enough information about himself to freely complain that his girlfriend was taking all his money and that he wished she were dead. He now claims it was merely jailhouse trash talk, just a way of blowing off macho steam.

But Lyle was caught off-guard by Peernock's reaction to his remark about wishing his girlfriend dead. He seized on the concept like a horny lifer snatching up a new arrival on the cellblock. Before long, whenever the two new pals could capture a moment of privacy, Peernock was exploring the idea of eliminating the opposition.

At first Lyle just played along as Peernock repeatedly broached the topic of hiring someone to kill "that bitch Doom" and Peernock's teenaged daughter, who was "lying her ass off to get at her father's money." Lyle kept telling himself that lots of people talk about revenge in the joint; most of it drifts away with the next hit of smuggled weed. But this Peernock guy was pressing the subject, such as, did Lyle know anyone who could set it up? And how much would it cost to *actually do it*? Not only was it becoming harder to steer Peernock away from the subject, Lyle soon realized that his was not the only doorbell Peernock was ringing.

Other guys were beginning to talk. One of the inmates on the black side had supposedly been hit up for the job. Another of the Mexicans bragged of being approached. So far these men were laughing it off, but Lyle knew that the size of some of the drug habits in the joint guaranteed that eventually Peernock would find someone who was desperate enough to do anything for cash, even seek out a man's terrorized daughter, identify her by the scars covering her face, and finish her off once and for all.

Lyle couldn't believe it. The irony of his position was breaking his face. Here he was, feeling coated with shame over the treatment he had inflicted on his own daughter, while the man he had befriended as a part of this attempt to turn over a new leaf in life was asking him to arrange for *his* daughter's death.

Lyle might have been twisted but he wasn't stupid. As he explained it later, he could see from that very moment that life was messing with him.

He decided that this time old Lyle wasn't going to take the bait. Killing "some bitch attorney" was one thing. But helping Peernock to contract a whack on his own flesh and blood? "Hey," he explained to Fisk, "at least when you screw them they can survive to go get therapy."

No, Lyle concluded, he had starred in a few too many of his own personal tales from the dark side. And when he thought about Peernock trying to make Lyle his private flunky in this evil deed, Lyle started to get mad. He wondered, did Robert give a damn about Lyle at all or about whatever might come around in Lyle's life because of this? Right. Lyle could see that Peernock had no respect for him; the man just wasn't coming from the heart.

Clearly, it was time to give Robert Peernock a chance to make his own decision about whether he would step any farther into hell or not. Lyle had made his.

And so, two weeks after checking in to the L.A. County Jail, Lyle took a guard aside on his way back from mealtime. He talked fast. Keeping his voice low, he muttered that he had information for the detectives on Peernock's case and *somebody* better talk to him *soon* and, hey, this is no bullshit.

Then he headed back to his cell, moving fast but casual, acting like nothing was up. To simply be seen by another inmate talking to a guard without some clear, valid reason was enough to turn the others on you, get you branded as a squealer. But to actually be heard leaking information on somebody was a sure guarantee of a bad death.

• • •

Steve Fisk knew all too well that there was a dire snitch situation over in County Jail. Some of the inmates would make up stories about their mothers to get a plea bargain or a shortened sentence. The courts never accept an isolated story offered by one con against another, not with so much special interest at stake. With a story like Lyle's, hard evidence is the only way to go.

Still, to Fisk this report rang true. It seemed perfectly plausible that Peernock wasn't through yet, not as long as his daughter was alive and willing to testify.

So on November 19 Fisk wired Lyle for sound and sent him back into the cellblock with a story about a fictitious hit man named "Jake." The plan was simply to feed Peernock a verbal noose and see if he hung himself on tape.

Murphy's Law being what it is, naturally the machine malfunctioned.

What Lyle brought back was a tale of how Peernock had made clear and incriminating statements during the bugged conversation, but that something bungled the connection on the microphone wire. Fisk wound up with zero. The pressure increased when Lyle assured him that Peernock was shopping for killers on other cellblocks, leaving Fisk with the possibility that Peernock might find one before Fisk could use Lyle to get the drop on him.

What would happen, Fisk wondered, if Peernock had a hired killer lined up already?

Fisk feared that Lyle might be getting buyer's remorse. Maybe the guy sabotaged the mike himself, Fisk thought. Speaking to Lyle so there would no chance of miscommunication, Fisk warned that if a young girl died because of any such sabotage, Lyle's life would fall face-first into the toilet.

Then Fisk had the audio experts wire him up again. He ordered them to do it so carefully that if anything screwed up this time, they would know for sure whose fault it was.

• • •

On November 24 Lyle went back into the cellblock wired for sound. The tape recorder functioned properly this time. Nevertheless the tape Lyle brought back was maddening, nearly impossible to listen to. Fisk strained his ears for more than half an hour, struggling to hear through the deafening background din produced by a rooftop basketball game, countless bickering jailbirds, and frequent unintelligible announcements blaring over what sounded like the world's worst loudspeaker system.

But then—toward the end, practically buried in the ball-court babble—there was that one section. Five minutes and six seconds that simultaneously chilled Fisk's blood and gladdened his heart.

Lyle had gotten Peernock to say it out loud after all.

On top of the jail, in the rooftop ball-court area, sprinkled in with inane bits of jailhouse ball-game chatter and questions about passes to see the chaplain, the ice-cold truth came out.

Lyle: "So I got one phone call before I got back. And, uh, you won't get hurt."

Peernock: "Is there a wire on you, by any chance?"

Lyle: [sounding crushed by the implication] "No, Bob."

Peernock: " 'Cause they'll do that."

[There is a rustling sound as Lyle pulls up his shirt to make it look like he has no wire. He manages to pull it up just high enough to bunch the fabric over the recording unit, which was taped high on his back between the shoulder blades.] "I don't mind. I don't have nothin'. I'm clean. I wouldn't let 'em do that. I don't mind, I'm glad that you're, uh, y'know, that you watch."

Peernock: [apparently satisfied] " 'Cause that's one of the only reasons why I came up here. I'm ver-y cau-tious."

[other inmates discuss the game for a while, then:]

Peernock: "I don't know when my attorney's coming this

week. But I've got the case starting Wednesday of next week. Which is the second.''

Lyle: "Next week?"

Peernock: "The second. We've got one weekend.''

[garbled words in the background]

Lyle: "Well, I got on the phone when I was up there.''

Peernock: "Say again?''

Lyle: "I got on the phone. When I came back? Just briefly, they got me off of it right away. I did get hold of Jake. He said he'll want to get some money but he'll take care of these things.''

Peernock: "Mm-hm.''

Lyle: "He said he'll be glad to take care of the situation. He lowered it to fifteen thousand.''

Lyle later testified that Peernock had chortled off tape: "If this thing works, maybe we should go after the district attorney and the lead investigator on the case.'' Lyle claimed that Peernock even discussed how lucrative it might be to go into the murder-for-hire business. Fisk knew that no one can deny that there are plenty of other arrestees who would appreciate the service of having inconvenient witnesses removed. Fisk also knew that Robert Peernock had always been good with money and seldom missed a chance to turn one dollar into two.

Robert Peernock was immediately charged with solicitation of the murders of Victoria and Natasha.

Lyle has been given a false name here. Whatever crimes he may be paying for currently, he neither requested nor received special privileges for his testimony about Robert's solicitation attempt. And he did not ask for early parole by risking himself for Victoria and Natasha.

Only Lyle knows if his remorse over the damage he inflicted upon his own daughter is genuine. But he saved two lives on the day that he dared to come forward.

• • •

Victoria received a call shortly after Peernock's jail-cell arrest for the solicitation of murder. Pam Springer, the deputy district attorney who had been assigned to Peernock's case, wanted Victoria to come in to Springer's office right away. But she wouldn't say why.

Victoria showed up fearing that something had gone wrong with Peernock's case, that she was about to be told that the charges against him would be dropped on some asinine technicality.

Instead she was greeted by a tall, attractive woman with short blond hair and cool blue eyes, who was every bit as expert as Victoria in keeping her feelings hidden behind a professional mask when duty called for it.

At the moment the mask told Victoria nothing.

Once inside Pam Springer's office, Victoria sat down and tried to read the woman's expression while the DDA took a seat behind her desk. Springer's slim face could look alternately sharp and cold or angled and pretty, depending on the light, the occasion, the mood. She gave Victoria the news with a soft voice and a dry smile.

"No point beating around the bush, really. We weren't going to tell you, since at this point there isn't much you can do. But in case he got to somebody else that we don't know about yet . . ."

"Please. Just tell me what this is about, if you don't mind."

"I do mind. But we have to let you know, and there's no easy way to do it, so here it is: Robert Peernock was tape-recorded in jail soliciting for a hit man to kill you and Natasha."

"What??"

"Seems there was some debate over whether they should firebomb your car or kill Natasha with a drug overdose and make you take the blame."

"No. You don't . . . this isn't . . ."

"Don't worry. The guy turned on him. We've got him. Strengthens our case against Peernock, actually."

"Strengthens your—?"

"But you might want to take extra security precautions. I mean, we're telling you this on the off chance that he got to someone else. Someone who might still come looking for you."

There was much more to the conversation, of course. Victoria was able to recall bits and pieces of it once she left the building. After she'd finished throwing up in the ladies' room.

Robert Peernock's response to the charge of solicitation of the murders of Victoria and Natasha was unequivocal. He cried out that the jailhouse snitch was a paid liar and that the DA's story was simply an excuse for the DA's office to justify freezing all of Peernock's money. To Peernock, this was proof that Victoria Doom was actively working with the prosecution to rig a conviction.

Victoria acknowledges that he was right about one aspect of his suspicions; she was certainly doing everything she could think of to help put Peernock away. The attempt on her life had given her the final element of legal power she had not been able to secure up to that point. Now all of Peernock's money was cut off to him. And since his assets were completely frozen, he could no longer afford private attorneys.

Deputy DA Springer and Victoria Doom decided not to tell Natasha about the hit man. Not yet, anyway. Peernock had no way of knowing his daughter had moved away, that she had married, or that she was in Hawaii. Secrecy was Natasha's best protection; Steve Fisk's caution in having had Natasha flown out under an assumed identity had paid off in spades. Naturally she would have to be told before her time to come back and testify, but for right now there had to be a limit to how much she was expected to cope with.

But Victoria received one of her Christmas presents a month early that year when her husband gave her a shotgun with the barrel cut down to the minimum length. So while Robert Peernock was being arraigned on the additional charge of solicitation of a dual murder, screaming that this "bullshit charge" was simply one more example of the governmental plot to destroy him, Victoria was keeping her new present propped in the footwell of her office desk.

She was also granted a permit to carry a concealed pistol. Since it was next to impossible to obtain such a permit in Los Angeles County at that time, the fact that she actually got one was a mark of just how highly the system had begun to assess Robert Peernock's level of potential danger.

Like the nurses who avoided telling Natasha about her mother's death, the attorneys in Los Angeles may have underestimated her ability to comprehend her father's animosity. After all, she had been there the first time he'd tried to kill her. Today she says she wouldn't have had much trouble comprehending the idea that he'd tried to hire a murderer to finish the job for him.

Nevertheless, the warmth she was feeling as a new bride in Hawaii came to represent a focal point she would badly need later on. She had no way of predicting the deeper challenges that lay waiting, because she had yet to meet the confusers or to hear the accusations and suspicions that would be leveled at her, one on top of another, by individuals eager for fresh interpretations of the events behind the night of slaughter. Even as she lived in the hope of a safer future, the gray cloud of despair she had dared hope to have escaped back in California was already approaching relentlessly across the sea, drawn magnetically by the pull of unfinished business.

She had one more dance with Daddy left ahead of her. This one would not last for a matter of hours, as the last one had.

It would go on for days.

CHAPTER
19

It was three o'clock in the afternoon on December 21 when the bailiff finally came out into the hallway and called Tasha into the courtroom. For her, the past two days leading up to her time of testimony at her father's preliminary hearing had been marked by a steady buildup of tension and a sick feeling of dread.

The return flight to California was an ordeal of apprehension as Tasha wondered how hard she would be grilled. Immediately on her arrival, the authorities told her about the hit man. There was no avoiding it. They had to explain why she was to be accompanied by two bodyguards twenty-four hours a day, why she was to be whisked away to a secret hotel for the duration of her stay, why she was not even to be allowed to step outside the room without a guard. There was even talk of placing a heavy bulletproof vest over her for the journey from the car into the courthouse.

She was relieved when they decided just to bring her through a back door of the court building, arriving with her each day at varied times. Everything felt bizarre enough already.

Pam Springer warned her that her father's attorney, Bradley Brunon, would probably do everything he could to cast doubt on her story. This was because in the past months, not a single piece of solid physical evidence had been found that could tie her father to the scene of the crime. The case so far had boiled down to her credibility against her father's.

Robert Peernock's explanations had grown more polished

with practice, his denials more emphatic. And although no one inside the system who had observed his behavior since his arrest on September 4 retained the slightest belief in him, any slip of Tasha's memory would be seized on by the defense and turned against her.

Now as she stood and slowly walked through the door into the courtroom, she settled the invisible blanket around her feelings the way she had learned to do at home years ago.

Tasha avoided looking around as she was sworn in. She knew her father was in the courtroom, but she was in no hurry to meet his gaze. She didn't want to feel any more of his energy. *Evil* was the word she had privately used to describe him ever since her grade school days, and the night of the murder only reinforced her conviction that he had somehow lost himself altogether to evil. And the evil always seemed to find a way to prevail, to push through any situation against any adversary.

As she took her seat in the witness chair, the fear flashed through her that somehow her father had managed to get his hands on some kind of weapon, perhaps bribed a guard with the money his girlfriend had pulled out of his heavily stocked bank accounts before Victoria sealed them. She wondered, if her father had resolved to finish the attack right inside the courtroom, did anybody here have the power to protect her?

Fortunately for her, Pam Springer was the first to begin the questions. That helped put Tasha at ease a little. Springer's cool, efficient demeanor and professional polish conveyed a sense that things were under the control of forces that could still overpower sheer evil. Tasha fixed her eyes on Springer, hoping that it was true. She didn't look anywhere else as the initial questions began. The easy questions.

Springer: "Do you know the defendant in this case, Robert Peernock?"

Natasha: "Yes. He's my father."

Springer: "Is he seated over here in the middle of the counsel table next to the phone?"

Natasha twitched in shock as her eyes flew open in surprise. She hadn't noticed the man sitting there and at first he didn't seem familiar. But as she took in his features, the eyes, the skin, the build, she realized he was her father indeed. "Oh. Yeah," she breathed in amazement. Since the arrest his hair had changed from bleached blond curls to straight, dark brown. His beard was gone. His chin was bigger, the skin around the eyes was tight. It finally hit her just how hard her father had tried to disguise his appearance with the plastic surgery. "He looks *way* different," she added, exhaling with a sound that was halfway between a bitter laugh and a shudder.

Tasha knew that Springer didn't want her to volunteer any comments, but the last remark slipped out. She wanted to go on, to rage at him, to demand that Robert tell them who the hell he'd been planning on fooling, by changing his face around like that. But she forced herself into silence. Springer had warned her how even the innocent volunteering of some little comment might be used to help the defense in some way.

Over the next few hours, the whole story slowly came out. Tasha never faltered, never broke down. She spoke clearly, sticking to the direct, simple sentences that Pam Springer had asked her to use. Sometimes when the questions elicited the most painful answers, her voice would drop so softly that the judge had to ask her to speak up and to repeat her responses. But she kept on without breaking, answer by answer by answer, building the huge jigsaw puzzle one tiny piece at a time.

Finally they got to the final moments of the crimes.

Springer: "What happened next?"

Natasha: "Then he stopped the car and put us both in the front seat."

"Now, who did he place in the front seat first?"

"My mom."

"He then placed you in the front seat?"

"Yes. On the passenger side."

"When he placed you on the front seat, was the hood still on?"

"Yes."

"Were you still handcuffed?"

"Yes."

"In the front or in the back?"

"In the front."

"When had he removed the handcuffs from the back to the front?"

"When I was in the bedroom."

"Before he carried you out?"

"Yes. I told him I couldn't feel my hands."

"When he placed you in the front seat of his car on the passenger side—"

"Yes."

"—Were your feet still tied?"

"Yes."

And later, Springer asked: "Natasha, had you ever driven that car before?"

"No."

"Did you like the car?"

"No."

"Did your mom drive the car?"

"No."

"Did she like it?"

"No."

"Did she, in fact, hate that car?"

"Yes. She thought it was tacky."

"Natasha, did your mom drink and drive?"

"No."

Before she could stop herself, Tasha raised her gaze to

meet her father's. Her heart immediately jumped as the old feelings of fear shot through her. She was face-to-face with the man who had turned into a demon before her eyes and destroyed her family. How much power did he really have? Was he going to lunge for her right now? He seemed to be capable of any kind of violence. She tore her eyes away and turned her head, but it took conscious effort. She knew she could never get through this if she let his eyes meet hers.

She didn't risk looking at him again for the rest of her testimony.

Upon cross-examination Bradley Brunon did everything he could to challenge her credibility. To make Robert appear supportive, he brought out the fact that Tasha's father had paid for her medical bills and dental bills. He brought up her horse.

Brunon: "Did he buy you a horse?"

Natasha: "Yes."

"When did he buy you a horse?"

"After he broke my arm."

"Is that the arm you told the doctors and everybody else you broke while falling?"

"He told them that."

"Didn't you also tell them that?"

"Because he told me not to tell anyone, and my mom did not want me to tell anyone."

"So, you told the doctors that you fell in your house and broke your arm, is that right?"

"Yes."

"That was a lie, wasn't it?"

"Yes."

"You continued that lie for approximately four years?"

"I didn't tell anybody else besides the hospital."

"You told numerous people at the hospital, did you not, including the doctors and nurses?"

"Yes."

"As far as you know they all believed you?"

"Yes."

"So, you were a persuasive liar on that point?"

And so it went, for three days. Brunon and Springer alternately attacked her and defended her credibility while she held tightly to her story. It was to be the easiest questioning she would endure in the case; there was much more to come. But at least for now it was over.

Her portion of the preliminary hearing ended on the twenty-third of December.

This was not a trial yet; Peernock's innocence or guilt was not to be determined here. But enough evidence was laid out, and the judge found Natasha's testimony believable enough, that the case was successfully bound over for trial.

Her testimony had just ended when the bodyguards took her aside into a small room down the hall from the courtroom. Tasha had complained bitterly about not being given any freedom to see anybody while in Los Angeles to testify, but the police were firm in their conviction that she simply could not be allowed to risk independent movement. So an artificial little reunion with her younger sister at the courthouse had been the best they could offer.

Moments after Tasha entered the room, her eleven-year-old sister was brought in. The girl was now living with her full-time foster parents and the two hadn't seen each other since before the crimes. The bodyguards stepped out to give them a few moments of privacy while they sat in two chairs facing each other in the barren little room. Later, even years later, the memory of the encounter would stick with her clearly.

There was an awkward silence as her sister looked strangely at Tasha, taking in her drastically changed appearance. Tasha wondered what she must look like to her and what she must be thinking. Finally the little girl spoke.

"Your hair looks really stupid."

It wasn't the best of circumstances for a fulfilling reunion.

So Tasha's Christmas present that year was the knowledge that she had successfully helped to put in motion the long process of forcing her father to answer for the crimes of that terrible summer. As the bodyguards escorted her to the airport, automated holiday carols were playing everywhere. But the weight of what she had just endured hung heavily on her, making her feel alone while the entire Judeo-Christian world was on a giant Muzak high.

The carols tolled in the airport while the ticket agents screwed up her tickets and the carols tolled in the police station where her bodyguards took her to wait for four hours while somebody in a command position figured out what to do and the carols tolled back at the motel where they finally put her up for the night.

The carols were still Muzaking away on Christmas Eve when Tasha's bodyguards finally released her to the next plane for Hawaii. I'll be home for Christmas.

Daddy had received a visit for the holidays from his supposed-to-be-dead daughter. And during this season to be jolly, Tasha had brought him the gift of a living, breathing souvenir from their last dance together on their final night in the Peernock house.

CHAPTER

20

As the year drew to a close, Victoria found her practice suffering severely. Even though she had farmed out most of her non-Peernock cases, she barely kept her head above the paper river flowing her way from Dern, Mason and Floum. She had even farmed out Natasha's civil cases to avoid any conflict of interest, concentrating on the probate settlements and the lawsuits against Robert's estate. Although that cleared her of any hint of conflict of interest on Natasha's behalf, it also lowered her prospects of financial gain from a case that had already sapped her resources to the breaking point. She was learning that no amount of work will maintain a sole practice when a lawyer is forced into court every day on endless rounds of motions, while her practice collects no money for the efforts and has to function solely in the hope of future compensation.

She went into the holidays in a miserable state, unconsoled by the early present from Richard, which she still kept propped in the footwell of her desk. Physically and mentally exhausted, she was finally beginning to face the thing she had feared most when deciding whether to take the case: she no longer saw how she could keep going against virtually unlimited resources fielded by an entire law firm bent on overwhelming her.

Confronted by the loss of her practice and complete defeat as Natasha's advocate, she spent the holidays discussing with her husband, Richard, whether or not she should let go while there might still be something in the case to save. Noble as it can sound to fight to the very last, such a strategy would not only leave nothing for her but could leave Natasha's next attorney with insufficient ammunition to salvage the case.

On the other hand, there was that "Agreement." The memory of it haunted her. She had long ago given it to Steve Fisk, but she could see it clearly in her mind's eye. A simple, plaintive request by a frightened woman, asking that her alienated husband not beat her or attack her elder daughter or verbally abuse anyone in the household.

There was still Claire's faith in her to consider, and of course Natasha's. The young client who'd started out simply as a name on a dissolution form had become a warm human presence in her life. Natasha's fears for the future, her hopes and concerns, had become familiar to Victoria. So was her pain. And Victoria knew that the grinding process Natasha was to endure under the wheels of the system had only just started. There were still civil trials, probate hearings and Juvenile Court hearings, not to mention the main criminal trial itself. She would be called to the stand many more times.

If Victoria walked away from this now, she had no idea how she could ever carry the guilt load should something go disastrously wrong with Natasha's claim on her share of her parents' assets. There was nothing else for a horribly injured girl barely out of high school to fall back on for rebuilding her life.

There was always some chance that Natasha might muddle through by herself, even if she wound up with nothing to help her. Others had done it in the past. But Victoria's years of watching the effects of severe family disasters on children of all ages whose support system failed them convinced her that those who made it through the trauma unscathed were vastly outnumbered by those who went down for the count, who fell into deep depression and succumbed to various forms of slow self-destruction.

Still, Victoria just didn't know how much more she could take.

It was in this frame of mind that she arrived early at the office on the first working day after New Year's to see what new assaults on her practice had arrived from Dern, Mason and Floum. She found what she was expecting right on top of the early-morning mail, a legal-sized envelope with the DMF logo.

She sighed heavily and sat at her desk to open the mail, suddenly feeling as if she had put in a full day already, as she tore open the envelope flap and pulled out the contents.

And there it was.

A substitution form from the excellent law firm of Dern, Mason and Floum, officially notifying her that they were withdrawing their entire squad of corporate attorneys from the Peernock extravaganza. No longer would the unending avalanche of legalese from the Century City firm's word-processing department bury her under opposition papers. Whether they were giving up the onslaught or whether their client had fired them, from now on Robert Peernock would be in propria persona. Peernock had chosen to represent himself in court against her.

She was about to go head to head with the Magic Pencil.

Yes, Victoria, the little voice sang in the back of her mind, *there is a Santa Claus.* She laughed out loud for the first time in days.

Oh, yes, there is indeed.

Tasha was aware that her new husband shared the love of football with his other Navy pals, so the fact that he was irritated at having to leave the television in the middle of the game to come to the airport and pick her up on Christmas Day didn't surprise her. She focused on how pleased he was going to be when he got his present. He had always loved to play computer games in arcades and would often stay for hours pumping coins into the machines. Now the latest Nintendo hardware-and-software combination was going to be her gift to him. She had already purchased it out of her dwindling insurance money. As they drove back to the apartment the thought of giving him the chance to play as much as he wanted to, as well as having him around the house more at the same time, made her feel happy.

It helped her to forget that her father, acting as his own attorney, had served Natasha with a subpoena to testify in Juvenile Court as a witness in a case challenging her sister's foster parents for custody.

In two weeks she was going to have to return to Los Angeles and take the stand again. This time Robert Peernock would be representing himself, which meant that the system was going to allow him to put her up on the stand. The man who had nearly killed her was going to grill her in open court.

CHAPTER

21

The California courts were in a unique position with regard to Robert John Peernock. The fact that he was awaiting trial for murder and was charged with twice trying to kill his daughter did not prevent him from access to the same rights as any other citizen, so long as he was not yet convicted. Since anyone has the right of self-representation in court provided that he or she cooperates with rules and required conduct, nobody could stop him from representing himself in his challenge for the custody of the youngest daughter. He was adamant that the little girl be kept with someone who remained under his control.

Tasha knew her father was going to try to manipulate her into sounding like a liar for speaking out about the crimes. She knew he was going to try to maneuver her into helping him get back out onto the street. She also knew that if she tried to ignore the command to appear in court, she would be held in contempt and left to face fines she could not pay, perhaps even jail time too bitter and ironic to endure.

On the morning of Wednesday, January 6, 1988, she sat in the gallery of Los Angeles Juvenile Court waiting to begin her testimony. This time, however, things were very different from before. As if by a strange form of magic, the nervousness and dread of her last court appearance had left her. Now in their place was a calm sensation, almost one of contentment. This feeling had puzzled her on the plane ride over.

She wondered why she shouldn't be full of foreboding at having to confront Robert in public.

It hadn't been until she was actually on her way into court, once again flanked by bodyguards, that the answer came to her.

He was going to have to do it out in the open now.

Since the point in her life years before when she'd begun openly thinking of him as evil, she'd had to endure his abuses in private. There was no winning in any conflict with him; he persisted until he overcame resistance. There was nowhere to run, to hide, to turn for reinforcement. Even when he'd shattered her bones by throwing her against the kitchen wall, Claire had asked her to remain silent, because at that point Claire hadn't found the strength to face him down.

But Tasha had already faced him down once before, back on July 21, the day his crime spree began. She had done it without protection, even though it had nearly cost her life.

So she told herself she could surely face him down again, surrounded by policemen in open court. Whatever he did to her, whatever lies he told, whatever accusations, insults, or scorn he heaped upon her, he was going to have to do it with witnesses this time. A court reporter would take down every word and file it in a safe place so that nobody could ever come back at some future point and try to make her feel stupid or crazy by insisting that something she'd clearly heard with her own ears had in fact never been said.

And so her father had unwittingly given her a chance to speak up for all of the Peernock family women and for years of his abuse. And this time he could yell and scream all he wanted to, but he couldn't hurt anybody.

She could see her father's back as he sat at the attorneys' table conferring with his co-counsel, ready to begin whatever it was that he had called her here to do. But just as her testimony was beginning, Natasha was astounded to hear the judge observe, out loud, that the trial needed to proceed in a timely fashion—because Natasha Peernock had just been *flown in from Hawaii.*

She couldn't believe her ears. This wasn't criminal court, but was it possible that this judge actually hadn't been told that she was under witness protection? And that her father, sitting right there, was the reason for it?

Robert was sitting as close to the judge as she was. She had clearly heard the judge give away her secret location, in full voice, in open court. Surely her father heard it too.

She nearly screamed in frustration.

Her mind raced. What to do? Should she speak up, ask them to stop, or was the damage done? Did anybody realize what had just happened? No one seemed to have reacted. The lawyers were having a discussion with the judge about some technical point; it had apparently just slipped out. Her father didn't react openly, but she knew he was too clever to do that anyway. No, she would just have to hope that it was a slip of the tongue and that the judge realized what he had done. She could only pray that Robert's attention was occupied with his notes and that he hadn't heard.

And then the judge said it again.

Not thirty seconds later. Something to the effect of "Let's wrap up her testimony so that she can *go back to Hawaii.*" She couldn't believe her ears. Her fear that her father might find a way to outsmart the legal system jumped up about a hundred notches.

And that was how her testimony began.

Today her memory of the details is blurred under the weight of the relentless probing she endured there. But she is crystal clear on one point; the psychological ordeal lasted for four days as she sat pinned in the witness chair under her father's machine-gun questioning, forced to go over every tiny detail of the night of the crimes, piece by jagged piece, while he labored to portray her as a liar.

• • •

Juvenile Court records are sealed under the law and cannot be quoted as matters of public record in the way that other types of civil or criminal action may be. There is good purpose to this law. It protects the minor children, both psychologically and physically, who are the subjects of the trials; some of the most impassioned and potentially abusive behavior people will display shows up in custody battles.

Without revealing the confidentiality of the trial or the names of the foster parents, Natasha can clearly recall her growing amazement that the court allowed her father to continue berating her, despite being continually warned that his questions were improper and that he was not sticking to the juvenile-custody issue, and despite the judge's expressed awareness that Robert was trying to address his criminal trial issues here in Juvenile Court. She remembers her father at one point openly taunting her, asking, "Did your mommy die in a car wreck?" The court scolded him but still he was allowed to continue.

Throughout the four-day ordeal she clung to the consolation that at least someone was hearing him, at least his coldness, his contempt, his flagrant disrespect, were being displayed for everyone to see.

But every day she climbed down from the stand feeling a little more drained. She tried to get to sleep at night but her sense of outrage hammered away inside her. It seemed incredible that nobody was stopping him.

By the end of the fourth day her grip on that consolation was at the breaking point. Fatigue had drained her strength. Her throat had gone raw, her chest was congested. It had become hard to swallow and her ears throbbed.

As if invisible tentacles of hatred had reached out from her father's maliciousness, she could feel, like a vampire's victim, the health being sucked out of her.

It began to seem that he was still working his evil, but that now he could do it invisibly.

At last, at the end of the afternoon on January 13, the judge decided that Robert Peernock had been given every courtesy by the system and had had ample opportunity to cross-examine Natasha. The four-day beating was finished.

She climbed down from the stand and walked out of the room without looking back.

Tasha had hoped to brighten up this trip to Los Angeles by seeing some friends, maybe going out to some of the old haunts. Instead, she went straight back to her in-laws' home, fell into bed, and stayed there for two weeks before she was well enough to get back on a plane and fly home.

But when she arrived back in Hawaii she found that a barrier had begun to form inside her marriage, and outsiders were not going to be able to help her deal with it. The consequences of marrying a young man she had barely known began to be felt as their opposite styles of coping with stress slowly drove a wedge between them.

When she tried to talk about what the trial had been like, her husband still refused to refer to the night of the crimes as murder, calling it "the accident" instead. She didn't like talking about it, but sometimes the subject just came up and she needed a mention, a comment, a comforting word or two from him to bring the thoughts hammering at her out into the light of day.

His responses were sullen, frustrating bouts of silence.

She cursed herself for having bought the computer game, as her husband began to lose himself in the brightly colored game world.

Not long afterward she awoke one night to hear him mumbling in his sleep. For a moment she feared he might be dreaming about a girlfriend, some pretty thing with no scars and no legal problems and no trauma. But it wasn't that. In his sleep, he was deep in the conflict of his newest software fantasy, the hero of a legendary battle game. Resentment flooded through her, but she didn't wake him up. What was the point of starting a fight? It would just make everything feel worse. Tasha told herself that maybe they just needed to get past the hump of this damned murder trial. And besides, what if he snapped and issued an ultimatum to her—where else was she going to go?

She still felt too scarred, too marked by the crimes, to attempt to face the world on her own. Her mother's fears that Natasha might end up dependant on a man had become reality, albeit by means no one could have predicted.

On January 26, 1988, Victoria Doom actually saw Robert Peernock for the first time at a probate hearing before Judge Fred Rimmerman. It was Peernock's first probate hearing since he had fired Dern, Mason and Floum and decided to represent himself.

Given typical self-represented status, he was allowed to come into the courtroom without wearing shackles or leg restraints, even though in his case this was being done despite the numerous Class A felony charges pending against him. The only law enforcement in the courtroom was a single bailiff.

Victoria watched in fascination as Robert stormed angrily into court with a bundle of legal papers under his arm, marched up to the attorney table, slammed the papers down, and glared at her with what she could only interpret as pure hatred. Moments after Judge Rimmerman opened the proceedings Robert began to interrupt loudly, haranguing the judge for several minutes with a list of accusations against the DA's office and Deputy DA Myron Jenkins, plus all of the judges appointed by former Governor Jerry Brown including Rimmerman himself, plus Judge Michael Luros, who had presided at the preliminary hearing in the murder case.

Judge Rimmerman sat quietly at first, allowing Robert to outline the vast conspiracy against him and the tidal wave of corruption that he claimed had him in its grip. However, Rimmerman began warning Robert that he was going too far when he began to make accusations against Victoria and Natasha for stealing his money and preventing him from using it to hire an attorney to replace Bradley Brunon, whose fee had only covered Robert as far as the preliminary hearing. Robert demanded the right to use that money to hire someone who could get him out of the morass swallowing him. He didn't want to hear anything about probate laws, which demanded the estate be shared by the survivors. He especially didn't want to hear anything about Natasha's right to protect the estate from being used entirely for Robert's defense, leaving nothing for the daughters.

Finally Rimmerman had had enough and ordered Robert to leave the courtroom until he could get himself under sufficient control to be able to function as his own attorney. But when the bailiff tried to escort him from the courtroom, Robert started struggling with him, refusing to leave, continuing to scream at the judge.

A violent struggle broke out, with the bailiff trying to call for backup while he restrained Robert, who continued struggling and shouting his conspiracy accusations.

The judge leaned under his desk and pushed the hidden call button to summon more officers to the courtroom. People in the gallery jumped up and began to crowd for the doors in panic as the situation quickly careened out of control.

It took two minutes, which felt more like two hours on adrenaline time, before another six deputies showed up with guns and subdued Robert completely, dragging him out of the courtroom.

The power of Robert's emotions stunned Victoria.

Within minutes of walking in, Peernock had worked himself into a self-stimulated Vesuvian eruption unlike anything she had ever seen in court. She sat marveling at what she had just learned about her adversary. While the power of his passion was undeniable, he seemed to have no clue whatsoever about the wisdom of projecting a reasonable image in court, whether that image is true or false.

After a few minutes to restore order, Judge Rimmerman called for the defendant to be returned. This time there were two armed guards kept in position at the main entrance.

Five more were positioned in a semicircle around Robert Peernock.

CHAPTER

22

During the time Tasha spent between trips back to L.A. to testify, Hawaii began to feel more like a trap than a paradise. Her appearance kept her from wanting to socialize and her artistic nature couldn't find much in common with the military wives of her husband's friends. She didn't feel able to attempt working yet, and a new sailor's salary doesn't leave much money for a young couple's entertainment.

Shortly after she'd returned home from her testimony in the juvenile case she began seriously to fear for her marriage. Even though it had been more an act of need than true love, it still felt wrong just to let the marriage go without a fight.

This was when Tasha realized she might have an opportunity to let her father be of some actual positive value after all the trouble he had caused. Perhaps the very real threat that he posed to her safety, plus the judge's slip of the tongue in court when he'd mentioned her home state twice in a row, might offer her a way to use her witness-protection situation to maneuver a transfer out of Hawaii for her husband. A change of scene might be just the thing.

She called Pam Springer to complain of her fears now that her father surely knew where to send his private investigators to look for her. The complaints didn't fall on deaf ears. Springer knew that Robert Peernock still had much to gain from his daughter's untimely death before the case came to trial. And Springer feared that Peernock's girlfriend, Sonia, might still believe in his innocence. It didn't take much of a stretch to imagine a scenario whereby Peernock somehow managed, with outside help, to hire another attempt on his daughter.

When Tasha began to sense that the system was going to try to help them, she was elated. She checked Navy base locations around the world and dared to hope that the DA's office might persuade the Department of the Navy to work out a transfer to some exotic faraway place. Someplace far from the courtroom madness, far from the reach of her enraged father and yet a place like Hawaii, sunny and inviting.

In April the orders came through for a transfer to Adak, Alaska.

She rushed to a map. She looked, looked some more, took turns looking with her husband, nearly ruined her eyes searching the map, then finally found it: a tiny spec of an island off the Alaskan coast, near the Russian mainland. *Close* to the mainland. It has a population of about five thousand military personnel and dependents, living on a chunk of frozen tundra.

The perfectly linear reasoning of military intelligence had indeed answered the call to find someplace safe for this young woman whose father seemed bent on destroying her. The army had simply marched in step with the witness protection program's main philosophy.

They can't hurt you if they can't find you.

The rules at Adak, as it turned out, were pretty simple. The guard/escort filled them in as soon as they arrived, talking fast to get his points across before the couple developed that glassy-eyed look people tend to take on as soon as they have the chance to walk around and see where they are.

"Relax," he told them. "Not a problem. We're a long way from Stateside; we don't stand on a lot of ceremony here. Hey, how much trouble can you get into, wandering around on frozen grasses and fifty-seven varieties of moss on a seabound hunk of tundra?

"Oh, and pets? Not a problem. Just keep the cats inside. We have a lot of bald eagles around here and they love to carry off cats to feed their young.

"Dogs are a little tougher, although still not a problem. That is, if you can find one. Don't get many strays here. In fact, if your dog escapes you only get one freebie from the dog catcher. Second time, they put the dog to sleep. Have to. Can't risk having them wander onto the airstrip. Tend to cause plane wrecks, very tough in a location where everything you eat, drink, and wear is imported by air. Definitely a problem.

"Hey, other than that, not much else to do but work on your tan. Heh-heh. We like to say that around here.

". . . You guys okay?"

By summertime Robert Peernock was on his third attorney. He had accepted no suggestions that he was mentally incompetent to stand trial or that he plead insanity. He maintained that any encouragement for him to do so was of course motivated strictly by orders from the state in their attempt to sabotage his defense. He remained confidant that at trial he would prove his innocence and expose the plot to frame him, to destroy his family and neutralize the threat he presented to the vast corrupt structure of the state government.

As for his daughter, Tasha was having such difficulty in her marriage that she managed a plane ticket back to Los Angeles for a visit and stayed for two months, agonizing over whether she should try to keep working at the marriage or throw in the towel and take her chances alone in California.

She contacted Victoria from time to time, hoping for news of some progress in the probate case that would allow a little of her mother's life insurance money to be released to her for living expenses, or even allow the sale of one of the houses. But Victoria had to keep repeating the difficult fact that while there was indeed some money in the family estate, it was tied up and would likely stay that way until Robert's trial was heard. What Victoria didn't tell Natasha was that she had been keeping up on the progress of the criminal case and things could have looked a lot better.

Because Robert's position appeared defensible.

Victoria had learned much about him and was convinced that whatever whistleblowing Robert had genuinely done, it did nothing to explain the crimes. This was insight gained from bits and pieces of personal history she had picked up by helping to sort through the household goods and getting them into storage for Natasha. Most of it was stuff the jury would never see.

Robert had explanations for the explosive rigging under the car, and since juries are inclined to believe in corrupt government officials and tend to side with the noble notion of a little guy against the system, Peernock actually appeared to have a real chance of getting away with his crimes.

Further, after the battle she had been waging against his access to the family estate, Victoria knew he was madder at her than ever. Any slip-up on the part of the court could result in Peernock's being free to come after her and Natasha once again.

She knew that Pam Springer had originally thought the case could be wrapped up in a year at the most. But that year was now ended and the trial was nowhere in sight.

Only Robert's daughter could connect him to the awful crimes, and Natasha had already endured six days of testimony during the preliminary hearing and the Juvenile Court hearing. She had been repeatedly attacked on the witness stand and made out to be a liar. As for Victoria, it could go much worse for her if Peernock's trial attorney decided to pursue Robert's pet theory about Victoria Doom.

Word had filtered back to her that this theory now entailed Robert's claim that when Claire came to Victoria for divorce advice and Victoria realized how much money the estate would be worth with Claire dead, Victoria and Claire's boss had conspired to create a plan whereby Claire would be snatched by hired killers and set up in a fake car wreck. According to Robert's theory, although the clumsy explosive apparatus was designed to frame Robert, its very clumsiness showed that Robert wouldn't have done it that way. He said Tasha had been included in the car wreck to raise the insurance value of the crimes, so that Victoria and Claire's boss could then use legal means to loot Claire's estate.

Since the estate would fall under Victoria's control upon Claire's death, as indeed much of it had done despite Natasha's control by name, this would allow Victoria to gain access to the million and a half dollars in insurance money and real estate that the family would be worth if both Claire and Natasha died in a car wreck and earned maximum payment on their life insurance policies.

And so the realization gradually pressed down upon Victoria; *Robert was maneuvering her into position to take the fall for his crimes.*

She had located a number of policies on Natasha, totaling $187,000 on her alone. Claire had numerous policies and one of them paid several times more in value if she died in a car wreck. But Victoria knew she could never prove that she hadn't known any of this before Claire was killed. In the eyes of a jury, if Victoria were psychopathic enough to kill for greed, she could certainly be portrayed as having the motive.

So the story was evolving that she and Claire's boss had conspired to murder Claire and Natasha, but had somehow convinced Steve Fisk to program Natasha into repeating a phony handcuff story while she was still in the hospital, drugged and impressionable.

Or else they had terrorized her into giving the story.

Or else they had bribed her by promising her a chance at

revenge against a man who had scorned her for years, plus a hefty piece of the eventual estate payout.

In this theory, Natasha Peernock knew that her father was innocent but was glad to forgive Victoria and Claire's boss for nearly killing her, for disfiguring her face, and for killing her mother—all in return for the chance to send Robert to prison and to get a share of whatever amount of his money might be left after all the court actions were finished.

Victoria wanted to laugh. It was so horrid even to think such things, it seemed absurd that any twelve people could be convinced of it.

And yet she knew that the prosecution had yet to find Robert's signature on any of the evidence.

PART

IV

A Checklist for Murder

This whole thing is rigged! It has to do with millions and millions of dollars on state contracts!

> —*Robert Peernock, moments before being hauled out of the courtroom*

Wouldn't it be nice if Mommy died in a car wreck?

> —*Robert Peernock to his ten-year-old daughter, according to the neighbor who swore that she overheard it*

CHAPTER

23

In April of 1989 Victoria Doom got the word that Robert Peernock had hired yet another law firm to help him try to pull money out of the estate funds to pay for building a defense. So far she had kept the accounts frozen, but now, twenty-one months after the crimes, she found herself back in court once more to answer Peernock's assertion that the funds were *his* money and could not constitutionally be kept away from him and that to do so deprived him of the right to his best defense.

It is a compelling argument for any defendant to raise. And it was the same issue he had put forth at his preliminary hearing.

"The court," he protested, "the State of California, has taken away all my property, all my possessions. I have not been convicted of any crime and yet every single thing I own in the world has been taken away from me. I *do* have enough money in my accounts to pay for attorneys. They have frozen all my accounts, yet I've not been convicted of any crime.

"This is a civil rights violation, and the state has done everything possible to make things as tough as they can for me.

"Now the court is choosing what lawyer I can have to represent me, even though I have money in my accounts to choose the attorney I want. Now, that's certainly improper and illegal, a civil rights violation."

Victoria found herself in Judge Rimmerman's chambers with Robert's new attorney, Marshal A. Oldman, who was there to formally request the funds. Victoria knew this was her cue to again take protective action in the hope that whenever the criminal case concluded, Robert Peernock's two daughters would have something left.

But this time she walked into the chambers more convinced than ever that if this new law firm successfully opened the floodgates, Robert would spend every penny of his daughters' future before he was through. After nearly two years behind bars, he had motivation to employ every available resource to get himself out.

No matter who suffered as a result.

And somehow after Natasha's testimony against her father, Victoria had a hard time visualizing Peernock doing anything to help his daughter get back on her feet, even if he actually managed to beat the charges against him.

The sticking point was that no matter how aggressively any attorney would try to defend Natasha's interests, Robert Peernock had the intelligence and skill to utilize every protection the constitution has to offer, right down to fine-print interpretations and subtle aspects of case law which most citizens wouldn't comprehend. The pretrial courts knew that if they took a position which truly denied him any of his rights, a conviction would be worthless; they would simply be setting the stage for a mistrial or reversal upon appeal.

Every consideration had to be given to him, no matter how absurd it might sound. Thus a position that seemed perfectly reasonable on its face was going to be even harder for Victoria to repel, such as his insistence upon being allowed to use the family's estate for his defense because he had to be presumed innocent until proven guilty. Today, as soon as the hearing got started, her senses warned her that it was not going to go well.

She argued forcefully to the judge that Peernock's access to funds could justifiably be limited because of the civil cases against the estate and because the end result of those cases partially depended on the outcome of the criminal trial. But her point was not as direct as Peernock's very simple reliance upon the basic constitutional guarantee of the presumption of innocence.

Beneath the legal reasoning was her gut feeling that the court should deny *all* access to his funds because this man, who had already tried to kill his own daughter twice and also attempted to have Victoria killed, just might be inclined to use the money to try again.

Her worst fears began to take shape shortly after the session began. Judge Rimmerman agreed with Peernock's position that if there were any funds held by the estate which legally belonged to him, they had to be released to him so that he could hire whatever attorney he wanted, especially since Peernock's constant disputes with the state-appointed lawyers were dragging the trial far beyond the original time estimates. Once again it seemed that Peernock's manipulation of the system's flexibility was working.

Marshal Oldman reminded the judge that Peernock was down in his cell insisting he now realized that Gerald Fogelman, Peernock's third criminal defense lawyer, was also working for the district attorney's office to help rig a conviction against him. Therefore Peernock had immediate and pressing need for funds to pay for a new attorney. Furthermore, he had located one through his own trusted sources.

Victoria sighed and informed the judge that her office had been collecting and saving rents from the three income properties ever since the arrest. Half of that money belonged to Robert's share of the estate. It would most likely come to around $40,000.

She affirmed that although she had seen Peernock's rage at her and had read his constant attacks on Natasha in his handwritten court pleadings, she could offer no concrete proof that if he got his hands on any cash he would use it to create more lethal mischief.

But it was at this point that Victoria realized, to her great chagrin, that her emotions had begun to overwhelm her. She could feel tears welling in her eyes. *Don't do this,* she ordered herself. *This is just the sort of thing that sexist male lawyers make jokes about female lawyers doing under stress. Do not do this.* She had never lost emotional control inside a courthouse, but it was like being a grade school kid all over again. She was without the slightest power to stop her eyes from filling up, hating her emotions for betraying her so bluntly. She stood in utter embarrassment as tears began rolling down her cheeks. "I tried to remain composed," she said later, "but I couldn't. I'd been fighting this case for too long without adequate resources. I just lost it."

Judge Rimmerman had known her for years and realized that this was extraordinary behavior for a woman with a reputation for being just as tough as any situation called for her to be. He paused a moment, then asked Marshal Oldman to wait outside.

"All right, Vicki," Rimmerman said once they were alone, "this isn't something we usually see in here. What's going on with you today?"

"I'm sorry, Your Honor," she replied, chagrined. "I really am. It's just that I can't do this any longer. There's nothing left. You can't practice law on air. I've had to deal with Robert's first attorney, Bradley Brunon, and respond to all of his requests while he was generating something like sixty thousand dollars in billed hours on Robert's defense. And of course Dern, Mason and Floum dragged me into court constantly. They generated enough opposition to justify billing seventy thousand dollars for about three months of work, most of which was used as ammunition to try to get at Natasha. All of it required legal responses from my office. Then Peernock went in pro per and started filing one motion after another from inside his cell because his meals are paid for and he has nothing better to do. And I could still handle that much, but now he wants to give this new attorney forty thousand dollars to do God knows what.

"Everybody seems to have unlimited funds to fight this thing. And I'm all that stands between him and Natasha. I'm not afraid to battle it out, but this case, this damn case, is killing me. It's killing me physically. It's killing me emotionally. And financially, forget it.

"In a year and eight months since I took Natasha's case, I've received a total of ten thousand dollars. It takes up too much time for me to handle much other casework, but my office overhead is five thousand dollars a month in staff salary and costs. If I throw in the towel and sub out the case, what about Natasha? What if the next attorney just uses her to run up fees and leaves her with nothing? We both know it's quite possible to do that and be perfectly within the law. I mean, her uncle told me that Claire Peernock would have wanted me to do this and I've come to feel so much loyalty to the girl. But now . . ."

She had to stop.

After a long pause, Rimmerman stood and admitted Marshal Oldman back inside. He quietly told him he could have $40,000 from the rent receipts, but only on the condition that Robert Peernock should agree that Victoria Doom could receive another $30,000 against her accumulated unpaid fees to pay her staff and catch up with her office expenses. If both sides were going all the way to the wall on this case, Rimmerman determined that they should do it on a level playing field, where the best legal position could win on its merit, not where one side simply spent the other into defeat.

Victoria sighed with relief as she left the courthouse. The new funds wouldn't really level off the playing field after so many months of volunteer legal work. But at least she would be rolling the boulder up a gentler slope for a while.

• • •

That night Victoria stayed late at her office, trying to figure out what her next step ought to be. She slowly sifted through piles of assorted papers that she had retrieved from the Peernock house on Natasha's behalf. As she did so, she realized that she hadn't come as close to being driven out of the case as she had feared; all these little remnants of the family's shattered lives were here in her hands, just as Natasha's future was.

She never could have let the opposition whip her into just walking away.

One of the papers she came across was a copy of a reference request that Tasha's fashion-design school had sent to her high school counselor. The counselor, who had known Tasha for nearly four years, had written his reply weeks before the night of the crimes, when he had no idea that anyone outside the design school would ever see it. And as Victoria began reading remarks that Natasha herself had never seen, she felt as if she were listening in on some secret conversation.

Appearance: Excellent. *Maturity:* Excellent. *Integrity:* Excellent. *Creativity:* Excellent. "Natasha is a motivated, intelligent, and mature individual who constantly strives to accomplish her personal and educational goals. Loyal, determined, and fun loving, her pleasant personality, sincerity, and compassion for others has been a shining delight to her peers and teachers. This outstanding and determined young lady will strive diligently to pursue her career goal of working in the fashion industry."

Victoria might have found the recommendation touching under other circumstances, but now it just made her angry. She got madder by the second as she thought about the characterizations leveled at Natasha in the court documents filed by Dern, Mason and Floum. They had essentially accused her of having made everything up to frame her poor innocent father, of inventing a horrible lie in the form of this story about her father being a killer. They not only implied that she was doing it in order to get her hands on her dead mother's insurance money, they had included Victoria in these valentines. They called her professional behavior deceptive, dishonest, done in service of some awful hoax.

The firm had asserted this position to the courts even though they were talking about a young woman who had lain trapped in the car's wreckage next to her mother's dead body while the pool of gasoline that the murderer had poured over them slowly ate away at her flesh.

Victoria clutched Natasha's character reference in her hands, gazing through it with a grim stare. How satisfying it would have been, she thought, if the excellent law firm of Dern, Mason and Floum had not yet left the case. She would have loved to take this character reference over to their offices high up inside the shining white towers of Century City.

And jam it down their throats.

Tasha's facial scars had healed enough that she was finally able to make herself get a job as a waitress at the base NCO club. Her flesh was still too raw to tolerate sunlight, but she wanted to try working indoors. The job helped to bring in a little money. It gave her a chance to go somewhere on her own, to have something to do even if it was just a service job. Most importantly, it helped to take her mind off the fact that her marriage was beginning to feel as if it had hit the same wall her father's Cadillac had been headed toward on the night of the crimes.

Piles of coins began accumulating on her dresser at home. They helped give her the feeling that she was finally able to accomplish something on her own. Still, every time she tried to imagine leaving, she got a sick feeling in the pit of her stomach. Leave and go where?

At least things were looking up in one sense; either people didn't stare at her so much anymore, or she had begun to develop a resistance to it. It made working easier. She mulled over the marriage while she hefted the heavy trays, glad finally to have something to do that got her out of the house on a regular basis.

She realized that when they had started out, her husband had barely been more than a kid himself. He had suddenly found himself saddled with a badly injured young wife and a witness protection program and stories of brutality that went far beyond the impersonal naval battles he was trained to fight.

She could see his side of the problem, all right. It just didn't give her any way of reconnecting their broken communication lines.

Back in Los Angeles as the second year of the case dragged toward a close, Pam Springer discovered she was being transferred to another division. The Peernock case, which the D.A.'s office had originally estimated would take only a year to complete, now found itself in need of a new prosecutor.

Springer admits that she left with definitely mixed emotions. She was hardly sorry to be free of the entanglements, but was still frustrated that she wouldn't be able to see it to completion.

Because by that point Robert Peernock was on his fifth defense attorney and his fourth pretrial judge, chewing them up like gum balls. He found every loophole in the system to drag out the proceedings month after month, despite blaming the delays on the system itself. He turned nearly every court appearance into yet another opportunity to plead his detailed conspiracy accusations.

Even today when she gives her thoughts about the personal experience of handling the case, her eyes harden. She lapses into prosecutorial mode, ticking off names and facts with the skill of an experienced senior prosecutor. Clearly, that part of her hated to walk away.

Only when the topic switches to her marriage and motherhood does Springer's smile fully open up. Her eyes suddenly glow, her face softens; the woman that her husband fell in love with is revealed. Her smile remains for as long as the topics focus on pleasant things.

It is still there as she begins to discuss Craig Richman, the-up-and-coming young prosecutor who replaced her. Springer knew that whatever the outcome of the trial, Craig Richman would be aggressive as hell in pursuing the conviction.

And by this point Pam Springer knew very well that whatever the outcome of the case, this new guy Richman was in for a treat.

"I came back from lunch one day and walked into my office to find several big boxes of case files on my desk," Richman said later. "There was a note from Billy Webb, my boss, telling me that the Peernock case was now my baby. I didn't have to ask who Robert Peernock was; by this point everybody knew. But I also knew that the guy had been having a lot of success at jerking the system around in circles. A couple other prosecutors who were senior to me had been offered the case and refused. One had been involved with Peernock before on his old battery case and didn't want to set grounds for conflict of interest. But nobody asked if I wanted it or not."

Craig Richman trained at the U.S. Air Force Academy in Colorado Springs and still describes himself as a soldier. Now he serves with the thousand-prosecutor army of the largest law office in the world. The battlefront is a courtroom, and here the bad guys have Craig's team heavily outgunned and severely outnumbered.

Asked whether it made him nervous to inherit an infamous and complex murder case, Richman replies that it did not.

But then he smiles and shakes his head. "I didn't know any better."

Richman was a radio announcer at the Air Force Academy's campus station. The background shows in his voice. He liked radio so well that after military service he spent several years working at stations in California and Arizona before settling into law school in Sacramento. He left his radio career behind when he joined the DA's office in 1985, but he describes trial work as being like radio drama. "The two are similar in a lot of ways. The jury is an audience; you have to draw them in and keep their interest. Just because they can't change the channel doesn't mean they can't tune you out."

On the day he inherited the Peernock case, Richman had just begun married life with a wife whose beauty matches his chiseled features so well that co-workers still refer to them dryly as "Ken and Barbie." He resolved to keep the case away from his off-duty time; he didn't want to blow the new homelife. But it didn't take long before the case began to bite deeper. Like Steve Fisk, Richman was born in Los Angeles and grew up watching his hometown become increasingly dangerous as the streets turned into shooting galleries and the neighborhoods into breeding grounds for bizarre psychotic outbursts.

Furthermore, as each twisted piece of the Peernock puzzle dropped into place, Craig Richman saw the fate of this tragic family as a particularly hideous example of the weakening of family ties, the loss of social cohesion. The codes of society are no longer strong enough to instill much respect for life or to teach restraint to the enraged. The Peernock file was a small and very personal example of how those large, abstract concepts manifest themselves in the intimate reality of a single family.

And like Steve Fisk, Richman also radiates the strong impression that he sees the killers who come up against him in court as having brought their business into his own backyard. The experiences haven't made him optimistic about any dramatic turns for the better in the near future.

"Consider the L.A. riots. If we don't get a handle on some level of mutual human respect in this city," he says with a grim sigh, "L.A. hasn't begun to burn."

So he attacked the case files hard, cramming research into stolen time, absorbing endless lists of evidence and interviews and two years' worth of Fisk's investigative work. Eventually he and Fisk began to spend whatever mutual time they could spare in the hunt for anything they could use to bring in a conviction.

His longstanding habit of heading straight for the gym before going home began to prove invaluable at working off stress, once he realized how difficult it might be to get that conviction.

Before long, despite Richman's motivation to go home early at night, something—perhaps the photos of the crime scene, or the emergency-room shots of Natasha that look more like coroner's photos, or the actual coroner's pictures of Claire—something was enough to push him to the limit in preparing for the case. The contents of the Peernock files began to seem like components of a huge Rubik's Cube, waiting for just the right twist before all the colors fell into place. He became convinced that somewhere, precisely the right twist for the giant puzzle cube lay waiting. Somewhere.

While the sweltering Los Angeles summer deepened into autumn, Craig Richman started wandering into the office on weekends. As often as not he was on his way back from what was supposed to just be a workout at the gym, dressed in a T-shirt, shorts, and sandals. Still aching from sessions with the free weights, he shuffled through the halls of the deserted office building, sorting through the files, calling Steve Fisk at home, bugging him about details.

Looking for the twist.

CHAPTER

24

There is no hard evidence that the final payment of $40,000 which Robert Peernock managed to get from his estate to pay for a private defense attorney ever went to create more murderous mischief outside the jail.

No one wanted to go on record with their suspicions. Still, stories swirled in the background about strange cars following people home late at night, about unusual people pacing sidewalks in front of other people's homes, of clicking sounds on telephone lines. By this point the case exuded paranoia like scent off a flattened skunk.

Perhaps harmless events were taking on deathly implications and people's suspicions simply began to run away with them. Or perhaps they don't want to come forward because they know that they can't conclusively prove what their senses tell them is true: that Robert Peernock hired private investigators to follow them, and perhaps ultimately to discourage potential testimony.

In the end, it doesn't matter whether or not any of the frightened people's stories have a basis in fact; the result was the same. Paranoia permeated lives at all levels of this drawn-out case. The fear was contagious, touching nearly everyone involved.

Even Peernock himself was not immune. As 1990 lurched to a close, he became firm in his conviction that he could not trust his fifth attorney, Filipa Richland, even though he had sought her out and hired her himself, using the money that he wrested from his daughters' future.

Filipa Richland was, he decided, just one more conspirator who was in on the plot to frame him.

Court records are jammed with transcripts of hearings where he showed up insisting that he be allowed to fire her. He registered one protest after another; she would not allow him to have private records in his cell, she would not take his phone calls often enough, she would not visit him enough, she would not take his orders on how to run the case.

He did not believe her explanation that she didn't allow murder clients to have private papers in their cells because the snitch situation there invited other inmates to peek at private papers and try to turn in fake evidence in return for shortened sentences. He was sure that she was only using that explanation as an excuse to try to prevent him from assisting with his own defense.

He complained that she refused to send investigators to interview the long lists of people he wanted her to involve in the case. This argument was not new. No matter who his attorney was at any given point, Robert Peernock never accepted his or her explanation that many of the people on his suggested subpoena list were simply witnesses from his old struggle against the Department of Water Resources, and were of little or no value against the murder rap facing him.

As with his other attorneys, he could not make Filipa Richland see that it was *all the same thing,* that his old battery case at the DWR and his fourteen lawsuits against the state government and his current charges of murder, attempted murder, kidnapping, arson, and everything else were all a part of the same struggle against corrupt monsters hiding in the darkness of smoke-filled rooms and secret meeting places, plotting against all the taxpayers Robert Peernock wanted so desperately to defend.

To Filipa Richland's credit, she lasted one year and ten months with Robert Peernock as a client, longer than any other attorney who tried to defend his long list of felony charges.

But in the end she stood in court and agreed that if he wanted her to substitute out to yet another attorney, and if the court was prepared to allow him still more legal wrangling before pressing the case to trial, she would willingly step aside.

That was all Peernock needed to hear. He jumped at the chance to dump what he claimed was another conspirator clearly out to rig a conviction against him. The state's persistence in maneuvering him into prison for life was not going to succeed against Robert Peernock.

He demanded nothing less than a full acquittal for himself and complete public exposure of the vast network of tax-paid monsters operating in the dark.

And so it was right after New Year's Day of 1991 that the Peernock case returned to Nevada for the first time since ''James Dobbs'' of Sacramento checked into Bally's and headed downstairs to scope out the feathered fannies at the *JUBILEE!* show. This time the case landed in the office of the man who would wind up actually bringing it to trial.

Attorney Donald Green has his own law practice in Las Vegas, but he keeps his bar dues paid in California as well. Since graduating from Southwestern University Law School near the top of his class, Donald Green has learned that anything can grow under the golden West Coast sun: oranges, avocados, homicidal rages. Every time he picks up the phone, it is yet another opportunity to hear a tale too bizarre to believe.

He sometimes finds himself hired to make a jury believe one anyway.

''I operate on a need-to-know basis. One of the first things I instruct a client is not to tell me that they're innocent and for God's sake not to tell me they're guilty. Proof is the

problem of the prosecution. As the defense, I'm in to provide
a reasonable doubt. Nothing else. If you try to play father
confessor to all the people you defend''—he pauses at this
point, sighs, shakes his head—''you will *absolutely* lose your
mind.''

Green was in the eighth year of his legal career in January
of 1991 when his phone rang with a call that would change
his life for years to come.

''I got a call from a client of mine who had been charged
with being a contract killer in the so-called Ninja Assassin
murders back in 1985 and was in L.A. County Jail for a long
time, where he became friends with another inmate who
spent a couple of years in jail defending himself because he
did not trust attorneys.

''And it turns out that this other guy was in the cell next
to Robert Peernock. They got to talking about lawyers. The
guy tells Peernock about this so-called Ninja Assassin who
I defended. So Peernock contacted me through this guy, re-
laying the message that his primary concern was that he locate an attorney who cannot be bribed by the system, who
isn't afraid to operate outside the system and against system
pressure, especially on a PC-187: first-degree murder.''

And so Green arranged a special visit at the L.A. County
Jail over the coming weekend. Then he flew to Los Angeles
to meet Robert Peernock for the first time.

He walked in the back door from the parking lot and entered the sour stink of the jail, handed the guard his California bar card and driver's license, did the usual b.s. about
why are you a California attorney with a Nevada address.
He removed his steel-toed cowboy boots before stepping
through the metal detector.

The heavy door slid open and Green was led down to the
jail's hospital ward to meet Robert Peernock for the first
time.

''Peernock came in, no handcuffs, no shackles, even

though he was being held in the Highpower section, which means he's in there with your biker maniacs, your hillside stranglers, your contract killers, that sort of thing. He comes in with two big expandable folders tucked under his arms. Stuffed with papers.

"I hadn't heard of the Peernock case yet and had no preconception about who Robert Peernock was. And when we met that first time my immediate reaction was that he was a man on a *mission*"—Green hits the word hard—"to prove that he did not kill his wife or do any of the crimes he was accused of."

After their initial two-hour interview he agreed to take Peernock's file back to Las Vegas with him, read it on the plane, and call back with his opinion on whether or not he could be of any help. Green knew that Peernock had no immediate cash to pay him, but that there were funds held in various family accounts. He could make application for them if he and Robert agreed to attempt the case together.

Hence he might get paid, he might not. "But my policy is that I never turn down a referral case on a major felony, regardless of the ability to pay. Money was never a consideration in taking this case either. Later that week I told him his case could be defensible and that I would represent him."

So Donald Green substituted in for Filipa Richland and became Robert Peernock's defense attorney number six.

The story took another ironic twist as Green got set to face off against Craig Richman; both men have strong military backgrounds. Green is a decorated Army veteran and frequently uses his special military license to defend courtmartial cases in the U.S. Court of Military Appeals.

Craig Richman raised hell. He petitioned the judge to refuse to allow Peernock to push the trial back once again so that yet *another* attorney could take the time to get up to speed, only to be deemed a co-conspirator as soon as the attorney

failed to obey Peernock's instructions. Therefore Donald
Green was forced to commit, in court and on the record, to
remaining on the case for the long haul and not to bail out
if things got tough. He swore to see the case through to
completion, no matter what.

As of January 10, 1991, Donald Green officially became
Robert Peernock's trial lawyer, in for the duration.

He recalls Robert Peernock as being completely coopera-
tive.

At first.

January was just as busy for Victoria. She made the final
move out of California and over to New Mexico, joining
Richard on the land they had purchased there the year before.
He had already moved their collection of animals and was
setting up the grounds with the necessary enclosures.

The decision to move had come after Pam Springer called
Victoria into her office to give her the news that Robert Peernock was soliciting a hit man to kill her and Natasha. That
news finally did what all the other stress factors of the city
had not yet been able to do; it convinced her to give up life
as a big-city lawyer. If the pollution doesn't kill you and the
traffic doesn't kill you and the stress of the job doesn't kill
you, Victoria thought, why, then there are always the paid
operatives of a jailhouse murderer to worry about.

By the time she threw in the towel on life in L.A., she
was packing a pistol to get herself to and from her car and
keeping a shotgun under her desk, losing sleep over bumps
in the night, and fretting over every detail of her part of the
Peernock case.

So finally she and Richard sat down and asked themselves
if this was really what their married life was supposed to be
about. He had recently taken early retirement from a successful career and wanted her to have a little more leisure in
her own life too. Richard thought it might seem especially

nice if his wife could avoid getting plugged in the parking lot by some monosyllabic junkie on a lunatic mission.

L.A. just wasn't worth it anymore.

So she stayed on in her Saugus office while Richard began getting their new home ready on a large patch of raw land several miles outside the little town of Las Vegas, New Mexico, which looks nothing at all like its more famous namesake. It had taken over a year to wind down her L.A. practice. She would continue to represent Natasha via phone and fax, flying back for hearings.

So the year opened with Victoria walking out the door of her Saugus office for the last time, moving to someplace where the zoning inspectors wouldn't get on her back over her fondness for strange animals and any new hit men in her life would have to work a little harder to get to her.

During that same January, Tasha's phone conversations with Victoria were keeping hope alive that at some point in the future this endless mess of her father's trial would at last be over and that the money her mother had set aside for her would be released. Then she could finish her schooling, take a breather from her endless rounds of survival jobs, and make a few choices about her future based on something other than the immediate need to cover the rent and scramble for groceries.

But sometimes the hope of all that seemed like nothing more than an illusion, another shell game from a legal world she had learned to distrust through all of the years that she watched her father use the system. Even though she had never clearly understood her father's methods, the very fact that he managed to use the courts to get his way made courtrooms seem like suspicious places to her.

Still, there was nothing to do but place her faith in Victoria Doom and hope that her mother had chosen wisely when she went to Doom's office in the first place.

• • •

As February drew near, Craig Richman got the word from his boss. From that moment until completion of the Peernock trial he would be relieved of any other duties, to afford him every opportunity of hitting the ground at full speed when the trial began.

He was grateful for the chance to focus entirely on the baffling case. To Craig Richman, Peernock was clearly guilty when all the evidence was taken together, but throughout the pretrial hearings Peernock had always offered explanations for every single piece of it.

Richman knew that all Peernock needed was for one juror to buy his conspiracy story. The question kept dogging him: what if one of the jurors turned out to have been the victim of some conspiracy at work and still held a grudge about it? Would he be able to differentiate between his personal experience and this case? All it took was that one juror to listen to Peernock's story, to hear the evidence and find he couldn't shake away that old reasonable doubt.

The trial had been postponed countless times, but was now scheduled for April, or early summer at the latest. The excuses for pushing the date back were running out and the feeling of inevitability was beginning to settle in over everybody concerned with the case.

Richman started finding himself getting to the gym later and later in the day as he pushed himself to uncover every angle that he could. His certainty of Peernock's guilt was based upon countless hours spent going over an avalanche of evidence time after time. He was far less certain that the same evidence could be passed in front of a jury once or twice and remain coherent to all twelve.

In the year and a half he'd spent sifting that evidence, he still hadn't found the twist that his senses had told him from the beginning must be there somewhere, something that would snap all the pieces of the giant puzzle cube into place.

And Peernock had gotten his statement straight so cleverly that Richman knew this twist might be vital in his quest to convince the jury. If Richman failed to do that, he could then stand back and try to tell himself that the disasters virtually guaranteed to result for Natasha and Victoria were none of his doing.

The trial judge was finally selected as the inevitable confrontation moved closer. Judge Howard J. Schwab would marshal the case through to completion. Out of all the judges in front of whom Robert Peernock had appeared since the day of his arrest, the selection of Howard Schwab could have been a lucky break for Peernock.

In fact, the arrival of Judge Schwab in Robert's life should have been his luckiest day. One glance at Schwab's resume makes it plain that this is not someone who will throw away his career on a bribe so that mysterious higher-ups can silence one of the government's endless list of gadflies.

As a history major at UCLA, Howard Schwab graduated with honors. After graduation from UCLA Law School he rose quickly through the ranks as deputy city attorney of Los Angeles to become California's deputy attorney general. In that capacity he argued and briefed what the notorious Charles Manson murder case and other related cases of Manson's family members.

As co-counsel to former California Governor George Deukmejian, he argued the landmark decision upholding the constitutionality of capital punishment in California.

He personally argued and briefed what was then the longest criminal case in California history, *People* v. *Powell,* the subject of Joseph Wambaugh's *The Onion Field.* He also argued and briefed the William and Emily Harris case, concerning the infamous Symbionese Liberation Army.

As for his personal style, Schwab's love of history, philosophy, books in general, and the law in particular shines through his demeanor in the courtroom. He astounds attorneys for both sides with an ability to cite specific case law on obscure rulings entirely from memory. His remarks in the courtroom are sprinkled with historical references and his rulings reflect the historical context from which he derives them.

Howard Schwab is absolutely the wrong judge for an unprepared attorney to try to bluff. Anyone planning to frame up an innocent defendant in Schwab's court had better approach the task with the highest intellect, unlimited research sources, and a vast supply of luck.

And so Robert Peernock could not have done better in his quest for a judge who would deal with his case strictly on the merits brought by the prosecution and by the defendant himself. This was just the judge to blow any manipulated conspiracy wide open, to resist any prosecution attempts to frame an innocent man, and to see to it that Robert Peernock got exactly the justice he deserved.

HON-EY-MOON—noun. [fr. the idea that the first month of marriage is the sweetest] A period of unusual harmony following the establishment of a new relationship.

—Webster's New Collegiate Dictionary

Honeymoons are short by definition. Conflict is inevitable.

By spring, Peernock was claiming that Donald Green had been bribed by Judge Schwab with offers of future lucrative courtroom assignments on behalf of indigent defendants. These cases can make appointed lawyers rich if they stay at the top of the court's assignment roster.

Peernock figured that Green's refusal to subpoena witnesses from old union struggles of a decade ago, plus Green's unwillingness to allow Robert to commandeer his California bar license and more or less run his own case, all served to prove that Donald Green was a puppet of government forces like the five attorneys before him. This would be despite the fact that Peernock himself had sought out both Filipa Richland's and Donald Green's services, despite the fact that Green had come recommended to Peernock by former defendants, and moreover that they had vowed from personal experience that Green would not respond to intimidation and that he could not be bribed.

None of that impressed Robert Peernock anymore.

The honeymoon was over.

CHAPTER

25

As summer of 1991 began, the case was finally proceeding to trial.

By this point Tasha couldn't make herself put the effort into settling into an apartment by herself. For the last few months she had resorted to staying with friends and acquaintances around Los Angeles. As the trial approached, she went to spend some time with Louise, her mother's friend of so many years, but though the familiar face was comforting she couldn't make herself open up to the woman. Tasha really only felt okay when she could keep herself busy and distracted, preferably with people who knew little or nothing about her background. Staying with Louise was a difficult reminder of the unfinished business she was about to confront in court for the third time.

By now the story seemed to come out by itself. She had lost track of the number of times that detectives and prosecutors and doctors had asked her about the night of the crimes. She would just go into her witness mode and let them pummel her with their endless questions, always with the implication that if they twisted a question around and asked it in enough different ways, maybe she would slip up and say something different. But this new guy Craig Richman had started to get all intense about the coming trial. And that was making her notice her own nerves.

He gave her portions of her preliminary hearing testimony from nearly four years before and asked her to read over it, to refresh her memory just in case there were any details she might have gotten fuzzy about during all the time that her father was dragging the case through the courts.

She protested that she didn't feel like reading about the crimes anymore. The whole thing was such a drag to have to dive into all over again. But Craig kept calling her and calling her, asking if she had read it yet, if she had any questions, if she had any new memories to add.

Finally he confronted her. It startled her to see how strongly he felt about the case.

"Natasha, I know you hate to go through this again, but the other side wants you to get up there and screw up. Don't you realize that? The preliminary hearing where you were on the stand for three days, the civil trial where your father grilled you for four days, all of that was only a rehearsal for this. *This* is the real thing. You're the only one who was there, so they want you to look like a liar. They want you to contradict yourself. They'll probably make a big deal out of the fact that when the ambulance picked you up you didn't know what you were saying. Now, we have doctors to explain to the jury how blows to the head can work on short-term memory, but it really all comes down to you."

Then Richman dropped the bomb on her.

"If the other side can portray you as some nasty little teenager who had it in for her father, and who somehow is doing all this against an innocent man, Natasha . . . he's going to walk out of that court free as a bird. Tell me, what do you think that means?"

Richman knew that his question had hit home. It showed in her eyes. The question punctured all of her resistance to having to get up and defend herself one more time. It got through to her where nothing else did because she had little doubt about the answer.

"He'll find a way to kill me," she answered softly. "And make it look like an accident."

She went home to study the transcript and make sure her memory was fresh on every detail.

On the eve of the trial, Craig Richman found himself alone in his office building, long after regular working hours. He already knew that he wasn't going to make it to the gym for his workout today. As the trial closed in on him, he couldn't shake the feeling that stones were still unturned. Even though he had no doubt, not a single doubt, that Robert Peernock was guilty of all the crimes, he also didn't doubt that there was still a chance that the guy could actually skate past the jury.

But the question kept haunting him—*what* could he have missed? He had flown up to Sacramento and interviewed the Department of Water Resources people who had worked with Peernock, as well as with people in Los Angeles from Network Electronics where Peernock had last worked as VP in charge of the testing of their pyrotechnic devices. Richman talked nonstop to anybody who could shed any light at all on Peernock's background and his efforts as a whistleblower.

He spent countless hours dealing with medical experts and toxicological experts and crime scene experts of every description. He pored over every bit of testimony from every pretrial hearing.

Richman would have loved to have the chance to cross-examine Peernock, but the defendant had been routinely disruptive in most of his hearings and was dragged out of the courtroom on several occasions. Because of that it seemed inconceivable that the defense would allow Peernock to take the stand. Richman would have to mount his case strictly on legal skill, even though he lacked crucial evidence to clinch a conviction. Still, there was little left that he could do to prepare for the most important trial he had ever undertaken.

So it was more out of his own work habit than anything else that he sat down at the large work table in the office copy room and prepared his little make-work assignment: going through a large box of papers that Steve Fisk had confiscated from Peernock's Datsun shortly after the car had been impounded. He told himself that it was just a bunch of junk, really. Hardly worth the effort. But Richman knew he would sleep better if he'd personally glanced over each piece of paper before he left the building for the night.

He opened the box and started picking up one piece at a time, turning it over to check both sides, and setting each one aside carefully before going on to the next.

It was soon clear that he was going to be there for quite a while. Peernock was a chronic, habitual list maker who catalogued reminders for every mundane activity in every day of his life. Grocery lists, laundry lists, hardware-store lists, banking lists, personal reminders. Many of them were dutifully labeled "To-Do" at the top, sometimes dated, sometimes not.

The chore began to capture Richman's interest. Peernock was compulsive, scrawling the lists on any scrap of paper, large or small. Some were in numbered order on blank pages; others were simply scribbled across corners torn from something else.

Fisk's investigators had just scooped the papers out of the Datsun and dumped them into the box, so they weren't in any particular order. But as Richman sorted them, a funny kind of structure began to emerge. Peernock's style was to make the list and run a line through each item as it was taken care of until the entire list was checked off. Then he discarded it and started another. Sometimes there were several for a single day.

Richman picked up one of the papers labeled "To-Do" at the top. It had been divided into two halves. The first half had four numbered entries and the second half had ten. They all looked like regular chores, each item dutifully lined through in pencil. "Hook up wire for sprinklers," scratched through, "Pick up all tools," scratched through, and farther down the page: "Call Meyers," followed by a phone number, scratched through.

Then something caught Craig's eye.

Under that last phone-number entry, item number four was a little drawing. It was followed by the word *stock.*

The little drawing looked like a large, hollow L, but the L had been turned backward, then laid over on its side.

The large, hollow, L-shaped drawing was sharply pointed on the long end. And that was all. A drawing of a sharpened, pointed, bent thing, followed by the word *stock.*

Craig ran his eyes down the rest of the page, but all the other items were innocuous little entries, notes about fixing air-conditioning on the rental properties, about a renter coming over at 4:30, nothing remarkable.

And then it hit him. He felt as if his blood temperature dropped twenty degrees.

The flat steel bar that had been bent into an L-shape and fastened under the death car had also been filed to a sharp point.

Just like the little drawing Richman was holding in his hand.

Craig considered the little drawing of the hollow, sharpened L and the word *stock.* He already knew that when you go to a metal supply place and order a thick bar of steel, you ask for a bar of stock. Bar stock. Bar stock is thick enough to be strong, but thin enough to be bent into an L-shape if you use a good vise and a large wrench.

Two large wrenches had been taken from the Datsun. A vise had been found in the hatchback section, wrapped in white plastic right next to the toolbox that had the guns inside.

And here on this list was this bizarre little entry, tucked in among all these other daily chores. The only date on the page was a reference to one of the renters' starting on June

3, 1987, so the list had been drawn up sometime during the seven weeks preceding the crimes.

"So," Craig muttered, "go out and buy a piece of bar stock and bend it into a right angle and sharpen the long end to a point to use in murdering your wife and daughter in such a fashion that it will look like they died in a fiery auto accident. Oh, and don't forget: a renter is coming over at four-thirty."

And if this drawing was not the cutter bar found rigged under the car by the gas tank, then what was it? What harmless thing could it be? *What innocent thing is described by drawing a large, hollow, sharp-pointed L—followed by the word* stock*?*

By now Richman's heart had started pounding. He snatched another handful of papers from the box and began going down each list. Still, most of them were nothing.

June 7, "Air pump from Datsun," scratched out, "rope," not scratched out. Apparently he hadn't gotten the rope he needed on June 7.

June 8, "Buy battery, 9 volt," scratched out, followed by two more lists on the same page, all for plain daily chores at the rental properties.

But here was one, labeled "To Do 5/14/87," and the very first item was "Call about window tint." Richman already knew that Peernock had taken the Cadillac in to have the windows tinted early in June, less than a month after this notation was made. But Peernock claimed that he rarely drove the car at that time. His girlfriend, Sonia Siegel, confirmed that he had nearly stopped driving it altogether. So why tint the windows? Besides, tinting makes it harder to see out at night.

And harder to see in.

But the other items on that list were just chores, right down to the last entry, an odd little item labeled number eight, "Take care of Foothill." It was the last item on that

page. It had not been scratched out. Peernock claimed in his
pretrial hearings to have been engaged in struggles with the
Foothill police over something or other concerning his ongoing whistleblower activities. So as of May 14 he had apparently not taken care of Foothill yet. But the wreck had
been staged inside the Police Department's Foothill Division.

Richman was tearing through the box now, scanning each
page quickly, rejecting most of them as meaningless, and
setting them aside before picking up another and still another. Check the sprinklers. Check the car. Check this. Check
that.

Here was an odd one: "Find Loc."

Location? Craig wondered. Find location? The item was
not scratched out. It dated all the way back to December 1,
1986, a short time after Claire had seen Victoria Doom about
the divorce. Peernock needed a location on that day and he
had not scratched it out. Also on that page was "Empty car,"
and "Buy Liq." followed by a number 2 inside a small circle. Buy two bottles of liquor? Peernock didn't drink and
everyone confirmed that Claire never touched hard liquor.
Since Peernock did not seem to have any friends, for whom
would he buy two bottles of liquor, *without bothering to note
what kind or what brand*?

That is, unless he needed a bottle of hard stuff, any kind
of hard stuff, to force-feed the women. And maybe a second
bottle to leave next to Claire's body in the staged car wreck?

Of course, that would have to take place after carefully
pressing her fingers against it to leave prints on the bottle. And
yet it seemed he had forgotten to press her fingers to the steering wheel; the controls of the car she had supposedly been
driving showed no trace of ever having been touched by her.

Craig Richman hadn't left his chair, but he had broken a
sweat. He wouldn't need an aerobic pump today; his heart
rate was right up there in the target zone.

And there now, on the same December page, set inside a

little hand-drawn box, was a sublist of seven numbered entries. To the right of that box were the abbreviated words "Bar thick 2 R. & Sq." Peernock's car had indeed been fitted with a thick bar that had been turned at nearly a right angle, squared off to the flat side of the bar. But this item was written six months before the June 3 list that had the L-shaped drawing. This earlier list didn't have such a drawing anywhere on it, just the item. Maybe Peernock hadn't perfected the design, back in December?

But it was the seven numbered entries on the left side that really jumped up off of the page. Written in terse abbreviations, the seven items looked confusing.

1. H.C.
2. Cl's Pur
3. Keys
4. W. Bott.s
5. Rags & Tissues
6. Liq
7. F.M.

At first the abbreviations made no sense. Then they began to translate themselves—

Within moments the items unfolded before Craig Richman's eyes.

Number two. Claire's purse? Peernock didn't live with Claire, they barely communicated. What did he need with Claire's purse? What else could this be? Richman asked himself. What harmless list of things would this be?

"My God," Richman muttered out loud. It had to be a "To-Do" list to murder Claire. Peernock had drawn up this list, working out the details, *seven months before he actually did the deeds*.

ONE, handcuffs, TWO, Claire's purse, THREE, don't forget the extra keys, FOUR, water bottles to clean up with,

FIVE, rags and tissues to wipe off with and for the fire in the trunk, SIX, liquor to pour into her and to leave in the car, SEVEN, either remember to set the car radio on FM, the way Claire would set it if she were really driving the car. Or maybe—

Don't forget the face mask.

He shuffled through more lists. Page after page. Here was another: "Flashlight," for obvious reasons, then "Rope & G"—rope and gas? "Tire replacement"—after removing the murder kit from the trunk at the scene? "Lq in Bot."—liquor in bottle? Peernock didn't drink. "Wat. in bot & rags," water and rags to clean himself up before leaving the dark location?

Beneath that was the underlined heading *"Bag,"* followed by the familiar "H.C." and "F.M." and also by "Rope" and "Gloves" and "Matches" and the note to "Put spark plugs in Cad."

Yeah, right, Richman thought to himself. *You certainly don't want the car you don't drive to be futzing out on you when you send it speeding for the concrete wall.*

On the same page was a separate section with the notations "W. in backseat + Ch. + cover." Wife in backseat, plus child, plus cover. If not that, then what? What harmless thing could it be, other than an idea to cover the kidnapped women with something so passing cars wouldn't see? Also "Bott liq & water & rags," obvious again.

And then came the most chilling notation so far:

"Test str. to what speed." Test straight to what speed? Got to make sure the car you don't drive goes straight at high speeds. Even if no one is holding the wheel. Straight all the way to the wall, assuming that by now Peernock knew about the wall—because this list had no date, but it also had no reminder to "Find Loc." as there had been on several other lists throughout the seven-month period.

By the time Peernock had made the notation of "test str.

to what speed," he was apparently no longer concerned that he needed to "Find Loc." The lists covered seven months of time and many of the more incriminating notations had been made over and over. Find location, find location, find location. It seemed that by the time he'd drawn up this one he had already found his location. That meant that by this time he knew about the wall.

Then all he would have to do is "test str. to what speed."

And finally, there at the bottom of the page, Craig Richman found the last list he would need. It consisted of nine items in all, sprinkled in with other routine chores that any landlord might perform, mixed in with perfectly understandable and harmless activities. The list began with the reminder to "move seat up." To hold Claire's body in place? Richman felt as if he was gazing into some madman's crystal ball, watching the carefully crafted crimes being rehearsed.

Then came the reminder "pur." Wouldn't want to forget to throw her purse in, as the purse indeed had been, to make it look as if she were really driving.

Then came the notation "keys," followed by a couple of unreadable scribbles.

Next was the reminder to "pull wires." The paramedics testified that light was a problem inside the car. The dome light was off even though the door was open. It seems that the reminder had worked and he had remembered to pull the wires.

The bottom notation was the reminder "plastic bag for rope and wire." Right, he thought grimly. Wouldn't want to put bloody equipment inside the getaway car.

Last of all, at the right of the page directly next to this final list, was a single notation "home contracts."

Natasha had testified several times that her father had told her, before Claire had arrived at home, that he was going to force her to sign papers. Craig had already recovered a scrap of paper written out in draft form in Peernock's handwriting, which said, "In lieu of anything, I accept $2,000 dollars." It had a hand-drawn signature line. Robert had printed Claire Peernock's name underneath the signature line.

But Claire had never signed it. Did she, Richman wondered, have that piece of paper waved under her face just before Natasha, lying bound in her mother's bedroom, heard the sound of bodies falling to the floor like little girls turning cartwheels indoors on a rainy day?

Richman knew that even though the courts won't allow a witness to testify to her gut feelings, Natasha was convinced that the loud thuds on the floor were the result of Claire's refusal to sign whatever contract Robert had handed her.

Craig Richman was holding, right here in his hands, a road map of progress showing the twisted journey Peernock had walked as he pursued the idea of slaughtering his family. Over the months that Robert Peernock had been compiling these lists, he had met with his family women, spoken with them, looked into their eyes, while planning their fiery deaths.

When the ominous items were culled from the harmless reminders and translated from their abbreviations, they formed an arm of incrimination that swung toward Robert Peernock as plainly as a compass needle showing magnetic north.

> Check underneath car
> Call about window tint
> Check straight to what speed
> Wife in backseat, plus child plus cover
> Liquor bottles
> Water bottles
> Rags and tissues
> Move seat up
> Claire's purse
> Handcuffs

        Keys
        Face Mask
        Find Location
        Find Location
        Find Location
        Get statement straight.

Craig Richman finally stood up from the table in the deserted office building, his mouth dry as parchment. He hurried to the nearest phone and dialed Steve Fisk's home number.

"Steve, Craig Richman. You're brilliant. Do you know that?"

"Wow. Thanks. You called at this hour to tell me that?"

"No. I called at this hour to tell you that a lot of other detectives would have decided that Peernock's car was full of bits of scrap paper that weren't worth anything and they would have let the papers get pitched out."

"You finally get around to going through that stuff?"

"Ohhh, yeah."

"What've you got?"

"Lists. The guy was writing little reminder lists, over and over, for *seven months*! There are about ten of them, but they're all part of the same thing. The same list.

"Steve, it's a checklist for murder."

When Craig Richman finally hung up the phone, it wasn't just the telephone receiver that he felt dropping into place. It was all of the pieces of the giant puzzle cube, dropping into all of the proper spots.

The way they do when the puzzle finally gets just the right twist.

CHAPTER
26

The fireworks began on the first day of trial. Before Judge Schwab allowed the jury to come in for the first time, Robert tried to fire Green and go in pro per as his own attorney. He had already been given this opportunity during the pretrial phase but had turned it down. Now Judge Schwab dismissed his motion as a stalling tactic. He cited the fact that trial was already beginning and emphasized Peernock's prior outrageous behavior in court as proof that he was either unable or unwilling to conform to court standards of behavior. When Robert's motion to defend himself was denied he blew up once again and was finally dragged out and put in the lockup next to the courtroom.

The jury had not even been called in yet.

There was a pause in the courtroom as Donald Green excused himself and visited Robert in the lockup. Green's shouting was so loud that his muffled voice could be heard inside the court. But a few minutes later Robert was escorted back in, subdued and somehow persuaded to remain calm.

Judge Schwab called for the jury to be buzzed in from the jury room and the trial of Robert John Peernock formally began.

In his opening remarks, Donald Green called allegations against his client a "Grand Illusion" consisting of unprovable accusations against a man who simply could not be placed at the crime scene by the prosecution. He promised the jury that they would soon see that despite the theory of

291

guilt against his client, there was no proof. There would be plenty of that golden commodity, reasonable doubt.

But then Craig Richman began. The experts came again as they had for the preliminary hearing years before. The paramedics, the doctors, the coroner, the evidence technicians. Piece by piece, the story was laid out for a jury who were hearing it all for the first time.

This time the new addition to the witness list was Sonia Siegel. At the time of the preliminary hearing she had still been convinced that Robert was innocent and had been embroiled in legal troubles of her own, facing charges of conspiracy in the crime. By now the authorities had concluded that she'd had nothing to do with the Peernock crimes but had been a silent victim that night. They believed that her love had been prevailed upon as a source of alibi and her trust manipulated to provide Peernock with an accomplice during his flight from arrest.

She was now a principal witness against him.

Sonia explained that it had been Detective Castro who had called her with the bad news on the day after the murder and asked her to have Robert contact the police—not Detective Fisk, as Peernock had claimed in his postarrest statements. Peernock had insisted it was Fisk who'd been on the phone during that call to Sonia's house and that Fisk had promised to frame Robert, saying, "This time we'll make it stick." She confirmed that in the years she and Robert had lived together he had never once stayed at Claire's house unless he was there with his youngest daughter. But he had left the little girl at Sonia's house that night.

She went through the checklist for murder with Craig Richman and sadly agreed that despite all of the many lists she had seen Robert make, she could offer no innocent explanations for what those ominous items might be.

Sonia's most poignant moment came when Craig Richman showed her a doctor's form that Robert had filled out for the plastic surgeon in Las Vegas. She went through all the fake information point by point, until they reached the date of birth. At first she confirmed that the birth date was accurate, then she paused and said, "Wait a minute, the year is right but the month and day are wrong." For some reason, the month and day that Robert had listed were not for his birthday. They were for hers.

With a sad smile, she added softly: "He remembered."

Tasha stood before the mirror on the morning of her first day of testimony and studied the strange reflection. She looked like somebody else. Friends had brought her a dress to wear in court, some pink feminine outfit that looked just fine on her except for the fact that she never wore pink and never wore this style of clothing. On somebody else it would have been a pretty dress; on her it was a costume.

But Craig Richman had been adamant that the jury would not have time to get to know Natasha, might not appreciate her artistic nature and her recent tendency to dress entirely in black. They might find it foreboding or intimidating. They might even wonder if black clothing made her a bad person.

What, after all, was she going to do if her father walked away?

So she stepped outside with the bodyguards who had come for her and she rode with them to the courthouse hoping that the weirdness she felt inside wouldn't show to the jury.

The bodyguards took her in by the back entrance. Reporters had the front staked out and there was still concern that a hired killer could be there among the journalists, the free-lance writers, the thrill seekers, and the curious observers.

But by now she was a pro at keeping cool under fire. She kept away the fear and the nerves and the dread by focusing on happy little things. She knew from Craig's daily phone calls to update her during the course of the trial that her father had been freaking out pretty regularly in court, getting himself thrown out. It seemed that people were finally seeing her father as she saw him, right there in open court. This time it wasn't taking place in some civil trial or some minor hearing, it was the main trial, the prime test of truth. And she knew that a lot of experts had been heard already and their testimony had all helped to bolster her story. It was a good feeling, all these strangers using their expertise to say that, yes, she must be telling the truth even though her own father kept saying that she was a liar, had always been a liar.

She smiled to herself, down inside where the guards waiting beside her could not see. Because she had lied to her father in the past about where she was going with friends, and she had lied to her mother about whether or not she had any homework to do at night. But this time she wasn't the one who had to remember the lies and keep the story straight. All she had to do was stay calm and say what had happened just as she had done a hundred times before. And try not to look like a weird, artsy-fartsy kid. She knew from experience that some people just hate those types. If one of those people was on the jury, he or she might be inclined to sit and wonder if she was actually capable of the horrible things her father claimed about her. All it would take was that one juror to turn her father back out into the streets. And if he went free, how long would he let her live, knowing what she knew about him?

So she used one of the tricks she had learned many years before, when the fighting at home was unbearable but she couldn't leave the house and couldn't keep from hearing it and didn't dare speak up because it might draw the rage down upon her.

She sang.

Much later, she described how it worked. She sang silently to herself, out loud inside her head but not moving her lips, not even the smallest amount. The songs were her private mantra, leaping and spinning and dancing inside her head where no one could hear it except her.

The police bodyguards took care of her physical safety, but the songs took care of her heart. Warding off the outrage and the sadness and the dread, the song/mantras played on invisibly inside her.

This way, when they finally called her name and brought her into the grim-faced courtroom, and when they walked her down the aisle and sat her down in the witness stand, she wasn't smiling anymore. But she still felt strong enough to tell them all about it, one more time.

Hour after hour after hour.

For the next three days she allowed Craig Richman to gently pull the details of every event out of her. She held fast to her memories when Donald Green stepped forward to retrace every detail from a different angle, trying to expose some uncertainty on her part, some conflict of fact, some aura of dishonesty.

Shortly after she had taken the stand she noticed that sitting forward on her witness chair was the only position from which she could actually see her father at the defense table. If she leaned back, the corner of the judge's bench blocked Robert from her view. Not long afterward it turned out to be a handy detail. When the lawyers were called forward to the bench to quietly go over some technical detail, Tasha, sitting forward, felt eyes boring into her. Before she could stop herself she glanced up to meet her father's piercing stare.

He silently mouthed something to her, steadily burning into her with his gaze. She felt the natural reaction of trying to read someone's lips, but it was a response she immediately switched off. A little feeling of freedom burst through her as she realized that it didn't matter what he was trying to tell her anymore; she didn't have to figure it out. She didn't even have to watch.

She just leaned back in the chair while the lawyers continued haggling at the bench. Her father was blocked from
view, simple as that. Whatever little message Daddy had for
his girl was lost with that single movement. She turned up
the music inside her head and watched events play out before
her as if they were some odd passion play that she could
only hope would someday soon have very little to do with
her life.

She made it through most of her testimony calmly. The
mantra failed her only once, when she was led through the
details of being hog-tied and hooded and left to lie on her
mother's bed while she listened to the thudding impacts vibrating the floor of the family room. Tasha felt the invisible
wall that she had learned to hold up around her feelings turn
to vapor and leave her raw emotions exposed. She broke
down and sobbed quietly.

Finally the questioning paused long enough to give her
time to recover her composure.

Then it began again.

At the end of the third day, after Craig Richman had finished laying out her story for the jury and Donald Green had
gone back over it to try to cast doubt upon her testimony,
working to give Robert Peernock that one little slice of reasonable doubt that had to be found somewhere, Richman got
back up for the last time for a very short redirect examination. With it, he laid to rest once and for all any thoughts in
the jury's minds that Natasha Peernock had somehow conspired to set up her father for murder.

"Whether you know it or not"—Craig smiled at her up
on the stand—"you're quite the clever person." He pulled
out a pile of papers and showed them to her.

"Do you remember signing any of these documents?"

"No, I don't"

"Do you know what these documents are?"

"They're papers to release money for the funeral expenses."

"You signed these documents in order to pay for your mother's funeral; is that right?"

"Correct."

"And you used an insurance policy to do that, at least that's what these documents say; is that correct?"

"Yes," she answered softly. Talking about her mother's funeral seemed to turn off the music inside again. Now there was just the thick silence of the courtroom. She later spoke of feeling the jury's stares on her skin. She could almost feel their thoughts flying through the room as they sized up every word she said. *Is this true? Is that a lie? Do we believe her?*

Craig seemed to feel their thoughts too. And he was ready to lead them to the answers.

"Your father, as far as you know at least, he wasn't around to handle the insurance proceeds and to take care of the funeral and things like that; is that right?"

"Correct." She kept her answers short and sweet, as Craig had told her to. Don't confuse the jury with detail. Let the simple truths work on them.

"They came to you on July thirtieth to ask you to release your mother's body from the coroner's office so that she could be buried?"

"Correct."

"Do you think that would be something that a husband would deal with as opposed to a daughter?"

"Objection," Donald Green shot out. "Calls for a speculation."

"Sustained."

"But as far as you know, Father wasn't around to take care of burying Mother?"

"Objection. It's been asked and answered, Your Honor."

"Overruled."

". . . Did you arrange to have your father go to Las Vegas and register in a hotel under an assumed name?"

"Objection, Your Honor. It's argumentative."

"Overruled."

"Did you do that?"

"No."

"Did you arrange to have your father get plastic surgery to change his face?"

"No."

"Did you arrange the handwritten notes that were found in your father's car that the jury will decide whether or not they have anything to do with this murder?"

"No."

"Did you plant the insurance policies that were found in your father's house that deal not only with you, but with your mother?"

"No."

"That would be pretty clever, wouldn't it?"

"Yes."

"Did you arrange to have your father at the house that night as opposed to any other night—reminds me of a Passover service"—he grinned, shaking his head—"Did you arrange to have your father at that house that night?"

Natasha: "No."

"Did you arrange to have your father force-feed alcohol to you?"

"No."

"Thank you. No further questions."

And with that, Tasha was finally excused. The rest of the day went by in a blur: being taken out of courtroom and hustled through the court building by armed guards, being driven back to Louise's house.

Her emotions were in a shambles. There was no single feeling at that point, but among the mix was a small, quiet sense of simply being glad that Craig had laid it out for the jury so clearly. It had been completely unlike the last time on the stand during the civil case, where her father had been his own attorney and had managed to combine cross-examination with sneering insults and mockery. This time her portion of the testimony was kept simple by Craig Richman and dignified by Donald Green. This time she finally had the chance to tell it as clearly as possible.

And with that her participation in the four-year process of courtroom nastiness came to a close. As she left the building she felt hungry to rub the soiled energy off herself, to get away from anything that might remind her of the case.

She needed to be among young people who didn't wear suits and who didn't know about this awful case and who wouldn't ask her the same endless, probing questions. The idea of dancing all night to very loud music tugged at her like the thought of a hot shower after a long and bitterly cold day.

If any of the guys she ran into in the dance clubs should be crass enough to ask about her facial scars, she could always give them the old car-wreck story—and then ask if they had come there to dance, or what.

A Prosecution Witness: "May I have a drink of water?"

Judge Schwab: "Bailiff, get the witness a glass of water, please."

Donald Green: "May I have a drink, too, Your Honor?"

Judge Schwab: "Certainly. Bailiff, please bring Mr. Green a glass of water, or some tea if he prefers."

Donald Green: [mutters] "Actually, I was thinking of something a little stronger."

CHAPTER
27

Victoria Doom found out that she was going to be the very last of the dozens of witnesses called by the prosecution. By the time her turn came, trial had been going for nearly two months and the case had dragged out for more than four years. Up to that point she had kept up with progress reports and with Peernock's evolving alibi stories through phone calls to Craig Richman.

She had already become slightly acquainted with Craig Richman a few years earlier when he was a novice prosecutor in the Newhall DA's office and when she worked for the public defender there. Now, as she drove to the courthouse early on the morning of her testimony, she thought back to the beginnings of their relationship. They had once squared off against each other on some case she no longer remembered. Before proceedings began, Victoria noticed that Craig had brought a little stuffed donkey into the courtroom and had it sitting next to his legal papers.

"What's that thing?" she asked him.

"Oh, that?" he responded innocently. "That's the Donkey of Justice, here to make asses out of your clients."

She laughed and went back to her last-minute preparations before the judge came in, but later, after she had dragged out the proceedings to her own advantage, Richman leaned over to her and whispered that if she didn't speed things along, the Donkey of Justice was going to crap on her case.

She had just laughed it off, but for a long time after that, whenever they ran into each other, she used to ask him how the Donkey of Justice was doing. He would always grin and say, "Just fine," until one day he groused that some jerk had ripped off his Donkey of Justice and that now he was just going to have to get convictions on his own.

The memory of the little donkey story made Victoria smile and helped her breathe a bit easier as she headed for the DA's office to check in with him.

"Craig," she told him nervously, "Peernock keeps saying that I somehow set this thing up just to get my clutches on Natasha and to get at his money or something."

"Don't worry about that, Vicki, just keep your answers short and sweet. I'm the lawyer in this thing today, you're just a witness. Lawyers are always the worst witnesses."

"Yes, but the jury will know I'm an attorney. A lot of people hate attorneys. They want to believe any bad thing about us that you can think of. What if they accept his story that I'm some kind of a—"

"I'm telling you, trust me. And keep it simple. Don't think you can improve upon my work by giving some kind of a speech. You'll just make a bunch of little messes that I have to go back and clean up."

"You haven't answered my question, Craig. What if they decide to believe him and think that I'm actually behind all this? My God, this man twists facts like they're made of Silly Putty."

"Relax." Craig grinned at her. "If you wind up being charged with any of these crimes, I promise I'll tell the DA we're friends. He'll just have to get some other prosecutor to convict you."

"Gee, Craig, thanks a heap," Victoria grumbled. "I feel so much better."

And so she was surprised and relieved when her time on the stand seemed to go without a hitch. Richman kept the questions focused on the legal aspects of Claire Peernock's attempt to divorce Robert. He had Victoria draw out the details of the civil actions and probate actions pending in the family's estate. Then he just finished up. Victoria was surprised that it was so simple.

As Richman sat down, Donald Green spoke up regarding the whiskey bottle that had been held in evidence since the day it was recovered from Claire Peernock's car.

"Your Honor, in light of the fact that we have been in trial almost two months, I would certainly like to renew my motion to have that Seagram's bottle opened up and maybe passed around."

"Even though I'm a teetotaler," Schwab replied, "I'll take it under submission."

Then Green rose to take his turn at her. *So much for the easy part,* Victoria told herself. If there was going to be serious trouble, if she was going to be accused of having been complicitous in Claire's murder, it would surely come now.

But it didn't. And Victoria couldn't believe how easy her cross-examination was. Green basically just went back over her testimony, are you sure about this, are you sure about that. No accusations, no sly hints that she was the mastermind of Natasha's tragedy and an evil manipulator who had controlled Natasha's part in the conspiracy against her poor father.

She walked out of the building in a daze, accompanied by her former law clerk, Elke Schardt, who had since become a lawyer herself and taken over Victoria's old office in Saugus.

"My God, Vicki," Elke marveled, "did you see the jury?"

"Are you kidding? I was too nervous to look at them. I didn't want them to think I was sucking up to them or something."

"Well, *I* watched them the whole time. Their body language was incredible! Whenever Richman was speaking, they looked open and relaxed, but when Green got up to try to pick your testimony apart, their positions changed completely. They crossed their legs, folded their arms, they scowled. Some even looked in the other direction!''

"You think they like me, then?"

"Oh, hell, no. You're an attorney. But Craig has them eating out of his hand."

"Ah. Thanks."

"He might actually get a conviction."

"Sure, he *might*. But what if he doesn't? I mean, what if the jury just doesn't get it? What if they actually believe Peernock didn't do this?"

"Well"—Elke   smiled   sweetly—"there's   always you. . . . ''

The prosecution finally rested its case. Now, after four years of pretrial jockeying for position and nearly eight weeks of the prosecution phase of the trial itself, the defense of Robert Peernock was about to begin at last.

And Donald Green felt as if he were being led to his own execution.

Only days before the trial began, he had received a phone call from Mary Grace Ball, who had been running his office for years. She reluctantly brought news that a new complaint had been served by mail. Peernock was actually suing Green for malpractice *while the trial was still in session*. He was charging Green with having been bribed by the prosecution to throw the case. Now in addition to Green's work on the defense phase of one of the most difficult trials he had yet had to face, he would somehow have to make time to plan his own defense against the very client he was trying to save.

Peernock was handling the malpractice suit as his own attorney, which gave him almost nothing to lose and a case that cost him next to nothing to pursue. If he somehow made his charges stick it could easily mean the end of Donald Green's career, even though he was still in his thirties and had a new family to support.

And then, as if the gods of stress had decided to place a few bets on how much the Las Vegas attorney could take, another unforeseen element entered the mix. Mary Grace called again to tell him it appeared that someone had sent private investigators to find the exact location of Green's hotel room in Los Angeles. She had received calls to the Las Vegas office from mysterious "investigators" who claimed to need Green's hotel-room number because they had "important new information" that could only be given to him.

But they would not say who they were.

Donald didn't like paranoid thinking and hated to believe that his own client might try to get a mistrial by having his attorney drop dead at the last moment, but the accusations being leveled against him by Peernock did nothing to reassure him that his client might not resort to the same sort of thing he had been accused of trying on Victoria Doom and Natasha.

Green knew that any inmate with money can arrange to have someone on the outside killed.

Is this man that desperate? Green asked himself. *Or am I just getting tired and picking up on everybody else's paranoia? Could there be some natural explanation?* But who else, he asked himself, would send unidentified "investigators"? It took effort to push the thoughts out of his mind.

Leaving the courthouse, Donald returned to the Mission Hills Inn, where he had been staying during the trial, feeling as if he had iron weights strapped to his shoulders. His wife, Samantha, was waiting up in the room, ready to handle his paralegal work for him and do whatever she could to get him ready to mount his case, but with this malpractice suit hanging over him, he hardly knew where to begin. Peernock was demanding the right to testify on his own behalf, despite the months of arguments that Green had given him against taking such a risk. Now the malpractice suit was a club in Peernock's hand forcing Green to let his client have his way in order for Donald to prove that he was doing nothing to hinder the case. But he suspected that to allow Peernock to get on the stand and be subjected to Craig Richman's verbal laser beam could amount to the same thing as simply throwing in the towel.

And then the hotel clerk stopped him at the front desk with the news that two men calling themselves investigators had been there earlier in the day, trying to get Green's room number.

"You didn't give it out, did you?" Green asked in alarm.

"No. I told them it's not our policy. They took off."

Green hurried up to his room. Samantha had recently delivered their first child and was accompanying him on all his trips for this trial so they could have their off-time together with their new daughter. Both would have been up in the room at the time these two men were looking for the room number.

He heaved a sigh of relief when Samantha greeted him at the door and happily held their little girl out for Daddy to kiss.

In the last few months Samantha Green had trained herself to become a skilled legal assistant. If that was what it took to make this marriage work, she had no objection to being listed as an office expense. Of course, she'd had no idea when she started helping her husband get up to speed that she and her daughter might be placed in personal jeopardy by the case. But she knew that Donald was trying to represent this Peernock guy without being paid anything up front, despite the $10,000-per-month cost of maintaining his office back in Nevada. In addition, Donald's own investigators were growing increasingly disgruntled over payment they hadn't received, even though their arrangement with him was that they wouldn't get paid until Donald himself got paid.

So she helped. It kept them together when work would otherwise have kept them apart and it held expenses down. Besides, she had thought, if the facts of the case were anything like the way Peernock described them, then it would be good to know that she and her new husband were working together to keep an innocent man from being convicted for a horrible crime.

But after Donald had paced nervously for a moment, he told her that they were going to have to move to a new hotel immediately.

"Why? I thought we were going to work on the case some more tonight."

"We are, but first we're moving. Right now."

"What's going on?"

"Mary Grace has had calls at the office from people trying to find out where I'm staying, and the clerk downstairs saw two men today who were . . . Jesus, Samantha, I think Robert might have people trying to find us."

There was a silent pause. It did not last long.

"I'll start packing."

She handed Donald their daughter and let him take care of the formula bottle while she gathered the baby's things.

She had begun this case thinking that it would be good to help her husband free an innocent man. Now, as she carried their daughter down to the car and Donald dragged out the heavy suitcases, Samantha Green found that everything about the situation felt much different to her.

Victoria's former law clerk, Elke Schardt, drove back to New Mexico with Victoria to spend a couple of days and offer a little moral support after Victoria's portion of the harrowing trial was finished. They combed the stores in Santa Fe where local artisans sell handmade goods to tourists. In one store they came across a huge display of tiny carved stone animals called fetishes, traditional charms against all kinds of disasters, evildoers, and evil deeds.

One was a little stone donkey.

"Look." Victoria laughed. "It's the Donkey of Justice!"

"The what?"

"Never mind. Think we've got time to get to the post office and send an overnight package to Los Angeles?"

"What for?"

But Victoria was already hurrying to the front of the store with the new Donkey of Justice in her hand.

CHAPTER

28

Donald Green called only two defense witnesses before Robert Peernock took the stand. Each witness was relatively minor. Both were neighbors of the Peernock family and offered testimony that proposed to cast doubt on facts presented by various prosecution witnesses. One claimed to have seen Robert Peernock with his youngest daughter on the evening of the crimes, but he became confused on the witness stand and could not be certain if it had not in fact been the evening of the previous day.

The other witness claimed to have seen Robert Peernock's car at the house at 2:00 A.M. on the night of the crimes, but on closer examination he agreed that it could have been 3:00 A.M. or even 4:00 A.M., and while he didn't think the Cadillac was at the house at that time, it turned out that he couldn't be absolutely sure of that either. Nothing either neighbor said did much for Donald Green's client.

Robert John Peernock was going to be the star of the show.

From the moment that Peernock took the stand and Green began to question his witness, it was clear that this was not a relationship based on trust. The honeymoon had been over for some time now. Green could get no cooperation from his client, even with the simplest point of the early establishing testimony.

Donald Green: "On or about September 4, 1987, were you arrested for the murder of one Claire Peernock?"

Robert Peernock: "I was arrested."

Green: "On that same day were you also arrested for the attempted murder of Natasha Peernock?"

Peernock: "I was arrested on that day."

And so it went, as Robert Peernock jockeyed for position in the attempt to show the jury that he was an innocent man being set up for murder and one who was simultaneously evading the attempt of his own attorney to trick him into saying something that might be used against him.

Green asked him all about his various bank accounts. This at least was the one part of the testimony that no one questioned, since it was all a matter of record. That was when the explanation came up for the suitcase Peernock had purchased just after 9:00 A.M. on the morning after the crimes, at the time when he was supposed to have been on his way to the police station to meet with Detective Ferrand.

Peernock claimed that Claire had agreed earlier in the week to accept $50,000 to settle their divorce. She wanted the money in cash because she was afraid of Victoria Doom, who claimed he was trying to use Claire at that time to get at Robert's money. So he bought the suitcase to hold the cash, which Claire wanted in small bills, because he did not yet know she had been involved in the wreck. Thus when he had gone to the bank a few hours after Claire's murder, it had simply been to withdraw cash to put in the suitcase that he would later buy so he could give a pile of small bills to Claire as a divorce settlement to avoid a drawn-out court battle.

Green took Robert through each of the events as Natasha had described them: the choking, the handcuffs, the face mask. Robert denied that any of it had ever happened. The truth, he swore, was that Claire had come home that evening and gotten into an argument with Natasha over the fact that Natasha had gone to a party where marijuana had been used the night before. Later that evening, Claire and Natasha had sat at the kitchen table and spent several hours drinking hard liquor together, which disgusted Robert so much that he went out to the backyard to paint his new bookshelves. During that time, Claire and Natasha decided to steal his car because, as he had overheard, they wanted to go out and meet some drug dealers and purchase drugs.

He then went through some of the items on the infamous "To-Do" lists which both he and Donald knew were going to be the highlight of Craig Richman's coming cross-examination. Each item, he claimed, was a harmless detail on a host of reminders based upon his maintenance work on the rental properties that he and Claire had owned jointly right up until the moment somebody bashed her skull in with a heavy metal bar.

Judge Schwab had to call Green and Richman up to the bench for sidebar conferences every few minutes as matters of strategy kept popping up. Peernock would not stop editorializing, and Richman objected strongly to allowing him to sit there and preach. But Green was unable to prevent it. When he would ask his client a simple question requiring only a yes or no answer, Peernock would launch into another long explanation and continue despite Green's instructions, despite Richman's objections, and finally despite the orders of Judge Schwab himself.

Donald Green was determined to keep Peernock's conspiracy theory from being blurted out for the jury, because he felt sure that his client's credibility would go straight out the window and a conviction would immediately follow; Craig Richman also wanted to keep it out for tactical reasons of his own. But Robert Peernock was determined to tell the story of his many years spent tilting at the windmills of state bureaucracy and the heavy cost it had laid upon his life once the dark forces inside the government buildings had singled him out for neutralization with a trumped-up murder charge.

So after Peernock explained the suitcase and his trip to the bank, Donald Green ended the initial questioning period before Peernock could do heavy damage to his case. But Green knew that Craig Richman was stomping at the starting gates and that the real test of Peernock's ability to stay cool under fire had not yet come.

Green had done what he could. Now he could only have a seat and cross his fingers.

Although Craig Richman had initially resisted the idea of having Peernock enunciate his conspiracy theory, he switched his strategy once he saw Peernock's adversarial performance on the stand under the softball questioning of his own attorney. Now Richman went straight for the jugular, beginning with Peernock's statement on the night of his arrest when he said that they might as well kill him and save the taxpayers a lot of money.

Peernock immediately asserted that it had never really happened. He said that his sworn declaration had been faked to make it look as if he'd signed it to acknowledge that the statement was true.

"Why would it be a fake?" Craig asked innocently, offering the bait he was now sure that Peernock would take. Peernock snatched it right up.

Donald Green, Peernock explained, had tricked him into signing a blank piece of paper and later typed in the declaration itself. Green had done that because he was trying to assist the state in rigging a conviction.

Craig Richman began to prompt Peernock for more detail, goading him to tell the giant conspiracy theory and all of its countless dark connections. It wasn't hard to pull the story out of him; it was hard to get him to talk about anything else. Ultimately Peernock's entire conspiracy saga was trotted out and paraded in front of the courtroom, stamping and snorting and switching its tail while the stunned jury looked on.

The "famous Foothill police," as Peernock called them in

reference to the Rodney King videotape case, had acted through their homicide detectives to join in the statewide conspiracy to silence Robert Peernock the whistleblower.

Every one of his six attorneys, whether they had been privately retained or court appointed, had joined in on the conspiracy against him.

All of the seven judges involved in four years' worth of hearings concerning the night of Claire's murder and Natasha's torture had also joined in on the conspiracy to convict this innocent man.

Natasha was lying.

Patricia was lying.

Victoria Doom was lying.

The neighbors were lying.

The prosecution's seven weeks' worth of witnesses had been bribed or threatened into lying.

The jailhouse informant who swore that Peernock tried to use him to hire the death of Natasha and Victoria was lying.

Peernock's own signed statement admitting that he had said that the police might as well kill him and save the taxpayers the money on the night of his arrest was a completely falsified statement.

The deputies who took him to and from jail were beating him regularly and lying about it.

Detective Steven Fisk had somehow arranged the murder at the behest of Victoria Doom and both of them were lying to cover their tracks.

Craig Richman: "Mr Peernock, before we recessed you criticized me for my phraseology [that we 'celebrate the fourth anniversary' of the death of] Claire Peernock during the course of this trial. Do you remember that?"

Robert Peernock: "Yes."

Question: "And you indicated that you were quite saddened by the occasion or the event. Is that—"

Answer: "Of course."

Question: "Of course. It was your wife; is that correct?"

Answer: "Yes."

Question: "You wouldn't want anything to happen to her; is that correct?"

Answer: "Of course not."

Question: "And if something happened to her you would have wanted to cut off your arm to prevent that from happening. Wouldn't that be a fair statement? Or maybe kill yourself instead; is that correct?"

Answer: "Certainly I did not want anything to happen to her."

Question: "Tell me, Mr. Peernock, what's the *JUBILEE!* show?"

Answer: "I don't understand the question."

Question: "What's the *JUBILEE!* show at Bally's?"

The Court: "In Las Vegas?"

Mr. Richman: "In Las Vegas."

The Defendant: "I don't recall."

Mr. Richman: "Do you recall going to the *JUBILEE!* show at Bally's in Las Vegas?"

Answer: "Yes. But I certainly wasn't paying attention. . . . "

The next day, Craig Richman turned his verbal laser beam onto the lists found inside Peernock's car when it was impounded near the L.A. Airport. The time had come to probe the defendant regarding the checklist for murder.

Question: "Do you remember being shown several documents by Mr. Green?"

Answer: "Yes."

Question: "Handwritten documents written by you?"

Answer: "Yes."

Question: I'd like to show them to you if I could, please . . . initially, the preliminary question: Is that your writing?"

Answer: "Yeah, it looks like it is. It may be—some things may have been changed on it, I cannot tell. Some of it looks like it's my writing, some of it may not be my writing."

Question: "What's been changed?"

Answer: "I cannot tell at this time. Do you have a magnifying glass so I could look very carefully?"

Question: "Well, the other day when you testified to it, you looked at the 'FIND LOC' part of it, the FIND L-O-C."

The Court: "Mr Peernock, a magnifying glass, sir."

Mr. Richman: "Oh, thank you, Your Honor."

The Defendant: "Thank you. You're talking about the 'FIND LOC' and beneath that it says, 'See Linda for address'?"

Question: "Correct."

Answer: "See Linda for address."

Question: "No, 'FIND LOC.' I don't care about Linda. Do you see that?"

Answer: "Yes."

Question: "Was that changed?"

Answer: "No, it doesn't look like it is—well, it looks a little bit different. It may or may not be."

Question: "It may or may not be; is that what your testimony is?"

Answer: "Yes."

And later in the day—Question: "You admit it's quite a coincidence that the date July twenty-first is on this second piece of paper, you have to admit that?"

Answer: "No, I don't think it's a coincidence at all. It's very easy to put the pieces of paper together like that and have somebody staple it."

Question: "Well, whether it's stapled or not, July twenty-first [the day Natasha's torture began], it's quite a coincidence that that date is on this piece of paper?"

Answer: "Only in your mind."

Question: "Yeah, that's my job."

The Court: "Mr. Richman, please."

Mr. Richman: "Sure, Your Honor."

And later in the day—Question: "Is that your writing?"

Answer: "It looks like it."

Question: So you're not questioning that portion as being authentic, are you?"

Answer: "I don't know if I'll question it or not, depending upon what you're going to come up with."

Question: "That's a good response, Mr. Peernock. Thank you."

And later in the day—Question: "How about the lock cutter part, which is the part that you know I'm going to concentrate on. Was that changed?"

Answer: "Probably not. I believe that was some sort of a wrench I was using to put in some piping underneath the sink. I don't recall exactly, but some sort of a device. Above, it [the list] had a red large wrench. I have "RED LARGE WRENCH," and then underneath it I have "LOCK CUTTER."

Question: "Now, you've heard the expression, haven't you, being an engineer—you are an engineer; is that correct?"

Answer: "Yes. I worked as an engineer; that's correct."

Question: "Of locking something into place. Have you heard of that, into place?"

Answer: "Like locking a car, locking a door?"

Question: "Locking a loan into place, have you heard that expression?"

Answer: "Of course I've heard that expression. Now we're going to hear your interpretation of it in your imagination. Go ahead."

Question: "You've heard the expression before of locking a part into position. Haven't you heard that expression before?"

Answer: "I guess everybody has at one time or another."

Question: "All right. Thank you. That's fair enough."

During the P.M. *recess, before the jury was brought back in:*

Peernock was too intelligent to have failed to realize that by this point his case was in deep trouble. If he was going to pull his testimony out of the fire, he would have to act fast. He was running out of opportunities to make some kind of saving move.

The Defendant: Your Honor, I want to be allowed to explain to the court. Every piece of paper has been taken from me. I'm prevented from putting on any defense whatsoever. All my papers have been taken away, all my papers. All my legal materials have been taken from me."

The Court: "The record should reflect that you have full access to any papers Mr. Green has."

The Defendant: "Mr. Green does not work for me. I fired him long ago. He isn't putting on any defense. I want to be able to have access to my materials and be able to introduce some documents."

The Court: "Anything you wish to bring up this time out of the presence of the jury?"

Mr. Green: "Not from the defense, Your Honor."

The Defendant: "See, he doesn't in the least defend me at all."

The Court: "Anything, Mr. Richman?"

Mr. Richman: "Nothing, Your Honor."

The Defendant: "This is all a plot. The whole thing is rigged."

The Court: "Mr. Peernock."

The Defendant: "He does not represent me, Your Honor. I want the record to be very clear on that. I have very important documents to introduce to prove I'm innocent."

The Court: "Mr. Peernock, please be quiet."

The Defendant: "He will not introduce any documents or

anything. He does not represent me, and the jury should know that he does not represent me in the least.''

The Court: ''Mr. Peernock, sir.''

The Defendant: ''This whole trial is rigged! It's a farce, it's a sham! All my papers have been taken away from me, everything. I cannot prove I'm innocent because they won't let me!''

The jury was brought back in and testimony resumed. Later:

Mr Richman: ''Now, there were several documents found in [Sonia's condo] that had nothing to do with you, but had to do with your wife and your daughter; isn't that correct?''

The Defendant: ''I don't know, because the Foothill police—the Foothill detectives went in there and did anything they wanted to with my property. They nearly took over my houses, they nearly took over the condominium, and also threw Sonia Siegel in jail for eight days.''

Question: ''Interestingly, there was a document from Amex Life Assurance Company dated December 1, 1986, which deleted you from coverage on her insurance policy that was found in your possession. Do you remember that?''

Answer: ''Do I remember the document or do I remember somebody testifying to it?''

Question: ''Let's ask both questions. Do you remember the document?''

Answer: ''I recall it here in court, yes.''

Question: ''But you didn't have that document in your possession?''

Answer: ''The document, the way I understood the testimony, was found at the condominium.''

Question: ''Yes, that's where it was found. Did you put it there?''

Answer: ''That particular document, I don't think so. But what I was trying to do was find out what was going on with the insurances. There was no reason for Claire to be taking out those insurance policies. I was very concerned about that.''

Question: ''You don't think you put that document there?''

Answer: ''I did try to gather some documents on the insurance to try and make a file to find out what was going on. It didn't make any sense.''

Question: ''To find out what was going on, or to make sure that you had all her insurance policies so that you could make claims on them?''

And later: Question: ''Why did you have Natasha's insurance policy dated May 27, 1987, at your house?''

Answer: ''Well, I'm not a beneficiary on that policy. I did not take out that policy. Just as all those other policies, I did not take them out. There's a very few of those policies I did take out. The policies I did take out were in '83 and '81.''

Question: *[taps the microphone]* ''Is this working? Why did you have Natasha's policy of 5/27/87 at [Sonia's condominium]?''

Answer: ''I don't know if that policy was there or not.''

Question: ''So, the police are framing you for that as well?''

Answer: ''Absolutely.''

Question: ''Okay.''

Answer: ''Sir, I blew the whistle on corruption on the state contracts. Since then they've tried everything to bring false charges against me. I was also writing a book that was exposing state contracts costing the taxpayers millions of dollars. I won lawsuits over those issues. They've spent a lot of money trying to file false charges against me, and that's what's going on now.''

Question: ''Why didn't they just kill you?''

Answer: ''If you look at the transcripts in the court records, there are six attempts all involving police officers to injure me or kill me, and I won, and proved those issues already."

Question: "Detective Fisk could have just killed you that night. In fact, according to your testimony, he wanted to."

Answer: "Yes, sir, he did. The only thing that stopped him was the fact that there was other police officers."

Question: "That would have saved the taxpayers a lot of money, wouldn't it have?"

Answer: "And as he said at the time to his partner, Knapp, 'Why don't we just kill him and take the money?'"

Question: "And it says—"

Answer: "And they only took $2,000 and shoved it in their pockets."

Question: "Why didn't they just take the rest?"

Answer: "Evidently Vicki Doom is the one that got the rest."

Question: "Why didn't they just take it that night?"

Answer: "All my money was taken."

Question: "Detective Fisk, he doesn't dress that well."

Answer: "They never returned the $25,000."

Question: "He could have used the $2,500 bucks for a new wardrobe."

By Mr. Green: "Objection, Your Honor."

The Court: "Sustained. Sustained."

By Mr. Richman: "You had separate bank accounts from Claire Peernock; is that correct?"

Answer: "Sir, the arrest warrant says clearly $28,000 was recovered. Only $25,760 was put into property."

Mr. Green: "Your Honor, motion to strike. It's not responsive to the question."

The Court: "I am granting your motion to strike."

The Defendant: "The records, the *police reports* say that!"

The Court: "There's no question pending, Mr. Peernock."

The Defendant: "Sir, Mr. Green does *not* work for me! He works for *you*! I fired him *numerous* times!"

The Court: "Mr. Richman, sir."

The Defendant: "He provides me *no help at all*!"

The Court: "At this time, ladies and gentlemen, you may now exit the courtroom, and this is the end of the testimony of Mr. Peernock. You may leave now."

[The jury begins filing out of the courtroom]

The Defendant: "The jurors should know that Green does not work for me in the least! This whole *thing* is rigged! It has to do with millions and millions of dollars of waste on state contracts! Sir, I move for a mistrial!"

[The jury exits the courtroom]

The Court: "The record should reflect that the jury and alternate jurors have left the courtroom.

"Mr Peernock is acting in an obstreperous manner. He kept on rambling and ranting and raving despite my warnings and my requests.

"I've warned him, warned him, and warned him. He refuses to desist in engaging in disruptive behavior. As such, his testimony is ended. He will be removed for the remainder and balance of the proceedings.

"Please set up the hearing device. We have ended Mr. Peernock's testimony, and you may comment on Mr. Peernock's obstruction on the stand as consciousness of guilt. . . . "

At numerous hearings over the years Peernock had been warned that he could not get away with shouting in court and hurling insults and accusations. So far the most anyone had done was make him sit in a lockup and listen in over the speaker system.

But this time he had cost himself his perch on the soapbox.

CHAPTER

29

"Lawyers work so hard
to win their cases.
Why do clients work so hard to lose them?"

—*Ancient Litigator's Riddle*

Don Green watched with mounting anguish during the days of Robert Peernock's testimony as Peernock became more and more belligerent on the witness stand, raising his voice louder by degrees, ignoring Green's motions to strike dangerous portions of his testimony, ignoring the judge's orders to answer questions as they were asked, ignoring questions that caused him any serious difficulty. Green looked on in helpless horror as Peernock finally began to lose all self-control, shouting out loud in front of the jury, showing no ability to restrain himself despite his own lawyer's efforts to contain him.

When Peernock finally had to be dragged out of court, still shouting that the trial had been rigged against him, Donald Green was sick at heart for having had to sit powerless while this scene played out before him. He later said that he felt as if he could have broken down and cried.

But there was nothing he could do to stop the runaway train.

Craig Richman, for his part, could smell victory at the moment the bailiff seized Peernock and took him away. But he also knew that with a jury there is never any guarantee until the final verdicts are read. Now he pressed his tactical advantage like a hound with the hare clearly in sight. As soon as Peernock was in the lockup next to the courtroom and the listening device was turned on so that the trial could legally resume, Richman jumped to try to drive in the final nails.

"I'm not sure if there's a reasonable solution to this problem," he told Judge Schwab, "but I ask that the court consider not allowing any further defense witnesses to testify."

Moments later, Green spoke up, fighting back the heavy feeling pulling at his insides. "I'd like to advise the court that, based upon what Mr. Peernock has stated in court today, whether it has been accepted as testimony or whether it was subject to a motion to strike, for the record, the court knows my reasons of why he was advised against testifying in the first place . . . the removal was obviously seen by the jury today.

"The jury just prior to the opening of the session this afternoon heard the rambling of Mr. Peernock on the stand about how a conviction has been rigged. I believe that based upon these factors; that is, the removal of Mr. Peernock, I guess by his own actions—"

Judge Schwab interrupted and asked whether Green conceded that Peernock's manner in court had made it mandatory to remove him before the proceedings totally unraveled.

"I understand, Your Honor," Green replied. "My point is that I, in my experience, in my seeing a number of jury trials, in my having my clients—"

"The bottom line is what do you *want,* Mr. Green, under the law . . . what am I to do, Mr. Green?"

"Your Honor, based on the irreparable harm, which has been caused by Mr. Peernock—"

"To himself," Schwab added.

"To himself, as has been noted by the court . . ." He knew

what he had to do at this point and it galled him. But the legs had been cut out from under any defense strategy that he could have mustered the moment his client exploded in the courtroom and offered the jury members a personal look into his psyche.

"The defense . . . will rest."

The words sat on Donald Green's tongue like rusted tin.

There was a moment of silence as everyone absorbed that. Finally, Judge Schwab spoke again.

"I would note for the record, Mr. Green, that you have tried in a most valiant effort to defend your client. Your client has fought you every inch of the way.

"For some reason, your client has determined that this courtroom shall be Golgotha, and crucified himself on the highest cross."

A few moments later the jury was brought back in. It was announced that the defense of Robert John Peernock had ended.

The next day, out of the presence of the jury, both sides met again before Judge Schwab regarding the stunning end to the defense. Craig Richman knew that the tide had turned decisively in his favor, but he also knew it was too soon to do anything other than press every advantage.

In support of Robert Peernock's being removed, Richman said, "I think that the record needs to reflect that it was apparent by Mr. Peernock's action that he would do anything to get off the witness stand at that point in time, including to strike out physically against either the bailiff, the court itself, or myself."

Howard Schwab nodded his agreement. "I am certain by Mr. Peernock's actions that he acted with full intent and knowledge of what he was doing and that he was disruptive in order to terminate the cross-examination in which he appeared to be faring badly. And I would also note for the record, Mr. Green, you observed Mr. Peernock testify and I know you begged and pleaded with him not to testify. You felt it would be to his disadvantage tactically to testify and yet despite your pleas he refused to listen to you; is that correct, Mr. Green?''

"That is correct," Donald replied heavily, "... because of the fact that certain events and circumstances had not been fully developed by the police when Mr. Peernock made certain statements, remarks, or writings, it was my considered opinion that for him to take the stand at that time, or take the stand at any time, would have caused irreparable damage to the defense.

"I believe up to the time that—of the presentation of the defense, and I still believe to this day, the people of the State of California could not put my client anywhere bludgeoning or beating anyone. I tried my best through the past couple of days by my objecting to the answers and sometimes the questions posed by the state, my objections to Mr. Peernock's answers were not to create a conflict or an adversarial position between Mr. Peernock and me, but only as a sound tactical move to get him to shut up, to answer the question yes or no and to leave out the editorial comments or to leave out other information which I believe led Mr. Richman, the prosecutor, into other areas of questioning which I felt were damaging.''

Moments later Judge Schwab summed up his understanding of Green's position. "And so by not calling these other witnesses, for sound tactical reasons, you are trying to basically salvage some credibility in an attempt to defend your client?''

"That is correct, to—while we still have the issue of reasonable doubt on the table.''

". . . Very good. I want the record to be clear about this, that any harm done to Mr. Peernock was done by Mr. Peernock himself only.

". . . And the court does take note that Mr. Peernock is attempting to act 'crazy like a fox,' in an attempt to disrupt the proceedings, hoping to receive favorable appellate review. And I again further find that Mr. Peernock's disruptive activities yesterday were performed purposely in order to prevent the continuation of cross-examination because Mr. Peernock was faring so poorly under the questioning of Mr. Richman.''

A few days later, after the final procedural matters had been resolved, closing arguments were presented to the jury. Donald Green and Craig Richman both came in to fight with everything they had.

The prosecution goes first. Craig Richman stood up from the table and prepared to address the jury directly for the first time since the trial had opened months before, knowing that by this point every deputy DA in L.A.'s huge army of prosecutors had their eyes on the outcome of the Peernock case. If Craig failed to add the finishing brushstrokes, if he somehow created a loophole for Robert Peernock to slide through, the list of potential victims would be long and the young prosecutor's career extremely short.

The jury did not see Craig Richman reach into his pocket and brush his fingertips over the strange-looking little carving of a donkey that he carried that day; he simply looked them each in the eyes, cleared his throat, and launched his summation. His trained voice constantly pulled the jury's attention into their own imaginations, inviting them to visualize the events as he drew the word pictures.

"The defendant has seen to it that we will never be able to hear Claire Peernock's version of the events that took place prior to her death, because the defendant has decided that for whatever reason she doesn't deserve to live.''

Richman moved through the evidence one piece at a time. When he came to the assorted components of the checklist for murder, he took the jury through the analysis of each one, tracing many of the same questions that he had planned to ask Peernock before the defendant turned himself inside out on the witness stand.

"... There is one other event that I really could not figure out how to place on this time line, and the computer wasn't any help, but it was a statement 'Wouldn't it be nice if Mommy died in a traffic wreck?' Remember [the neighbor] testified to that. Seemed like it got lost in the shuffle. [The neighbor] testified that she heard the defendant say that to his youngest daughter, six months to a year before Claire was found dead, the apparent victim of a traffic accident. 'Wouldn't it be nice if Mommy died in a traffic accident?'

"... Was he planning it to be soon? Yes. The problem was that Claire acted a little bit too fast. The divorce was filed on December fourth. The order to show cause was set on January eighth. The defendant was served on the fifteenth of December. 'How am I going to kill her that quickly? How am I going to kill her by the eighth? Gee, she filed for divorce. Are they going to think I killed her if all of a sudden she turns up dead?'

"So what are we going to do? We're going to have to buy more time. Let's get her to sign a contract where she agrees to delay the proceedings until August 1, 1987. 'Gee, Claire, I need to delay the proceedings until August 1, 1987, so I can have more time to kill you.'

"No, that won't work.

"Okay, how about this one. 'I would like you to delay the divorce proceedings until August 1, 1987, because I'm starting a new business and if you're gracious enough to agree to delay the proceedings until August 1, 1987, I will in turn promise that your greatest fear will be belied'—I think that's the right word—'that I will give you an uncontested, equal distribution of all property.'

"Vicki Doom [and] anybody who testified to that particular point indicated that Claire Peernock was concerned about the legal battle that she was going to have with the defendant, and all of a sudden she gets that carrot dangled in front of her. 'If you agree to delay this divorce proceeding until August first in order to give me more time to kill you, I will agree that if you survive that long I won't contest the divorce. You will get an equal distribution of property.'

"So she agrees. She signs the contract and she sends it to Doom. Ask yourself one thing: how many times do you think that the defendant looked through that house for that contract? He's got all these pieces of paper that he doesn't have any right to have in his house. How many times do you think he looked through the house looking for that contract? It reminds me of those old movies, not necessarily old movies, but the movie where the victim, right before they're being held at gunpoint or something like that, and they go, you know, 'If anything happens to me I sent a letter to the DA that says if I turn up dead, you did it.' Kind of reminds me of this. She outsmarted him. She didn't keep the contract in her house.

"She sent it to Victoria Doom.

"Safekeeping? It turns out that was the letter to the DA, 'If anything happens to me, the defendant did it.' She turns up dead ten days before this contract was supposed to expire. Coincidence or circumstantial evidence? You look at all the circumstantial evidence, coincidences are no longer coincidences. They become evidence to indicate that he did it. The order to show cause [in the divorce] was taken off calendar as a result of this contract.

"The next date that we have, or the next thing that indicates some sort of planning, is again a handwritten note by the defendant. It's dated April 22, 1987. Here's the date up on top. Now, remember, he's bought a little time, so he's got all the way till August now, so it seems that things have cooled off after a little bit for a while, but again on April twenty-second, we have 'FIND LOC.'

". . . And this 'location,' old San Fernando Road and Tuxford, it's like the perfect place. It's got the freeway overpass where you could beat somebody without somebody seeing. You've got these abandoned cars there, where if someone drove by and saw a car or two they wouldn't think anything about it. We've got the cement wall at the end of the road. So when the car hits the cement wall it's going to drive [the cutter bar] right into that gas tank. The fuse, gasoline rope, is going to light the gas on fire. All the evidence is going to be destroyed at the murder.

" 'Find location.'

"Mr. Peernock actually was kind of entertaining. *[He holds up a chart]* I don't know if you can read that, but that is actually an excerpt from the transcript that we have in this particular trial:

"Question: 'I ask you, is that your writing?'

"Answer: 'It looks like it.'

"Question: 'So you're not questioning that portion as being authentic, are you?'

"Answer: 'I don't know if I'll question it or not, depending on what you're going to come up with.'

"If that's not a commentary as to his credibility coming out of his own mouth, I don't know what is. This—you know I talked about a prosecutor dreaming of cross-examining a defendant on the stand; I don't even dream of answers this good. You can't ask for anything better. This shows that Mr. Peernock is totally incredible and will do anything to lie his way out of it. If that doesn't show a consciousness of guilt on his part, then there is nothing that will.

". . . Where do you think Mr. Peernock got the idea for this elaborate scheme on how to cover up his murdering Claire and Natasha for the money? He sat there at Network Electronics and tested those cutter devices for three years and watched those devices cut into vessels and cause those explosions, and that's exactly what People's 27 [the cutter bar] was supposed to do.

"... This isn't just something that was thought of on the spur of the moment, this was based upon Mr. Peernock's years of experience and patience in testing at Network Electronics, and months of at least planning on how to kill and cover up the killing of Claire Peernock and Natasha Peernock, planning that began, by evidence that we have, in December of 1986. Who knows when it started before that? That's all paperwork.

"... She [Natasha] was conscious; she just doesn't remember. But does that surprise you that she doesn't remember it? Common sense and what you know out of life. Does it surprise you that she doesn't remember? And if she's making this up, if she's making this whole thing up because the—whoever has gotten their hooks into her, as the defendant has testified to, why doesn't she just say, 'The defendant beat me. He took the tire iron and he beat my mom once, twice, three, four times in the head right between the eyes while she was just lying there and I cried, "Daddy, don't do it, don't do it," and then he turned and he did the same thing to me?'

"She's making this up? Why didn't she just go that extra step? How much more difficult would it have been? But she didn't, because she's telling the truth."

[And regarding Peernock's whereabouts through the day after the crimes, before he came home to Sonia's that evening] "Where was he during that entire period of time? Is he hiding? Is he scrambling? Is he cleaning up the house? I don't know. He knows, but he never let me ask him. Consciousness of guilt on his part. Remember that. He says he tried to get hold of Detective Fisk. [But] Sonia says, 'It wasn't Detective Fisk who called me. It was Detective Castro.' Why did he change [and] what does it matter?—Why did he lie about when those notes were written, if it *didn't* matter?

". . . The next morning, they wake up, Sonia says, 'Don't forget to call Detective Castro.' He calls and speaks to Detective Ferrand and they make an appointment. Detective Ferrand testifies that he gave him directions on how to get to the Foothill Division, but he doesn't show up.

"Where does he go? He goes to the bank.

". . . Claire's Grand Am tire. It was flat. Why was the tire flat? There was no reason for the tire to be flat. Was that to create an apparent justification as to why Claire Peernock was driving the Cadillac that evening? Probably. Who flattened the tire? The defendant.

". . . Mr. Peernock is crazy like a fox. Don't feel sorry for him because he seemed to be nuts on the stand. He knew exactly what he was doing on the witness stand. He knew exactly when he was getting into a position that he couldn't get himself out of, so he figured he'd go nuts so he could get out of it. And there he is, somewhere out in never-never land. Don't feel sorry for him. He killed Claire Peernock. He tried to kill Natasha Peernock . . . attempted, premeditated, deliberate, and willful murder. It has the same elements of murder, first degree murder, except that it has to be a direct but ineffectual act toward committing the murder. . . . A direct but ineffectual act is something beyond mere preparation. Ladies and gentlemen of the jury, her head was beaten in. How much more direct, but luckily ineffectual, can you get? He tried to kill her. He tried eight times to kill her, at least, but he didn't succeed.

". . . Did he lie to Sonia because he didn't go to the hospital and he was trying to satisfy Sonia? I don't know. Or is he lying here because he wants to make it seem like he had reason to be fearful? That there was this Grand Illusion that was referred to in the opening statement. Or is it a Grand

Delusion on the part of the defense—on the part of the defendant? Illusion, delusion, it's a fine line. But ladies and gentlemen, Mr. Peernock sat up here and he showed you. If I hadn't called any witnesses, you could look at Mr. Peernock and say, 'This is an evil man who will do anything he wants to kill anybody and get what he wants.' He showed it to you.

"How close was he to violence up on that witness stand? How close was he to hitting me? You can use that to decide whether Mr. Peernock is credible, whether he is exhibiting consciousness of guilt. Look at all the facts and you cannot possibly come up with any conclusion but that Mr. Peernock is guilty of all these crimes.

". . . And in the whole scheme of things, when all the circumstances are added up, you might as well have had somebody at the scene of this crime saying, 'Mr. Peernock did it,' because Mr. Peernock did it.

"There is not doubt."

The defense goes last. But as Victoria Doom had noted back in Judge Rimmerman's chambers two years earlier, you can't fight a case on air. Not only had Donald Green taken no money for himself in the defense of Robert Peernock, he had watched the defense dissolve in front of his eyes the moment his client was pulled off the stand.

Green made his closing remarks with passion, even though it was like trying to tap-dance on thin ice wearing heavy boots.

Still, he carefully and methodically went through each piece of evidence and offered explanations as to why they might deserve to be doubted. He emphasized the slightly confused or conflicting testimonies of various people who were testifying to what they had seen in the dark at 4:30 A.M. months or years before their testimony was given.

He wondered out loud if the police still thought Sonia was somehow involved, saying, "You have to ask yourselves why Sonia testified in court under a grant of immunity." But in the long run he was stuck with the task of creating reasonable doubt against the prosecution's scenario by trying to imply that some variation on one of these other explanations must be true:

1. One of the passersby who was at the scene for a short time after the car crashed and before the police arrived must have decided to take two women who were already unconscious and to smack them repeatedly in the head with a heavy metal bar, then pour gasoline over them, then rig up a wick under their car and light it, but *not bother to rob them,* and Natasha simply decided to take advantage of the situation following all of this by lying about everything that had happened in order to "get" her father; or

2. This had really all been set up by Fisk, Doom, and the police. Claire and Natasha were followed out there and the wreck was caused somehow by the cops and then rigged to look like Robert Peernock's doing, but Natasha somehow isn't aware of all that, even though she remembers everything that happened up until the moment her beating began; or

3. Natasha has been intimidated into lying and is only doing so because the crooked police have her too terrified to tell the truth.

Today Natasha laughs out loud at the very suggestion of number three. There is not a trace of humor in her laughter. Thus the jury was left to wonder whether one of those bizarre scenarios could offer any sort of doubt that was, in fact, reasonable.

It took them less than six hours to review the many pages of detailed jury instructions, consider the hundreds of pieces of evidence, and convict Robert John Peernock on every single count.

By the time the convictions came in, Tasha was supporting herself by working in Hollywood. She had gotten a job passing out fliers for underground nightclubs with roving locations. It didn't pay much, but the people she ran around with were all pretty low key. Best of all, none of them were tuned into the big murder trial going on across town.

The word about Robert's conviction didn't reach her right away; she had learned to make herself difficult to find. It made her feel safer just in case Daddy had any more surprises for her.

When someone finally tracked her down with the news, she felt relieved but not really surprised. She had thought of him as evil since before her early teens. Once she knew that he had revealed himself to the rest of the world, it just didn't seem that they could really let him go. After all, they would have to walk the streets with him too.

She went out dancing that night, but not because of the conviction. Tasha had already had four years to work at putting it all behind her. She went out dancing because she'd already had plans to go. "I was busy at the time," she says. "I had a lot of other things to think about."

Better things.

Out in New Mexico, Victoria's rural telephone line had been down for most of the day. She paced the floor, fretting over the Peernock case, knowing it had gone to the jury but unable to find out whether or not there was any news.

Finally her fax line fired up and began rolling out paper.
A letter was coming in on district attorney stationery.
It was from Craig Richman.

Hey, your phone isn't working. Hope you get this.
Robert Peernock was just convicted on all counts.
    The Donkey of Justice strikes again. . . .

CHAPTER

30

Craig Richman got a call at home a few days after the conviction. It was the watch commander at the L.A. County Jail, informing him that a search of Robert Peernock's cell had revealed that the newly convicted murderer had somehow come into possession of a new checklist. This one had the names, addresses, phone numbers, and workplaces of every one of the jurors in his case. There were two copies.

Peernock also had the address of the place where Craig's wife worked.

Craig Richman's blood ran cold as he recalled sitting with Steve Fisk and playing the jailhouse tape recording over and over, listening to Robert Peernock discussing the price of contract killings.

Craig later learned that Robert Peernock had obtained the list after he contacted a private investigator, using the fact that Peernock was still representing himself in some of the civil actions surrounding his estate and probate issues. But he used the investigator to cull through public records to obtain other, darker information, even getting unlisted home phone numbers for several of the jury members.

Peernock's explanation was that he simply wanted to poll the jury and find out whether or not the authorities had intimidated them into convicting him.

The public is left to wonder if Peernock also intended to poll Mrs. Richman.

• • •

Readers' Personal Protection Tip: In the judge's chambers, the private investigator was forced to reveal his method of obtaining the private information. He said that he searched the county's voter registration records, which is legal. But he added that when many people sign the voting list at their polling place *they inadvertently add their home phone numbers along with their name and address,* even though the phone number is *not* required in order to vote. However, once that phone number is written into the voting record it becomes public information—whether the phone number is unlisted or not. All good PI's know this.

The sentencing hearing did not take place until October 23, seven weeks after the September 4 conviction, because Peernock once again managed to delay the inevitable through careful use of the system.

As soon as he was convicted, he filed a motion for mistrial based upon his theories about tainted evidence and a rigged prosecution. He also challenged Howard Schwab's impartiality, accusing the judge of also being a direct and deliberate conspirator in the Grand Illusion to destroy Robert Peernock for the crime of daring to care so very deeply about the well-being of the taxpayers of California. Peernock did not mention that those taxpayers also included Claire Peernock, Victoria Doom and Robert's bludgeoned daughter.

When the day of the sentencing hearing finally arrived, Tasha decided at the last minute that she would go. Throughout the trial she had been quite content not to be allowed to attend any portion except for her testimony. Now, however, it was time to see the four years of fear for her life and struggle to survive finally come to fruition. It was time to perform her last act of witnessing in this case as some small measure of reprisal come home to the Peernock family women against the man who had destroyed their household.

That was pretty much the only way she thought of him

anymore: as the man who had destroyed their household. Although Tasha had barely glanced at him during the course of her trial testimony, she could not help but notice that four years of jail had changed him far beyond the prior work of the plastic surgeon. For reasons both physical and emotional, the man toward whom she had cast furtive glances during the trial no longer appeared anything like her father.

He was just some awful stranger with the same last name.

She took a seat in the front, not realizing that the empty table before her was the place where her father would be seated. When the deputies finally brought him in, she was shocked to find herself only a few feet from him.

He glared at her as they sat him in his chair, but he did not speak a word. This time he didn't try to mouth anything to her either.

She began to have a sick feeling inside and wondered if it had been a big mistake to come. All these serious people going through their grim duties. What did she need to see it for? She had done all she could to avenge her mother, to give herself and her little sister some measure of justice. What good would it do to watch her father being crushed and humiliated? It was going to happen now, with her or without her. She considered getting up and leaving. But the show had already started.

Peernock tried again to speak out forcefully as soon as he was brought in. But Judge Schwab just as quickly demanded silence.

"Sir," Schwab called out, "let me tell you this right now. If you are disruptive today I'm going to have you bound and gagged. I'm not going to just have you put in the lockup, I'm going to have you remain in the courtroom, because at this time I feel you should be present to see the result of your foul crimes."

"Sir," Peernock began, undaunted, "I'm innocent of these crimes and I have a right to speak in court. If you check

the law you'll find out that I do have a right to speak and
Mr. Green hasn't represented my interests. I fired him a
month before the trial began.''

"Listen to me—'' Schwab began. But Peernock was already interrupting.

"I am asking for a sixty-day continuance and that I be
given the transcripts so I can prepare a motion for new trial.
Green is not my attorney!''

"Sir, I did not have you bound and gagged because, one,
I wanted to guarantee you a fair trial—''

"You did not give me a fair trial!'' Peernock shouted.
"Green purposely prevented me from calling witnesses!''

"Mr. Peernock, if you are not quiet I will have you bound
and gagged!''

But Robert was rolling and was not about to stop now.
This was his last chance to be heard in this court and he
clearly had no intention of being silenced.

"You have in your hand right now a declaration by Bobby
Adams—'' he bellowed.

"Bailiff,'' Schwab called out over Peernock's voice,
"have him bound and gagged!''

As the defendant was being dragged out, he continued
shouting all the way down the aisle.

"I want a sixty-day continuance so I can prepare a motion
for new trial!''

Tasha could feel her heart slamming inside her chest. The
atmosphere in the room took on an out-of-control, nightmare
quality. *My God,* she wondered in a sudden panic, *what if
he's managed to hire some cohort to come in here in a deputy's uniform and toss him a gun? How much power does
he really have outside his cell, anyway?* She held her breath,
half convinced that an explosion of violence would go off in
the next second.

There was stunned silence among all the witnesses in the
courtroom. A number of them, having testified at trial and

therefore not having been allowed to see any other part of it, had never witnessed one of his outbursts before. They had just had their first look at something Tasha knew all too well: the way Robert Peernock could go from dead-eyed calm to hot rage in split seconds. The crimes that she had described instantly became easier for everyone else to visualize.

When he was brought back a short time later he was gagged; the entire bottom half of his head was wrapped in duct tape. His hands were cuffed behind him as Natasha's had been four years before.

Now Judge Schwab ordered that all the sealed portions of the transcript should finally be unsealed, so that future courts and the attorney general of California could have the benefit of reading the many accusations that Donald Green and others had had to endure from Robert Peernock during sealed proceedings over the course of the trial. They are now public record. They are there for anyone who chooses to take the trouble to read page after page of every imaginable accusation of corruption and bribery, all leveled by Robert Peernock against anyone who would not do as he ordered.

Still, Green had continued to file one motion after another on Peernock's behalf and to argue passionately for him at the trial.

Later that day, just before Peernock's fate was read to him, Green pleaded for the lightest sentence possible. He asked the court to view Peernock's behavior not as consciousness of guilt but as the actions of a desperate man. He ended his pleas for leniency with a historical reference that was right in the domain of Howard Schwab's personal interest.

"One hundred and thirty-one years ago," Green began, "in a hot August summer in Washington, D.C., there was the famous Andersonville trial. This was the trial of Captain Henry Wirz, who was the Confederate commandant of the Sumter County prison camp for Union soldiers during the Civil War. And during his command between 1863 and the end of the war, some twenty thousand Union soldiers were starved, beaten, or otherwise killed.

"But there was not one person, not one person, who could actually say that Captain Henry Wirz killed any of those people. . . . There was one person who came in, in the middle of the trial. That person didn't even have a name. He was named by his cohorts in prison. His nickname was Chicka- mauga, and Chickamauga was the name given to him be- cause of a famous battle in the Civil War, at which time he lost all his memory of everything that occurred before the battle. But everything that occurred after the battle he re- membered in excruciating and lurid detail.

"And when Chickamauga was on the stand he couldn't remember anything about what happened before he got to Andersonville prison, but he did remember that one time when he was released on a work detail to go outside of the prison camp to gather firewood, to gather blueberries so that they could have additional foodstuffs, he remembered seeing Captain Henry Wirz on a horse and saying, 'Kill that union soldier son of a bitch.'

"And one of the Confederate soldiers shot him. . . . The moral of the story is, your honor, that Captain Henry Wirz was ultimately hanged in the decision of the court martial which sat in his judgment. And judgment was pronounced by General Lew Wallace, who later came to be the first ter- ritorial governor of the state of New Mexico—"

"And the author of *Ben Hur*," Schwab added with a smile, not missing a beat.

"And the author of *Ben Hur*, a religious novel."

"However," Schwab interrupted, "with all due respect, Mr. Wirz did not flee to Las Vegas and see a girlie show on the night of the homicide. . . . "

Green never really wrapped up the end of his story. Per- haps it is safe to assume that, with Howard Schwab's inter- ruption, Green knew that he was watching the stern of the

Good Ship *Peernock* sink beneath the waves for the final time.

However, just as Judge Schwab was preparing to dole out the sentences, he expressed his admiration for Donald Green's work, performed under a vise grip of pressure and without support of his client.

"I would note for the record that I find, Mr. Green, that you are an outstanding lawyer. You are a man of high integrity and you have defended your client to the best of your abilities, which are considerable. But I look at this case as a very, very strong case against Mr. Peernock. The evidence is overwhelming with and without Natasha Peernock's testimony. And I find here a man who murdered his wife and tried to murder his own daughter, his own flesh and blood, a most unnatural act, for nothing less than greed and money.

"To take your own future and cast it away for money." Schwab sighed, then continued. "As I've said before during the trial when Mr. Peernock was disruptive, I had him removed from the court for two reasons. One, I wanted to ensure Mr. Peernock a fair trial. That was very important to me. . . . Second, I felt it was unseemly that Mr. Peernock should be bound and gagged in front of the jury. But today I felt that if in fact the motions for a new trial were to be denied, that Mr. Peernock should be present in court to be able to see for himself the results of his foul crimes.

"And what he has done is inexcusable and inhuman. I find him to be one of the most dangerous men that has ever appeared before me in this court. I find him to be one of the most dangerous men that I have ever had to deal with in my career as an attorney, and I have dealt with many very dangerous and severe homicides. And as such I make the following sentence. . . ."

All those in the room held their breath for an instant. People often do at this point. It is the moment of justice boiled down to its smallest component.

Consequence.

"The motion for new trial is denied on all grounds," Schwab began. "Now I also notice—" He stopped, looking at Peernock.

Peernock slumped forward, as if passing out. But his nose was not covered by the tape gag. Was this, perhaps, a last little trick? Sentence cannot be pronounced on an unconscious defendant.

"Is Mr. Peernock having a problem? I notice he has placed his face underneath the desk. This is a court of law, I will not have him act like an animal in this court."

Schwab ordered a recess as Peernock was removed once again so deputies could see if there was a real problem. But moments later Peernock was brought back in, still bound and gagged.

"Probation is denied, of course," Schwab began once more, "the grounds being that Mr. Peernock is a tremendous danger to the community. . . . "

Then Schwab issued the first sentence, for the solicitation of a hired hit on Natasha and Victoria after Peernock's arrest. "The sentence will be twenty-two years, four months in prison."

The length of that sentence was Natasha's exact age at that time. The tone of irony that had begun the case years before, with Peernock claiming that he was guilty of nothing more than too deep a loyalty to society, now grew to a peak. Robert would serve the length of his daughter's life for having tried to have that life extinguished.

Judge Schwab further ordered that after Peernock had served the twenty-two years and four months for soliciting Natasha's murder, he would then begin a life sentence for his attempted murder and assault upon Natasha during the night of the crimes. And after he had served the twenty-two years and four months followed by the life sentence, if he were still alive due to some mediating factor of sentence reduction for good behavior, then whatever remained of Robert John Peernock would begin serving a term of life in prison *without possibility of parole* for the murder of Claire Peernock.

"I do this," Schwab explained, "because of the especially callous manner in which this crime was committed, almost a torturous, satanic manner, in which his daughter was tied up, hog-tied, had the mask put on her face, was force-fed with alcohol and drugs, in which he attempted to murder his own daughter, his own flesh and blood, an unspeakable act even in this day and age of unspeakable acts.

". . . I want the following placed in a minute order to go with Mr. Peernock's file. It is my most steadfast recommendation that Mr. Peernock never be allowed back into society, and I want this stated in the minute order that I recommend that no future governor ever parole Mr. Peernock. That if any future governor should parole Mr. Peernock, Natasha Peernock's life is in danger. Other persons' lives are in danger. And the blood of any person Mr. Peernock kills will be on that governor's hands.

". . . I further recommend, and I want this placed in the minute order, that he be placed, that Mr. Peernock be placed in a position of high security, the most high security prison possible, Pelican Bay if possible . . . that he be allowed to have as little contact with other persons as possible because of his danger to other human beings. So I want this also placed in the minute order that he is to be put in a high security module as much as possible, Pelican Bay if possible, and that he be watched carefully and never allowed to again wreak his evil vengeance for greed or any other untoward purpose."

And then Robert Peernock was taken away.

Deputy DA Pam Springer's light blond hair made her stand out in the crowd as she sat alone in a back row of the courtroom to watch Robert Peernock's sentencing. Even though she had been transferred away from the Peernock case two years before and carried her own heavy caseload, she had asked Craig Richman to tell her when the sentencing was to take place so that she could come and see for herself. She sat wordlessly through the bizarre drama of Peernock's explosions and through all of the heartrending comments that family friends delivered before the sentence was read. She listened to each judgment being read against Peernock, in which the word *evil* was used again and again.

Like Craig Richman, she describes how her work always consists of rushing from one hot spot to another, usually on an emergency basis. She says that the same is true for everyone on the front lines of the firestorm of crime that is blackening lives in every part of the largest city in the most populous state in the most powerful country history has ever known. And she shares in the frustration of a besieged population that cries out for better protection, safer streets, longer sentences for felons, more prisons to hold them—and lower taxes.

But Springer paused in her rush from one fire to another on the day of Peernock's sentencing because she felt the need to see for herself the moment of consequence for this man who had made a mockery of the very idea of family and who then had openly jeered at the system while it labored to bring him to justice.

When it was all over she paused long enough to congratulate Craig Richman for having pursued the conviction so avidly, as she had been certain that he would. Then she turned and hurried back to her own office, back to the latest fire. There had been no time to spare for her to attend the hearing to begin with, but as with so many other people involved with this case, her professional detachment had been penetrated by it. The specter of a father laying waste to his own daughter's face with a bar of cold steel was an image she couldn't shrug off.

Pam Springer had recently given birth to her first child, a baby girl.

Detective Steve Fisk offered a quick congratulation to Craig Richman too. But that was it. The day was still early enough for him to get back to the office and check on new developments in his latest landslide of homicide cases. As he began his twenty-fifth year as an L.A. cop, he knew all too well there is never time to rest on laurels. While the city's population tears away at its own flesh like some crazed animal caught in a trap, Fisk hangs on to his serenity as a born-again Christian. Others don't have his source of solace; old friends on the force are constantly dropping out on stress leave or taking early retirement.

Steve Fisk had only been able to build this case by putting in outrageous seventeen- and eighteen-hour days, sometimes working straight through the weekend. It's a pace no one can sustain indefinitely, but he'd been trying not only to give back some kind of justice to what remained of the Peernock family but to give back a little justice to the city he'd been born and raised in, where he has built his own family.

It was just one way to work at giving his kids some sense of hope for the future, a sense that if enough people can pull together hard enough, determinedly enough, things might not fall completely apart after all.

But he knew there would be a stack of messages waiting on his desk.

There always is.

"I don't do high-fives when I win a case, and I didn't do any then," Craig Richman said afterward. "This thing was a tragedy any way you look at it. Here was a man who had it all, and he threw it away. A mother is dead with young daughters she will never see growing up. Natasha was left to try to find some way to trust people again.

"It was definitely not 'Miller time.' But you take what satisfaction you can. At least Vicki and Tasha both have a better chance to live out natural lifespans without some hired psycho coming after them.

"Your reward just has to be the satisfaction of creating a little justice. That"—he grins—"and of course the fabulous paycheck of a public servant.

"I did get the rest of the day off, though. So that's something. There was just enough time to hit the gym on the way home."

Now that this case was wrapped up there would, of course, be another stack of files sitting on his desk the next morning.

There always is.

Donald Green left the courtroom that day feeling sure that he could have provided his client with the magical reasonable doubt if only the man had kept his mouth shut and cooperated. Green had earned the admiration of everyone involved with the case, but he headed for the airport having only the Ancient Litigator's Riddle for comfort: "Attorneys work so hard to win their cases. Why do clients work so hard to lose them?" He had taken the case determined to help prevent a man from being "framed for murder," as his client had presented the story to him. But Robert Peernock, as Judge Schwab eventually concluded, had come to court determined to make it his personal Golgotha.

So Green left Los Angeles still facing a malpractice suit by the client he had tried to save. It would be many months to come before the suit would be dismissed. Later, he would also be taken to court by the investigators who had worked on the case for him, despite the fact that he'd entirely used what little money the courts provided him in order to pay his investigators' fees. Even though the investigators initially agreed that they would get paid only when Green himself did, and Green got nothing for all his troubles, they took him to court anyway.

He eventually won the suit, but it would take him years to clear up the legal fallout from the Peernock debacle.

Remarkably, at the time of this writing Green has changed nothing about his way of carrying out his practice. He still will not turn away a referral client in need of defense on a major felony charge, regardless of his or her ability to pay. He kept his practice going despite huge monetary losses on the case. He still hates the idea of innocent people facing prison because they can't afford good representation. So cases continue to come through his door because the word is out that he fights hard and loves to win.

When his clients give him the chance.

Although Robert Peernock seemed to have been pulled from the courtroom a thoroughly beaten and traumatized man, the case record shows that he went back to his cell and hand-wrote a "Designation of Record on Appeal." It was many pages long and signed that same day. Before the sun was down on the day of his sentencing, the unrelenting jailhouse lawyer had already begun the process of setting his appeal in motion.

Tasha lay down that afternoon and went to sleep, something she rarely did in the daytime. But the day's strangeness had vacuumed all of the energy out of her. She was limp with fatigue. She hadn't spoken at the sentencing hearing, even though Craig had invited her to. Where would she find words to express her feelings as her father was locked away forever? The reporters outside the courtroom had hounded her for quotes, but she'd brushed past them and said nothing. She'd felt no need to see her name in the papers again and had no desire to make a soundbite for the evening news.

Writers had pressed business cards into her hands. She'd dropped them to the floor and kept moving toward the exit, hungry for nothing else than to be gone from that unhappy place for the last time.

She lay down to rest without thinking whether she wanted to or not. Her body had just run out of gas. Sleep carried her away.

She woke up hours later. It had gotten dark. In the first fuzzy moment after opening her eyes it seemed that everything, all of it, had been an endless, awful dream.

Then as she rubbed the sleep from her eyes, her fingers brushed over the indented bones above her cheek, the ones that ached and throbbed every time the weather turned cold. She was instantly reminded that all of it had been real.

The reminders would be there for the rest of her sleep-shortened days and throughout all of her long, wakeful nights. Clear and present monster tracks, they would keep the memories forever close at hand.

CHAPTER

31

Robert was shipped off to Pelican Bay, a super security high-tech prison whose renowned Secure Housing Unit, called simply the SHU, is a thing of dread among California prisoners. Some of the SHU's most hardened inmates are said to have gone quite literally insane in the enforced silence of its utter isolation.

Even the very toughest child-murdering, gang-banging jailhouse thugs are known to have begged to be released back to a life of hard labor at an ordinary maximum security prison after less than a year in the SHU. A few have been dragged away to mental units after resorting to extreme and irrational behavior within their cells, going so far as to smear urine and feces all over themselves as if in some bizarre form of performance art reflecting the devolution of their lives. But at the Pelican Bay SHU such behavior is rarely effective in earning a transfer to a padded cell; more often they simply end up chained to their one-piece toilet.

California opened Pelican Bay State Prison in 1989 high up in northern California, isolated in the woods sixteen miles south of the Oregon border. It was built in response to a spiraling pattern of inmate violence inside all of the state prisons. At one institution, California's Corcoran prison, the violence had climbed to more than twenty-one assaults annually for every hundred inmates.

So the state had an immediate need for a place to send its most violent offenders: prison gang members, inmates who try to kill guards, major prison drug traffickers, even prisoners who, like Robert Peernock, attempt to hire the paid murders of innocent people on the outside.

The SHU was designed specifically as a place to isolate and to completely control inmates who are so violent and unpredictable that not even the slightest moment of trust, freedom, or individual choice can be permitted them, a place where these highly toxic individuals can be warehoused in the strongest sense of the word.

Robert Peernock began the year 1992 with his arrival at Pelican Bay, where he got his first glimpse of the stark white Secure Housing Unit and its dark blue gun towers. The tinted windows give the place the appearance of a movie set from some particularly foreboding piece of science fiction. Pelican Bay has been called the Alcatraz of the 1990s. Inmates call it "the dog pound." But inside, the place looks more like a windowless space station than any earthly scene that might come to mind.

By the time Peernock's prison bus rolled past the large electronic security gates and stopped at the back door of the SHU, much had changed in the California penal system. The inmate assault rate had dropped in the prior year to less than five per hundred at Corcoran prison. It was even less at other state prisons.

At Pelican Bay SHU it was down to less than one percent. Peernock could instantly see why. He stepped down to face a reception line of prison guards standing at attention in their jumpsuits and combat boots. Their billy clubs were drawn and ready, while the head guard kept his Taser drawn and poised to fire.

In a standard welcoming ceremony at the SHU, a new inmate is advised to look one last time at the outside world because it will be a very long time, if ever, before he sees it again.

As the reception ceremony continues, two prison guards step in front of him and two in back. They sternly advise him that from now on, any bullshit he might contemplate starting will in fact be finished by the staff.

By whatever means necessary.

Robert Peernock's waist chains were removed and his hands were cuffed behind his back, as Natasha's had been. He was ordered to bend over while a portable metal detector was run over his buttocks to be certain that he wasn't carrying any grappling hooks or hand grenades in his rectum; then it was run over the rest of his body to be certain he didn't have any skeleton keys or prison knives in his mouth, his ears, his hair, his nostrils.

During his final moments outside it was pointed out to him that the SHU is surrounded by a wide gravel "moat" covering a special weight-sensing grid that will set off alarms if touched by anyone weighing more than forty-five pounds. Potential escapees have serious dieting to do.

Then he was ushered inside through the heavy steel doors. Security cameras followed his every move. As he was escorted down the metal hallway, two guards holding 9mm assault rifles trailed his movements from the industrial screen floor of the overhead gangway, their eyes fixed on him every step of the way.

While being moved about the unit, he was ordered never to stop, never to talk unless answering a guard's question, and never, *ever* to turn around during the escort process, or he would be "immediately taken to the ground." The word *ground*, of course, is a misnomer; Peernock was finished with the ground. In truth he would he immediately taken down—hard—to the steel.

Locked inside those cells are over a thousand of the worst offenders society has ever had to face, kept in single-cell housing, confined for 23.5 hours each day to tiny windowless rooms where no direct sunlight ever reaches them. Cells are lined with opaque materials so inmates cannot see other prisoners. They can have reading materials, but anything passed to them is hand-checked and X-rayed for contraband. Inmates can watch TV or listen to the radio, but they must wear headphones to maintain silence.

Prisoners are fed in isolation inside their cells. If an inmate ever refuses to return his tray or his utensils or even the aluminum foil wrapper on his coffee creamer, a team of six to eight officers dressed in full riot gear will storm into his cell and attack the prisoner en masse, carrying riot shields and wearing face visors, armed with Tasers, billy clubs, and guns loaded with gas pellets and rubber bullets. They take the offender to the ground, to the steel. Hard.

Sometimes they hog-tie him. They may leave him lying hog-tied for hours at a time.

Who would do such a thing?

Robert Peernock's opportunity to begin deepening his study of irony began upon the moment of his arrival.

As his reception was completed, he walked down a concrete pathway that runs all the way around an elevated control station while the guard within it watched his every move. He was ordered to stop before the door of his new cell. The door slid open automatically. More guards followed him as he walked into the cell and the remote-controlled door slid shut behind them. A guard opened the locked cuff port in the cell door, then ordered him to back up and slip his hands through the hole. They always remove the handcuffs only *after* an inmate is secured inside the cell behind a locked steel door. Peernock was strip-searched, then they left him alone.

Other inmates have counted the holes in the steel mesh of the cell door and found that there are 4,094. Perhaps Robert Peernock saved that project for later. He had a cell to get organized, stowing away his towel, two sheets, and a blanket, plus the tennis shoes that were handed in to him after being X-rayed, as well as his yellow jumpsuit that ties in the front with ten little bows.

The cells are grouped eight to a "pod," with each pod sharing one high-walled, twenty-six-by-ten-foot exercise yard roofed with steel mesh and Plexiglas.

Peernock could see the guards pacing overhead on the steel mesh screen. He could see the speakers on the walls that can monitor conversations between inmates. Later, when it was his time to go along into the tiny exercise yard, where he was never going to be trusted with workout equipment, he would again be strip-searched before being allowed to step out into the bare concrete box.

The Pelican Bay SHU strip-search procedure is to guard the inmate with assault rifles while the inmate removes the jumpsuit. One officer stands gun-ready while another feels every inch of Peernock's clothing. Peernock is ordered to open his mouth, wag his tongue back and forth, turn his head to both sides, and show the back of both ears. Then he will run his hands through his hair, spread his fingers apart, and display both his palms and his armpits.

Robert Peernock then lifts his testicles and brushes his hands underneath them to prove conclusively for the State of California that he carries no implements of destruction under the family jewels. He must also wiggle his toes around and show the bottoms of his feet.

For any inmate who feels that he has not been given sufficient attention throughout his life, this is his finest hour: still naked and visible to the other guards and inmates on the pod, he is ordered to turn his back, bend over, grab his buttocks and spread them with both hands, then do a series of three deep knee-bends while coughing hard at the precise moment of the downstroke. Meanwhile a guard shines a flashlight at the inmate's rectum to confirm that no knives, razors, pipe bombs, track shoes, or pieces of wall-scaling equipment are hidden there.

When it's time for recess out on the bare concrete floor amid the four high concrete walls, the inmate may pace, run in place, do push-ups, jumping jacks, or sit-ups. He can sit against the wall and briefly feel the sunlight.

He can, if so inclined, think about how he got there.

Half an hour after Peernock's very first recess out in the yard began, he was back inside his cell. The door was locked once more. The silence again enveloped him. Thereafter he would keep company only with his legal papers and a few writing materials. He would read with glasses made of unbreakable plastic, not glass. He would be allowed *one* book and *one* magazine whose metal staples are always removed before they are passed on to an inmate. Every item is constantly scrutinized for security purposes.

In this way Robert John Peernock quietly, very quietly, began serving his sentence of life without possibility of parole as California's guest in January 1992, joining Pelican Bay State Prison's population of about 3,500. They are housed at a cost to Robert's taxpayers of $80 million per year because every one of these individuals has proven himself utterly untrustworthy of even the smallest degree of personal freedom.

The high-tech penal technology into which he threw the remainder of his life is unquestionably a mark of how far our society has come. Many see it as a dreadful indication of where we are headed. Robert Peernock, however, could only view this place as home. There he began the first of many long nights to come, shadowed in isolation and silence within his earthbound space station, flying away from his hard-earned captivity only in sleep, when he dreams such lucky dreams.

Craig Richman and Victoria Doom both agree that everyone who hears about this case asks the same thing: "She wasn't really his *biological* daughter, was she?" In an age stuffed with acts of insanity, nobody wants to see this last fragile taboo broken, no one wants to imagine that we have come to the point where a man who seems so ordinary on the outside can render his beautiful girl helpless in the flower of her youth and spend months plotting to tear at her face with cold steel.

While there is no way of knowing for certain how many monsters were in the dark out on that lonely road where Claire and Natasha were forced into a savage dance with the devil, there was surely more than one.

And Robert Peernock has long begged for someone, for anyone, to hear him when he cries out that the prosecution was wrong in saying that the crimes were committed by a single attacker, or that he alone destroyed his family that night.

While he never used the phrase *monsters in the dark* to explain the crime scene, he has said the same thing in essence. And in that sense he is right; the darkness out there was full of monsters. But the evidence left the jury and anyone else who looked at it seriously with one inescapable conclusion: that Robert Peernock is the one who issued the gruesome invitations.

No one in the court system ever disputed that perhaps years ago, Peernock really did discover corruption in the awarding of state contracts. But after the debilitating effect of his years of struggle against the system, after years of visualizing what steps the enemy might take to retaliate against him and then visualizing what steps he in turn might take to resist, after all his years of confronting opponents at the job site and then replaying the conflicts in his mind, somewhere along the way, as his behavior on the witness stand showed, he had lost the ability to tell friend from foe. Eventually he could no longer separate opponent from conspirator, conspirator from monster, estranged wife from monster, angry daughter from monster, monster from monster from monster.

From the moment he wrote the first reminder "Find Loc.," followed by all the other horrible reminders, surely he no longer had his real family in mind. This may be the only answer to the listener's dismay upon hearing of a successful man's plot to commit savage violence against his beautiful wife and his own daughter.

If Peernock was not simply a demon in human form that night, if he was not Evil incarnate as the trial court deemed him to be, then the most charitable explanation is that he was planning to strike out against monsters who had left the confines of his inner world and who could now step in and out of his imagination at will.

When he finally lifted that steel bar and slammed it downward with full arm blows, he was no longer facing his helplessly bound wife and terrorized daughter. He was striking out at monsters bent on destroying him. He could look right at his wife and bludgeon her again and again and never once see the woman he had promised to love and cherish for all the days of his life.

He could look right at his daughter, touch her lovely features, even say her name, and then give her over to the very demonic forces from which most fathers would offer up their lives in protection of their children. All the while he might never truly realize, down inside whatever could be left of his heart, that this was the same little girl he'd run along beside as he taught her to ride her first bicycle.

There were indeed monsters in the dark out on that road that night. Robert Peernock went after them with a vengeance. But he was trying to kill the movie by slashing at the screen.

All of his best-laid plans in response to the taunting of those hidden monsters simply led him to the darkness of his maximum security prison cell. There he found himself alone, with a lifetime to spend in battling them through every waking hour.

Perhaps by now he even fights the monsters in his dreams. Robert John Peernock is nothing if not a determined man.

The Grandfamily

The Final Chapter

Robert Peernock and I corresponded for months as I attempted to arrange an interview. At first he readily agreed, but also insisted that I sign what he called an "ironclad agreement" promising that I would say nothing to even *imply* that he may be guilty.

I declined the "ironclad agreement," but told him that since he had spent years claiming that the legal system would not let him speak, I would guarantee him in writing that he could tell his story without censorship—provided that he first answered certain questions. First of all, my chief concern was his response to the question of what he was doing on the night of the crimes when Patricia came to the house and couldn't get anyone to answer the door. Secondly, what were his *detailed* actions throughout that night, if indeed he had nothing to do with the crimes?

He ignored the questions and instead sent me hundreds of pages taken from his old lawsuits against the Department of Water Resources, plus passages from his grilling of Natasha while he was acting as his own attorney in the Juvenile Court case. He also sent pages of complex formulae concerning the rate at which dead bodies cool, purporting to prove that his wife died long before the "crooked cops" say that she did. He failed to mention that he had based his figures upon a body-cooling rate of one degree per hour, when in fact the rate of cooling can be two degrees or more, depending on body weight and air temperature. He failed to explain how his countless civil court actions prove he is innocent of the crimes. He spoke passionately about the continuing waste of taxpayers' money, but still did nothing to answer my simple questions about his activities on the night of the crimes.

Toward the end of our correspondence, I offered him an entire chapter's worth of unedited written statement if he would stick to the topic of his specific activities on that night and answer the original questions I had sent to him. He agreed, saying, "I will definitely take you up on the offer," but still failed to answer the questions.

Finally, with time running out, I wrote to tell him that I would fly to his prison and interview him on tape, but that he would still have to answer my original questions about his whereabouts that night. I had no desire to hear more tirades against the state while questions about his own activities went unanswered. Instead he sent me more copies of legal documents of all kinds from his prior lawsuits against the state, none of which said a word in answer to the questions I had repeatedly posed to him.

But the harder I pressed him to stick to the issues, the more hostile he became. It was a chilling reminder of his performance on the witness stand when Craig Richman pressed him to explain the checklist for murder. When I told him he would not take over my publishing contract for his own devices any more than he'd been able to take over his attorney's license to practice law, he wrote back with his revelation that I, too, am a hired shill for the government forces who are out to silence him.

He still never said why he hadn't answered the door for Patricia. He didn't detail his actions of that night. He never continued his explanations for those items on the "checklist for murder" that he'd been prevented from explaining on the witness stand because he'd gotten himself pulled out of the courtroom.

Instead, he finished up his correspondence with two more thick packets filled with detailed computations of time and temperature scales offered in complex proof of his innocence while still ignoring the simple questions. He packed his last letters with threats and accusations against me, Victoria Doom, Steve Fisk, Craig Richman, and Donald Green.

He doesn't accuse Natasha anymore, though. He says he just wants her to keep repeating the story she has been "programmed" to repeat so that the cops won't "hurt her anymore." I called Natasha and read that part to her. There was a pause, then she made a sound that was something like a laugh, but it was heavy and sad.

"Gee," she replied, "I'm *so* glad to have his permission now."

I asked her if she wanted to make any statement to him for the book, or maybe write him an open letter. When I asked her what she might want to say, her voice became very soft.

"I would just ask him if he has any idea what he has done, ask him why . . ." Then she stopped. It took her a few moments to continue.

"On second thought I don't really want to say anything to him. And I don't want to ask him any questions. What could he say? What difference would it make? He probably doesn't even know what the truth is, anymore. I really wouldn't even want to hear it."

So I informed Peernock that I was tired of his threats and accusations and that he had squandered his chance to speak. The PO box used for communicating with him was then disconnected.

Later, as I packed away his bundles of rambling correspondence, hundreds and hundreds of wasted pages generated by a man with nothing else to do to fill the slow drip of the years, I paused to glance again at a small line of print stamped horizontally at the sides of the pages.

It struck me as a kind of final epitaph to the sincerity of his whistleblower claims.

"Copied at taxpayer expense."

THE GRANDFAMILY

When Claire Peernock selected Victoria Doom as the one to whom she would entrust her future as well as the future of her children, she wove the first invisible stitch in an unseen network of connected choices. Each of those choices was made by someone determined not to let the forces of evil operate with impunity in their lives, regardless of the degree of sacrifice and determination required to make those choices stick. This invisible network would eventually grow to encompass dozens of strangers. It linked them together, indelibly altering each of their lives.

When such a web is composed of choices made with the highest levels of courage and moral conviction, made in spite of fear or laziness or countless temptations, then each person behind those choices becomes one more link in a unique human constellation that is described here as a Grandfamily.

The Grandfamily in this story is the thing that ultimately defeated the dark collective genius of all of the monsters who prowled the darkness unseen during the Peernock family's night of tragedy. The Grandfamily began with Claire's moment of choice to visit Victoria Doom and grew to become the engine of the Peernock story itself.

Claire made a choice of excellence, based in honesty and in fairness. She did not seek out a courthouse shyster to help her rip off her husband; she sought out a woman reputed for fairness who would understand Claire's position and help her find the strength to pursue an honest half of the family's property, but nothing more than that. When she avoided the temptation to seek someone who would bulldog the divorce into hateful negotiations of greed and revenge, she set the energy impulse into motion.

That choice put her in touch with an attorney who combined the ability to fight tooth and nail for the right verdict with a personality that responds strongly to situations in which someone is treated unfairly or is outrageously abused. With Victoria the first full link in this new Grandfamily was formed.

Detective Steve Fisk was at the crime scene before the car's engine had cooled, and the absolute wrongness of the situation went straight to his personal desire to keep the streets free of psychopathic killers who behave as if there are no laws but their own. When he met Natasha the next day and realized that what had been done to this family could just as easily have happened to his own neighbors, he began booking unpaid overtime six and seven days a week at a point in his career when many other officers are looking for easy assignments.

He could have put in regular workdays and never been censured by anyone. He could have let Peernock walk and just chalked it up to the luck of the draw. He could, perhaps, have read later, in the newspaper, a story about Natasha's being tracked down and killed by an unknown assailant, and shrugged it off as life in the big city. Steve Fisk had never heard the term *Grandfamily* and never pictured any invisible energy lines linking him with a woman he met only in death and an attorney he would not come to know until later. But Grandfamily connections don't require anyone to use the term or to see any connections. All anyone needs is the right strength of heart.

Fisk simply knew that he wasn't about to tread water on this one and that he stood ready to put whatever energy it took into getting some justice back into this demonically wrong situation. And so another link in the Grandfamily was made.

No one forced Craig Richman to put in so much extra time and energy; he could have left the job at the office and earned a fair wage and nobody would have faulted him. You win some, you lose some. Except for his strong need to see justice done, he could have stayed out of law enforcement altogether. In his first chosen field of radio broadcasting, he would almost certainly have made better money and would definitely have worked easier hours.

In his case research, no one was pushing him to search every tiny piece of scrap paper forgotten in the storage boxes until he found what would come to be called the "checklist for murder." But his own sense of excellence compelled him to chase down the case relentlessly. So another link in the web was formed.

By this point, actions of the other members were ricocheting back and forth like lightning. A domino effect of action and reaction was altering their lives steadily and changing them forever.

Howard Schwab was one of half a dozen judges involved in Robert Peernock's criminal escapade. He could have been Peernock's greatest ally. He is widely recognized as a judge who does not permit defendants to be railroaded, especially a man noble enough to risk his career to expose massive government fraud and waste. Schwab's drive for excellence is known throughout California by people who have stood both with him and against him, and it was also evident here. His tendency to do exhaustive case research before coming into his courtroom enabled him to cut through the poses and deal with the facts. Despite Peernock's constant accusations of courtroom corruption, despite his successful use of the system to subject the judge to examination by his peers for improper behavior, Howard Schwab pursued the case determined to offer a fair trial. After Peernock's conviction and claim that Judge Schwab had cooperated with a frame-up, Schwab was cleared of any hint of any bias and his handling of the case was fully supported by the court of review.

But by that point in the story, Robert Peernock was not just up against a legal system; he was up against a Grand-family of people united in their need to do the right thing even if it seemed the hardest choice, the least popular choice, the most time-consuming choice.

Thus, in the end, Robert Peernock turned out to be right about unseen connections existing beneath his murder conviction.

However, he was all wrong about the quality of the energy.

And he missed out entirely on the excellence.

An observer searching for some evidence of a Grandfamily connection somewhere in the life of Natasha Peernock during the days following the end of her father's trial could not be blamed for wondering if it had somehow missed her. A deepening depression that had been making life steadily more difficult threatened to envelop her completely. It appeared that the monsters were not through with her yet.

When Victoria was finally able to arrange for Tasha to receive her first small check from the estate's insurance money, minus the staggering sum that her father and his girlfriend had spent before access could be shut down, Tasha left L.A. altogether. Her marriage had ended with her husband stuck in the Aleutians and her stuck in Los Angeles. She hoped now to remedy the last part, and arrived down the coast in the town of Laguna Beach as a completely unknown visitor. Like some solo alien landing her flying saucer back behind the courthouse in the dark of night.

But even there, amid beautiful scenery, she found herself lost in a community of strangers. Her feelings boiled inside her as if in an overheated pressure cooker. Every time she turned in some new direction for relief, the heat only seemed to intensify.

How much loneliness, she wondered, how much of a sense of isolation, was considered tolerable? There was just no escaping the sensation that something was going to have to give. In her continued state of isolation, Tasha kept returning to the question of what her next move ought to be. But her thoughts beamed outward, bounced off the stars, and came back again and again with no answer.

She could only wonder—how much is life on this planet supposed to hurt, anyway?

As summer ended in the tiny town of Las Vegas, New Mexico, the Old Courthouse Building near the town square was playing host to the new office of Victoria Doom, attorney at law. The move away from Los Angeles had served to restore her zest for work, especially with her new life among all the exotic animals that she and Richard had gathered into their lives. Local cases began to come through her door as she juggled work between her new office in town and her home office on the ranch.

The only drag on her line was the nagging doubt about Natasha's ability to find a life for herself following the resolution of the long trial. Victoria had forced herself to take a step back from Tasha's life after beginning the first modest estate payouts to her. Victoria knew that her own protective nature could easily run on overdrive, but she kept reminding herself that Tasha was no longer the traumatized teenager she had first met, but an adult in her early twenties with every right to run her life as she chose. And for understandable reasons, the young woman wasn't big on adult authority.

But worry nagged at Victoria anyway. It followed her around the ranch as she visited the monkey cages and the birdcages and it stayed with her as she fed the llamas and tended the horses. It nibbled at her as she drove to the office in town, and most of all it snapped at her at night while she lay in bed trying to sleep.

She realized there was no way Claire could consciously have known that Victoria would be the type to risk her life and her practice to stand by Claire's brutalized daughter after the awful crimes were over. But the woman seemed to have had clear premonitions about the manner of her death; how much more had she sensed accurately? Victoria couldn't escape the nagging sense that this leftover feeling of connection to Natasha was part of something Claire had intuitively known about Victoria's nature.

But she kept reminding herself that there was nothing else left for her to do. She knew that she had far outpaced her professional and moral obligations, had perhaps lost her objectivity altogether.

So why didn't it feel finished?

She knew she had no right to intrude on Natasha and start telling her how to live her life. Most lawyers would have let it go long before this. Still, she lay in bed at night and fought a sense of concern that she could not rationally explain or justify. If she talked about it at all, she couldn't say much more than that the damn thing just didn't feel finished.

Robert Peernock was also far from finished in his battles with the legal system. It took him until August of 1992, but he finally got himself transferred out of the Pelican Bay SHU. He did it by using court records from lawsuits had filed against employers many years before documenting his long-standing claim that he suffers from "sleep apnea."

And so in August of 1992 Robert Peernock blasted off from space station Pelican Bay after snagging a transfer to the much more tolerant atmosphere of the California Medical Facility, located in Vacaville between San Francisco and

Sacramento. CMF was built with a design capacity of 2,168 inmates in the far less high-tech year of 1955. By the time Peernock arrived in 1992, the population was running at 150 percent of capacity with 3,293 inmates.

Whether he truly suffers from sleep apnea and has it severely enough to warrant medical concern is a matter for prison doctors to decide, but presumably they are doctors who will never see the crime scene photos, the autopsy photos, the emergency room photos, the checklists, the cutter bar. They will most likely not read the transcripts of endless hearings in which Peernock jeered at the system's ability to keep him down. They are surely far too busy to take time to note the long, long list of self-filed lawsuits Peernock has run over many years that demonstrate his ability to manipulate the legal system. They are unlikely to have enough information to weigh against the likely truthfulness of Peernock's supposed medical complaints.

Even if his sleep apnea condition is real, it cannot justify the general "walkabout" status he has been given, for inexplicable reasons, inside the overstuffed prison. He now mingles with a population of felons, some of whom are presumably murderers for hire.

He is allowed access to the telephone.

Peernock has a small prison bank account. Regular deposits are made into the account by "outside sources." Despite his claims of concern for his daughters, he settled a small lawsuit with a large life insurance company shortly after arriving at Vacaville but never sent a penny to Natasha. The money is no longer in his prison account. Where did it go?

He has found a woman in Pomona who is listed as "next of kin" in his prison file and who is allowed visiting privileges with him. Presumably she never saw Claire's autopsy photos or Natasha's emergency room photos.

And surely she has never spoken with Sonia Siegel.

Many women are attracted to lifers for reasons an entire squad of psychiatrists would have to explain. It may be safe to say that most of these women have also not seen the chilling evidence that their jailhouse hubbies have often left behind like monster spoor. But a woman in love can be very handy to an inmate stuck inside. She brings things in, she takes things out. She runs all kinds of errands the prison system has no way of monitoring.

And while their jailhouse partners wait behind bars, the women are safe from harm at hubby's hand, for the time being. They do not have to fear such things as the blunt end of a steel bar. For the time being.

Therefore when a convict has help on the outside and when he is allowed to roam free among other killers on the inside, when he has a bank account and access to the telephone, and when he is already serving time for trying to hire killers to do his dirty work, *is it unfair for others to be just a bit suspicious of his intentions?*

How cheaply can a man have the death of his daughter and her attorney/mentor arranged, when he has a whole range of felons to chose from and when he has spent several years getting to know the ropes of the jailhouse code? Would a man have discretion enough to avoid mentioning that the girl is his own flesh and blood, just in case another assassin is squeamish about such things?

As for Robert Peernock, he continues to jeer at the system, crowing that he is steadily working his way back out. He has a list of sworn enemies reaching all the way up to Judge Schwab, whom he openly threatened in a letter sent from behind bars shortly after his sentencing. Given Peernock's history, no one takes his threats lightly. He remains completely unbowed and is still doling out threats and accusations, forming them into the strongest terms legally allowed to him as a convict, and then sending them out in letters from his Vacaville cell.

Peernock has other dark connections. He has kept at least
one private investigator (one of those who allowed themselves to be used in Peernock's criminal case) constantly on
retainer even after he went to jail. During the months of
Peernock's murder trial, when the investigator was ordered
to gather the name and address lists, he cooperated.

Consequently, did Robert Peernock know that his daughter
had been living in Laguna Beach that summer?

Tasha kept up a running dialogue with herself as she steered
her car out of California and began to head north. The Ca-
nadian border was a long way off. She knew she would be
doing a lot of self-talk to keep up her courage for the trip.

Among all the people she had met in Laguna Beach,
among all the young men who might have been attracted to
the lovely young woman who kept to herself and radiated a
strange mixture of charm and isolation, she had never felt
connected even to one.

"I wasn't stabilized inside myself yet," she says. "People
don't prevent you from feeling lonely if you're not stabilized.
They just sort of rub you the wrong way and keep you reminded that things aren't okay."

It took her a long time to decide to approach her mother's
family up in Quebec. The idea of seeking out a group of
French-speaking strangers in another country seemed impossibly foreign. But the sense of isolation was killing her.
Whatever might happen next in her life, Tasha knew that she
couldn't keep trying to fly solo.

But while she drove onward the highway seemed to stretch
out farther and farther in front of her. It was almost as if the
car itself were fighting her, as if she had to press the accelerator harder just to keep up the same speed.

The trip seemed necessary but it felt wrong.

She asked herself what the problem could be. The plan
was so simple: drive for days to a place where you don't

speak the language and the climate is about the same as
Alaska's, barge in on a bunch of strangers you're supposedly
related to and then use pidgin English to join their clan when
you're not at all sure that you want to do that anyway.

"Vicki?"

"Tasha, is that you?"

"Yeah . . ."

"Well, hi! How are you doing?"

"Oh . . . Not too good."

"What's wrong?"

". . . Nothing."

"Mm-hm. Where are you?"

"Well, I'm in Arizona."

"Arizona. Okaaay. *Why* are you in Arizona?"

"It's kind of a long story. Listen, could I come and visit
you for a little while?"

"Just you?"

"Uh-huh."

"Sure. Sure you can. In fact, that would be really nice.
Richard and I finished the house, so you can have the mobile
home all to yourself. How soon will you be here?"

"I'm going to drive straight through."

"Well, there's no hurry. You know, you're allowed to eat
and sleep on the way if you want."

"No. I'm going to drive straight through."

"Oh. Okay. Can you find Las Vegas? It's the one in New
Mexico, you know."

"I'm just lonely, I'm not retarded."

"That's right. I remember now."

"So it's okay?"

"It's absolutely okay. You don't even have to drive
straight through. It will still be okay whenever you get here."

"No, I'm driving straight through."

". . . I'll stock up the fridge."

• • •

Either Tasha managed to arrive at dinner hour or Victoria managed to have dinner ready upon her arrival, but there was just enough time for Tasha to dump her bags in the mobile home parked twenty yards behind the house and then come back down for their first meal there together.

She explained the aborted Canada trip and about her need for some peace and quiet. Victoria said the mobile home was stocked up, the extra pickup truck was full of gas, and Tasha could come and go as she pleased. When she asked Tasha how long she planned to stay, Tasha replied she wasn't sure. Victoria told her to get comfortable and stay as long as she wanted to. Then she and Richard added the magic ingredient.

They left her alone.

Meals were usually held with everybody together around Victoria's kitchen table, but Tasha often stayed inside the mobile home for whole days at a time. She read voraciously from the large collection of books that overflowed the main house and were kept stashed in the new "guest house."

She marveled at the private zoo, cages full of gibbons and monkeys and exotic birds, huge kennels full of Irish wolfhounds. Horses ran free all over the grounds, thundering around the place like wild animals but tame enough to nuzzle up to the back door and nicker for carrots. Horses from the fantasies of a girl who had grown up loving horses and riding them every chance she got.

The wind across the mesa tops was musical. Animal sounds carried through the night. She still sat up late by herself, but her heart began to rest easier.

One of the dogs, a Labrador retriever named Black Dog, was as big and as capable of being scary as any other Lab can be, but he bonded with Tasha instantly. She still breaks into a fond smile and gets a goofy tone in her voice when she talks about him. She and Black Dog began to explore the countryside in earnest.

They walked for miles, day after day, up in the hills beyond the large mesa that guards the back of the ranch. For the first time since Niko and Queenie had been torn out of her life, Tasha had the chance to give over her affection to the unconditional love of an adoring dog who was generally enthusiastic about anything Tasha might feel like doing at any hour of the day or night. Their unspoken deal was that Black Dog could take the exercise if she could take the slobber. Their endless hill hiking required different muscles than Tasha's dancing but it burned calories just as well. She began to feel ready to have a dog of her own again.

Before long she found her way into town to attend a pet fair in search of a nice potbellied pig, one of the few kinds of animals not already at the ranch. The girl at the pig booth had the sad duty of explaining that all the pigs had been snapped up by local pig connoisseurs, who apparently had earlier sleep habits than Tasha's. But did Tasha want to see a really cute puppy?

"... A puppy?"

Tasha arrived back at the ranch deep in major-league love with a six-week-old Rottweiler male. She had already named him Magic. It fit. The relationship was perfect from the moment they laid eyes on each other, from the first slurp of a sloppy puppy tongue no bigger than a slippery postage stamp.

The tiny dog had taken one look up at this giant human female and felt the soft, buzzy cloud of her energy enveloping him. He seemed to know instantly, deep down in his heart, that he had just stumbled into Jackpot City.

Little Magic may not have realized that the huge female human he was staring up at had never been able to consider owning another dog since that time when she'd been too young and too badly injured to stop Niko and Queenie from being torn out of her life; but some ancient canine instinct seemed to tell him that he had just latched onto a bodyguard who had absolutely no intention, ever, of letting *anybody*

separate them. Tasha never stood a chance with Magic; he
was a pro. He had all the right moves. He looked up at her
with huge puppy eyes and made inexplicably cute little yip-
ping sounds. Magic whined beautifully, but not too much
and not too loudly. He struggled around, puppy style, just
enough to invite help but not so much as to appear pitiful.
He was utterly shameless about letting her feel his fat tummy
as much as she wanted to. He even had that extra, magical
little something that only a gifted few young animals have:
the ability to urinate all over you and somehow communicate
the fact that, hey, its nothing personal.

And so at the tender age of only six weeks, a little Magic
arrived back at the new guesthouse. Magic didn't know it
yet, but from the moment he succeeded in capturing Natasha,
he had discovered Permanent Alpo Recess.

Tasha never got to Canada, of course. Victoria kept her as a
guest for nearly three months and describes watching with
growing approval and quiet satisfaction as Tasha seemed to
change before her eyes with every passing day. That rest-
lessness that had been a part of Natasha Peernock from the
day Victoria first met her was slowly dissolving. A gentle,
trusting young woman began to appear from behind the fa-
cade. The intensity of the urban street scene gradually left
her. Her face took on a peaceful, rested look. Her gentle
laugh began to come out more and more easily.

Finally one day Tasha came to Victoria and asked if they
could travel together to an area far away. She had decided
to invest the money her mother had left for her by buying a
house and putting down roots to begin a real life for herself.

Victoria was delighted. This was starting to feel like something she had awaited for a long time now. So they got into
Tasha's car and drove for two days until they came to a place
where Tasha and Victoria were strangers to everyone and
nobody had any idea about Tasha's background.

They looked at houses until they found one that felt just right to Tasha, where she could see herself digging in for the long term. There was a big fenced yard for Magic and a sunroom for lots of plants. Victoria helped her through the paperwork and soon Tasha was moving her things out of storage in Los Angeles and into her new home.

She joined a local health club and enrolled in the community college. She began working toward starting her own business. She keeps a horse nearby now, has her dogs outside for protection and her cats inside to cuddle. She maintains a constant lookout among the local population for that glint in the eye, that ironic twist to the smile, that might reveal a fellow stranded traveler on the planet. She has begun to slowly gather friends. There is no hurry; she's in for the duration and fellow tribesmen always seem to know one another, no matter what disguises they are forced to wear.

As for Victoria, by the time she returned to the ranch with Tasha to gather her things out of the mobile home and then make the final trip back to the new house, she realized that something felt different inside. When Victoria saw Tasha's delight at finding the house and now, at having a home of her own in which to build a solid new life, it put something to rest within Victoria as well. The nagging sensation that had haunted her throughout the years of this case finally began to ease. The relationship with Tasha would continue, but the Peernock case was finished.

And that was it; the damn thing finally felt finished.

I was deep into the research for this story when I called Tasha one night to tell her I was having some trouble. When she asked what was wrong, I told her that despite all the research I had done on her family background, I couldn't find her. Where did her gentle personality come from?

After all, Robert Peernock's fate may be regrettable, but it is not that difficult to understand. The field of psychology is replete with case studies of vicious killers. Much can be inferred from his own family background, about a childhood that produced a man capable of such sustained and murderous coldness. If he is not simply to be dismissed as an incarnate demon, then he, too, has his story of abuse and of neglect sufficient to snuff the humanity in a growing boy and set him on course for actions so horrible that the only service he can now perform for his beloved taxpayers is to offer insight into the mind of a killer and into his methods for attempting to thwart justice.

But where, I asked his daughter, did Natasha come from? Was she simply her mother's child? Had she received so much nurturing from Claire that it insulated her from damage at Robert's hand? But Tasha was honest in revealing that Claire had not been some shielding saint. Indeed, Claire had cautioned her to tell none of Robert's hurling her across the room, and shattering her bones. The two women got along well enough in a kind of uneasy peace, but clearly this was not where Tasha's sweet disposition had begun.

Psychological texts predict dark futures for many children with a background of violence and rage coupled with a dominating parent who fills them with fear and suspicion. So, I asked her, where *did* you get your spirit? Why is your energy so fine, why are your mannerisms so graceful? She just laughed.

But some of Tasha's defense mechanisms are easy enough to see. She learned early in life to separate her self-concept from her troubled family image by thinking of herself as a complete outsider, outside her own family, her school, the neighborhood, the planet. If she sees herself as some temporary visitor here, an alien with a wrecked flying saucer, then she doesn't have to identify with those years in the monster house. It was just a dark, innermost cave through which she has passed and to which she does not have to return.

Still, as I reviewed Peernock's habit of tape-recording practically every aspect of his life, I wondered how she managed to keep the past from haunting her more than it does. For example, many of the family belongings are now in Tasha's hands by court order. Among the things she hasn't thrown away are stacks of those tape recordings, accumulated over the years by her father. One tape was made when Tasha was a baby, at two and a half months of age. The tape consists of her infant sounds as Robert pesters her endlessly to "say something" for the microphone. With a music box playing Brahms's "Lullaby" in the background, he begins with a sickly sweet cooing, urging her on. But when she doesn't speak (at ten weeks), he badgers her to say something, say something, with growing intensity until she eventually begins to cry. He refuses to pick her up and comfort her until she "says something," leaving her to cry louder and louder until the child is eventually wailing at the top of her lungs. Robert leaves the tape rolling, on and on. It is apparent on the tape that he does not pick her up. Little Tasha's mouth stays right next to the microphone while Robert can be heard moving around in the background, doing nothing to comfort her because the infant won't "say something." Her punishment for saying no to Daddy had already begun. After a long time Robert's angry voice finally says, "I don't think I like that," and the machine snaps off. He nevertheless saved the tape as a souvenir, for all those years.

I mentioned the tape to her and told her it was only one reason why I was having so much trouble finding the source of her quality of spirit. There were countless others. She sighed and her voice grew quiet, but she began to explain. We talked about my question over the course of several days and the answer slowly came forward as she offered her understanding of herself.

Natasha Peernock grew up in California, in an environment rife with spiritual viewpoints of every kind. She sees this lifetime as one of many she has had in this world. This time, as a little girl, she was given the maximum strain anyone could possibly carry, but as a result now she has the chance to make the maximum growth in herself. If Robert Peernock is indeed simply the end product of a long line of his own family's abuses that grew in ferocity until a monster emerged, then it has fallen to a spirit with Tasha's depth of serenity to overcome the power of that evil.

From her refusal to give in to defeat on the night of the crimes to her stubborn insistence upon taking charge of her own recovery, Tasha took the lead in speaking out for the Peernock family women and in restoring what measure of justice she could.

It's just that it took everything she had, that's all.

Tasha finished by saying that she is determined to reap the peace and contentment due to her now, but given her past in this life, she hopes that this might be her last go-around on this particular planet. Even though she has a strong taste for adventure, she would like to try someplace else next time.

After I had already spent months interviewing her for this book, night owls burning up the long-distance lines at two in the morning, I made my last trip out to see Natasha in person. We had become familiar with each other, comfortable in one another's company. And so, as we sat up one night going over some of the hardest personal issues in the story, she took my hand and brought my fingers up to the side of her face, gently running my fingertips over the bones that were shattered around her eye socket, her cheek, her forehead.

"Can you feel that?" she asked softly.

She didn't need to ask. It is the track of the monster, left behind like a horror story written in Braille. It must be an indication of the plastic surgeon's skill, that her face can look so good while the bones feel so broken under the flesh.

We left it at that and went on to other things. I can feel those bones under my fingertips every time I think of it, as clearly as if I were touching them again. Yet even though the monster track will be there all her life as a reminder of the monster's passing, Tasha readily agrees that her survival itself is a larger reminder of the track of the Grandfamily that formed around her when everything might otherwise have been lost.

The people in Tasha's Grandfamily only knew that they had found a time and a place where doing the right thing in the best way they could was the only alternative acceptable to them. For all they knew at the time, they were making those choices alone and they would never see a moment of victory from it. But each one found that he or she had to do it anyway.

Someday some genius in an attic lab somewhere will make special goggles that let the wearer see the millions of lines of glowing energy flashing back and forth among the Grand-families of the world like magical webs of light. Until then we can only track their invisible presence by the healing they create, by the strength they give, by the lives they change for the better.

If that mad inventor had had his magic goggles ready back then, any one of us might have been able to put on a pair and see the energy lines of this story's Grandfamily connections flashing through the air. As the actions of all its members reacted upon one another, they snatched power from demonic hands and restored a measure of justice in the aftermath of evil. Having seen it then, we could have gone on to watch the same process every day with the connections linking our own lives to the lives of countless like-minded people, whether they are strangers or not.

But maybe imaginary goggles work as well. Seeing it in

our mind's eye might be enough to encourage any one of us to make the tough choices when lesser parts of us would rather take an easy way out. It might be enough to give us heart.

Because we all know the monsters are out there. If we are to believe the toxic news coming nonstop over the media tubes, the monsters are growing in number, prowling the streets with impunity, tapping at the door, scratching at the windows. Nobody needs to invent special goggles to see the monsters. We all know that they are walking free among us, loud in their contempt, bold in their disrespect.

But if we could just get Tasha's flying saucer repaired and take it for a joyride, high up over the stratosphere, out there where the cold-eyed engineer/astronauts have those life-changing spiritual revelations that cause them to land, grinning ear to ear, talking crazily about the Big Picture, and if some beautiful mad scientist actually did issue sets of those magic Grandfamily goggles right before our own takeoff, then we could peer out of the view port and gaze back down toward the little ball hanging in space and see millions of lines of glowing energy flashing back and forth over the surface of one lonely planet as it rolls through the endless darkness.

The aftermath of the Peernock story is proof of how strong that power is, whether we can actually see any Grandfamily connections around us or not. It is proof that although a society whose values appear to be crumbling in all directions can never endure without a return to higher levels of personal responsibility, the true believers are quietly making their stand. And so there is good reason to dare to be full of hope, to dare to be strong in the determination that we can yet make the world as we know in our hearts it ought to be.

Meanwhile it probably couldn't hurt to keep those goggles handy.

SELECTED REFERENCES

Brazelton, T. Berry. *Families: Crises and Caring*. Reading, Mass.: Addison-Wesley, 1989.

Fontana, Vincent J. *Save the Family, Save the Child: What We Can Do to Help Children at Risk*. New York: Dutton, 1991.

Layman, Richard. *Child Abuse*. Detroit: Omnigraphics, Inc., 1990.

Moran, Richard (Special Editor). *The Insanity Defense*. The Annals of the American Academy of Political and Social Science, vol. 477. Beverly Hills: Sage Publications, Inc., 1985.

Noguchi, Thomas T. *Coroner at Large*. New York: Simon & Schuster, Inc., 1986.

Sarason, Irwin G. *Abnormal Psychology: The Problem of Maladaptive Behavior*. Englewood Cliffs, N.J.: Prentice Hall, 1984.

Strean, Dr. Herbert and Lucy Freeman. *Our Wish to Kill: The Murder in All Our Hearts*. New York: St. Martin's Press, Inc., 1991.

Swanson, David W. *The Paranoid*. Boston: Little, Brown & Co., 1970.

Willwerth, James. *Badge of Madness*. New York: M. Evans & Co., Inc., Philadelphia: distributed in the U.S. by J. B. Lippincott Co., 1977.

and if nothing else works . . .

Pawlicki, T. B. *How to Build a Flying Saucer*. New York: Prentice Hall Press, 1981

AUTHOR'S NOTE

The names of certain individuals who are not central to this story have been changed to preserve their privacy. A few small details that have no bearing upon the story's truth have also been altered, once again in the interests of protecting the privacy of those who have done nothing to warrant the dangers of public exposure.

Concern for this level of privacy is based upon the fact that elements of lethal threat behind this story remain all too real at the time of this writing.

ACKNOWLEDGMENTS

The emotional courage of those who agreed to be interviewed on the record for this book is truly admirable. Others spoke only on condition of anonymity, with reservations that were either personal or due to legal restraint. But they also served to round out the truth of the story.

Mark Renie from the American Film Institute gave invaluable commentary upon the early drafts.

The indefatigable Mary Lu Murphy, official court reporter on the Peernock case, was most gracious in allowing access to many volumes of her court transcripts.

Literary agents Al Zuckerman and Todd Wiggins of the Writers House in New York City matched my belief in this story with their own, then performed their prestidigitation in the marketplace with such élan as to make it look easy.

Editor Shawn Coyne gave the story an enthusiastic home. He applied keen editorial skill and his knowledge of the true-crime genre to the honing of the final manuscript. Jacob Hoye shepherded it into galley form and finally on to publication.

And evergreen thanks to personal counselors Laurel Rose, Lynn Benner, Ken Olfson, and Joan Lightfoot, as well as to writer Stewart Stern and to psychology instructor Bill House. Along with Elva Johnson and her magical kitchen round-table, their generous expressions of belief and support created miniature versions of themselves who became perpetual residents in my own inner gallery—an unseen circle of fellow travelers who showed up just in time.

A better Grandfamily is not to be found.

PARTING THANKS

to Napoleon Tunafart and The Flashy Boy
for demonstrating jail-break techniques,
to Miss Kitty
for her sensuous lap dancing, and
to Ellie 'n' Sham
for lovely background vocals
throughout so many of those long, long nights.

Happy trails